JUNG IN THE ACADEMY AND BEYOND

JUNG IN THE ACADEMY AND BEYOND
THE FORDHAM LECTURES 100 YEARS LATER

Edited by
MARK E. MATTSON
FREDERICK J. WERTZ
HARRY FOGARTY
MARGARET KLENCK
AND BEVERLEY ZABRISKIE

PUBLICATIONS IN JUNGIAN PSYCHOLOGY
www.springjournalandbooks.com

© 2015 by Spring Journal, Inc.
All rights reserved.

Spring Journal™, Spring: A Journal of Archetype and Culture™, Spring Books™, Spring Journal Books™, Spring Journal and Books™, and Spring Journal Publications™ are all trademarks of Spring Journal Incorporated. All Rights Reserved.

Published by:
Spring Journal, Inc.
New Orleans, Louisiana, USA
Website: www.springjournalandbooks.com

Cover image:
International Extension Course in Medical and Nervous Diseases, Fordham University, New York, Sep. 9 to 18, 1912 (http://digital.library.fordham.edu/cdm/ref/collection/PHOTO/id/7)
By permission: Archives & Special Collections, Fordham University Library, Bronx, New York.

Editorial and production assistance:
Erica Mattingly, eemattingly@gmail.com
Cover design, typography, and layout:
Northern Graphic Design & Publishing
info@ncarto.com

Text printed on acid-free paper

Library of Congress Cataloging-in-Publication Data Pending

Table of Contents

INTRODUCTION
Mark E. Mattson, Frederick J. Wertz, Harry Fogarty, Margaret Klenck, and Beverley Zabriskie 1

PART I
JUNG'S LECTURES AT FORDHAM

CHAPTER ONE. JUNG'S BREAK WITH FREUD REVISITED:
METHOD AND THE CHARACTER OF THEORY IN PSYCHOANALYSIS
Frederick J. Wertz 15

CHAPTER TWO. ENERGY AND EMOTION:
C. G. JUNG'S FORDHAM DECLARATION
Beverley Zabriskie 37

CHAPTER THREE. THE 1912 INTERNATIONAL EXTENSION COURSE
IN MEDICAL AND NERVOUS DISEASES:
THE INSTRUCTORS AND THE FORDHAM CONTEXT
Mark E. Mattson 51

CHAPTER FOUR. CARL JUNG, BEATRICE HINKLE, AND
CHARLOTTE TELLER, THE NEW YORK TIMES REPORTER
Jay Sherry 65

PART II
JUNG: SCIENCE AND THE ACADEMY

CHAPTER FIVE. JUNG, SCIENCE, GERMAN ROMANTICISM:
A CONTEMPORARY PERSPECTIVE
Joseph Cambray 77

CHAPTER SIX. JUNG: ROMANTIC, MODERNIST,
AND POST-MODERNIST:
DISCUSSION OF DR. CAMBRAY'S CHAPTER
Martin A. Schulman 101

CHAPTER SEVEN. THE FADING OF C. G. JUNG IN THE ACADEMY
Frances M. Parks 115

CHAPTER EIGHT. A TALE OF TWO INSTITUTES:
RESEARCH-LED TEACHING AND TEACHING-LED RESEARCH IN A JUNGIAN/
ARCHETYPAL STUDIES DOCTORAL PROGRAM
Jennifer Leigh Selig and Susan Rowland 121

CHAPTER NINE. JUNG AND LABORATORY ETHNOGRAPHIES:
LAB AS LOCUS OF TRANSFORMATIVE RESEARCH
Farzad Mahootian and Tara-Marie Linné 131

PART III
JUNG: THE HUMANITIES AND BEYOND

CHAPTER TEN. JUNG, PSYCHIC REALITY, AND GOD
Ann Belford Ulanov 165

CHAPTER ELEVEN. DISCUSSION OF DR. ULANOV'S CHAPTER
William J. Sneck, S.J. 187

CHAPTER TWELVE. UNBARRING SHEOL:
UNCONSCIOUS ILLUMINATIONS ON THE HISTORY, FORM, AND RECEPTION
OF THE HEBREW BIBLE
Tiffany Houck-Loomis 191

CHAPTER THIRTEEN. THE *DEUS ABSCONDITUS* AND THE
POST-SECULAR QUEST
Amy Bentley Lamborn 203

CHAPTER FOURTEEN. REVISITING CARL JUNG'S *SEMINAR NOTES*
ON THE IGNATIAN *EXERCISES*
Harry W. Fogarty 215

CHAPTER FIFTEEN. A FEELING OF KINSHIP WITH ALL THINGS:
ANALYTICAL PSYCHOLOGY, DEEP ECOLOGY, AND PHENOMENOLOGY
Teresa Arendell 223

CHAPTER SIXTEEN. A JUNGIAN PERSPECTIVE ON THE MOST
IMPORTANT ISSUE OF OUR TIME—CLIMATE CHANGE
Dennis L. Merritt 233

CHAPTER SEVENTEEN. HOW THE TREASURE OF COMPARATIVE MYTHOG-
RAPHY WAS LOST IN LATE TWENTIETH-CENTURY HUMANITIES
John Davenport 245

CHAPTER EIGHTEEN. WALKING THE STREETS:
NON-JUNGIAN REFLECTIONS ON THE JUNGIAN SUBJECT
Gustavo Beck 259

CHAPTER NINETEEN. JUNG AND CHINESE CULTURE:
    COMMENTS ON TRANSLATIONS OF CLASSIC CHINESE TEXTS, JUNG'S
    COMMENTARIES AND CONVERSATIONS
    Geoffrey Blowers 277
CONTRIBUTORS 289
INDEX 299

Dedication

This book is dedicated to Eugene Taylor, Ph.D. (1946–2013).

Introduction

Mark E. Mattson, Frederick J. Wertz, Harry W. Fogarty, Margaret Klenck, and Beverley Zabriskie

In September 1912 the *International Extension Course in Medical and Nervous Diseases* took place at Fordham University in the Bronx, New York. A featured speaker was Dr. Carl Jung, the eminent psychiatrist and psychoanalyst from Zürich. Fresh from the heart of the psychoanalytic movement in Europe, Jung challenged the participants to understand the science and psychological nuance behind psychoanalysis. Little did anyone know that these lectures signaled things to come, not only Jung's career development but also the dawning of a century of Jung's analytical psychology. These were influential lectures, delivered by Jung along with several other important presentations, seminars, and meetings in New York, Baltimore, and Chicago on that same visit to America.

In October 2012 Fordham University, in collaboration with the Jungian Psychoanalytic Association of New York, held a conference entitled *Jung in the Academy and Beyond: The Fordham Lectures 100 Years Later*. This conference honored the 100-year anniversary of these nine historic lectures, and also challenged *our* participants to look both back to the intervening years and ahead to future potential understanding and re-inclusion of Jungian psychology in the Academy and the larger psychology world.

Our conference took as its inspiration the fact that Jung and his analytical psychology have been missing from the scholarship of psychology for some years. How do we explain that Jung was slowly squeezed from the psychology departments of the Academy? We sought to lift this question into consciousness, explore why and how it happened, and bring together scholars and analysts to begin to bridge the gap.

The historical context of Jung's trip to America is important. At the time of the Fordham lectures, Jung was a thirty-seven-year-old psychiatrist and psychoanalyst, a star of the Zürich school, the president of the International Psychoanalytic Association, editor with Freud of the influential *Jarhbuch* journal, and Freud's anointed son and heir. He had been the face of the psychoanalytic movement in Europe.

Jung had also been struggling with the theory underlying psychoanalysis. He had set out to confirm Freud's ideas, but kept finding that he could not always do so. It was a tremendously charged time, culminating in his emotional break with Freud just three months after the Fordham lectures were given.

Upon returning from America, Jung sent this report to Freud:

> Dear Professor Freud,
>
> I have just gotten back from America and hasten to give you my news. … Altogether, the ΨA movement over there has enjoyed a tremendous upswing since we were last in America. Everywhere I met with great interest and was favorably received. I gave 9 lectures at the Jesuit University of Fordham, New York—a critical account of the development of the theory of ΨA. Naturally I also made room for those of my views which deviate in places from the hitherto existing conceptions, particularly in regard to the libido theory. I found that my version of ΨA won over many people who until now had been put off by the problem of sexuality in neurosis. As soon as I have an offprint, I shall take pleasure in sending you a copy of my lectures in the hope that you will gradually come to accept certain innovations already hinted at in my libido paper. I feel no need to let you down provided you can take an objective view of our common endeavors. I regret it very much if you think that the modifications in question have been prompted solely by resistances to you. With me it is not a question of caprice but of fighting for what I hold to be true. In this matter no personal regard for you can restrain me. On the other hand, I hope this letter will make it plain that I feel no need at all to break off personal relations with you. I do not identify you with a point of doctrine. I have always tried to play fair with you and

shall continue to do so no matter how our personal relations turn out. Obviously I would prefer to be on friendly terms with you, to whom I owe so much, but I want your objective judgment and no feelings of resentment. I think I deserve this much if only for reasons of expediency: I have done more to promote the ΨA movement than Rank, Stekel, Adler, etc. put together. I can only assure you that there is no resistance on my side, unless it be my refusal to be treated like a fool riddled with complexes. I think I have objective reasons for my views.[1]

Clearly, much was at stake for Jung, for Freud, and for the Psychoanalytic movement itself in the Fordham lectures.

The Fordham lectures offer a great deal to study. One gets a sense of Jung, his earnest brilliance, and his willingness to push an idea to its conclusion. They give us some of his bedrock and emerging inclinations, both clinical and theoretical. These ideas and theories are also extremely relevant today, especially as they articulate and demonstrate the then radical ideas about trauma, neurotic dynamics, and the prospective nature of symptoms.

Jung accomplished four things over the course of nine lectures:
1. He elucidated the theory of psychoanalysis, the new and revolutionary theory that was widely misunderstood, to an audience of doctors and psychologists, and brought the Americans up-to-date with the latest from Europe.
2. He confronted the critics of psychoanalysis directly, showing where their objections were un-scientific and/or culturally prejudiced mis-readings of the theory.
3. He articulated his own thinking, areas within the theory where he had grown to disagree with Freud, most especially Freud's purely sexual interpretation of libido. Jung had a dawning understanding that libido could be understood as descriptive of psychic energy more universally.
4. He demonstrated, using clinical examples, just how the theory worked.

One hundred years later, there is much at stake in our revisiting these lectures and their legacy in regard to the state of psychoanalysis today and the clinical work of psychoanalysis and analytical psychology.

The partnership between Fordham University and the Jungian Psychoanalytic Association can serve as a template for Jungians and scholars to collaborate, challenge, and move beyond historic splits and begin to incorporate all that is potentially intellectually exciting and clinically useful in our newly opened discourse.

Most of the conference sessions were held on Saturday, October 27, 2012 in Duane Library. The first talk was an invited address by the late Eugene Taylor on "Jung and His American Psychotherapeutic Milieu: 1912." His death in January 2013 was a great loss to his family, his colleagues, and to the field of the history of psychology. Taylor had not prepared for this book a written chapter based upon his presentation by the time of his death. We are hoping to digitally publish a version of his presentation as well as the other three presentations that are not, for a variety of reasons, included in this book.

Frederick J. Wertz (**Chapter 1**) was the discussant for Taylor's paper and expanded his comments especially for this book. Wertz explores the role of the Fordham lectures in the Jung-Freud break by examining the communication between the two thinkers around the event in light of a close reading of the lectures. He finds that although Jung warned Freud of his plan to criticize Freud and present his own theories in the lectures, Freud's uneasiness changed to admiration when he read the content of the lectures. Wertz finds that although the lectures contain the core of Jung's theoretical differences from Freud, they express a more fundamental sharing of scientific methodology that allows for theoretical critique and change. Wertz details the characteristics of the little known psychoanalytic research method and suggests that it provides a basis for unity among divergent schools of psychoanalysis throughout history and in the present. This chapter introduces the first part of the book which focuses on Jung's lectures at Fordham in 1912.

Beverley Zabriskie (**Chapter 2**) explores the original, forward-moving theory presented by Jung at Fordham University and draws out its divergence from Freud's approach and its anticipation of contemporary research on emotion and neuroscience. Zabriskie places Jung's ideas about psychic substance, dynamics, and energy as well as his analyses of complexes and the transference in the historical context of his mentors, including Freud, Bleuler, Janet, Charcot, James, and Nietzsche. She pays particular attention to Einstein's influence on Jung's theory of psychic energy, and documents Jung's teleological point of view, detailing how his emphasis on the primacy of emotion and the mind-matter continuum anticipated current views of emotional regulation and relational enactments in research and psychotherapy, inside and outside psychoanalysis.

The last two chapters in this section are historical, relating Jung and the 1912 International Extension Course to their local contexts of Fordham University and New York City. The instructors at the 1912 International Extension Course are introduced by **Mark E. Mattson (Chapter 3)**. The short history of Fordham's Medical School was the local context for the Course and Jung's lectures. **Jay Sherry (Chapter** 4) connected Jung with the New York avant-garde through Beatrice Hinkle and Charlotte Teller, who interviewed Jung for the New York Times.

The second part of the book covers Jung in science and the Academy. The conference began with an invited public lecture in Keating Hall on Friday, October 26 by **Joseph Cambray (Chapter 5)** that focuses on Jung and science, particularly the Romantic view of science of Alexander von Humboldt. While one stream of Jung's writing shifted from the scientific style of his contemporaries, as in the Fordham lectures, to a dramatically different style, as in *The Red Book*, Jung continued to believe he was being scientific. Cambray locates nineteenth-century Romantic and early twentieth-century influences on Jung's thinking. Especially relevant to Jung in the Academy, Cambray finds Jung's more holistic view of science on the rise today in areas like non-linear dynamical systems and epigenetics. Discussant **Martin A. Schulman (Chapter 6)** adds Jung as Modernist and Post-Modernist to Jung the Romantic scientist, along with his experience of the Freud-Jung split as editor of *The Psychoanalytic Review*.

In the domain of clinical practice, **Frances M. Parks' (Chapter 7)** "The Fading of C. G. Jung in the Academy" discusses the emergence of evidence-based practice and its influence on the world of mental health training and practice; she underscores the importance of Jungian analysts' participation in the dialogue surrounding this issue. As new research is demonstrating the superiority of analytic treatment for some disorders when measured over a span of years, she urges that Jungian training institutes adopt the consistent format of Pragmatic Case Studies in Psychotherapy (PCSP), so that the influence of Jung's theory and the rich work that has followed is included in psychology studies and practice models. **Jennifer Leigh Selig and Susan Rowland (Chapter 8)** also place Jung in the Academy, specifically at Pacifica Graduate Institute. Selig contrasts the development of Pacifica with the development of the C. G. Jung Institute in Zürich, and suggests that Jung's work is not more widespread today because it has been narrowed in definition in academe to a type of therapy, in contrast to its founder's much larger agenda. Rowland explains how her teaching and research at Pacifica are informed by teaching Jung's idea of active imagination and close reading as a methodology in literary studies.

Moving from culture, nature, and practice into the laboratory, **Farzad Mahootian and Tara-Marie Linné (Chapter 9)** explore the potential impact of analytical psychology on post-positivist scholarship in science, chiefly in the fields of Science and Technology Studies (STS). The authors review the alternative epistemologies of laboratory ethnographies from the perspective of physicist Niels Bohr's application of complementarity. They perceive its epistemological limits as congruent with Jung and Freud's dyadic methodologies. They discuss a laboratory ethnography case for the broader methodological implications that arise from the mutual interaction between Analytical Psychology and STS.

The final part of the book on Jung in the humanities and beyond begins with the third invited address by **Ann Belford Ulanov (Chapter 10)**. Ulanov first lifts up and explains the tensions between psychology and religion in the Academy. She then goes on to examine how "Jung finds the psyche is the medium through which God speaks to us," and tells us of Jung's conviction that "man's vital energy or libido is the divine pneuma." Highlighting Jung's notions of the personal equation and the bridging functions of symbol and imagination, Ulanov looks to *The Red Book* as a vehicle not only for Jung's inner journey, but also as a model of a way to encounter ourselves and our internal god-images. Ulanov calls us to see that our own psyches are the vessels through which we encounter God and symbol and that through struggling with such encounters, both conscious and unconscious, we and the world are transformed. **William J. Sneck, S.J. (Chapter 11)** responds to Ulanov's chapter with warmth and generosity. He speaks about ways in which Jung has indeed been excluded from the Academy but also reminds us of the larger world of thought and teaching, in which the influences and intentions of Jungian psychology are clearly felt.

Tiffany Houck-Loomis (Chapter 12) challenges the current field of biblical scholarship to include Jung's understandings of psyche. She looks at the fears of many in the biblical field in acknowledging the reality of the unconscious and suggests that those fears control the scholarly conversation. She urges scholars to see a parallel between their delving into the unknown of sacred texts and the unknown in themselves, stressing the need to use the images and symbols as bridges between the known and unknown. With this attitude, the symbols can once again become living, and scholars can then bring all that has been left out into the conversation: the repressed and marginalized, the feminine, and the numinous. This, for Houck-Loomis, creates a *new kind of knowing*, one she urges those in the biblical field to explore.

In their chapters Arendell, Beck, Fogarty, Lamborn, and Merritt offer fresh perspectives on the interface between Jung and our worlds—inner and outer. **Amy Bentley Lamborn (Chapter 13)** explores various moves for seeking the Deus Absconditus, God who has put off the images from which we adorned, and considers the Open, the Other, and the Chora. Elegantly, she weaves together contemporary writing on these motifs within theology and Jung's work, allowing us both a fresh clinical perspective and a fresh theological view on the movements of unknowing, or undoing, so we may more closely encounter the uncontainable all-living.

In an exploration of the interconnections and central affinities of Jung's thought and the Jesuit tradition of Fordham University, **Harry W. Fogarty (Chapter 14)** revisits Jung's 1939 *Seminar Notes* on the *Spiritual Exercises of St. Ignatius of Loyola*. Fogarty finds a deep convergence in the psychological and spiritual praxes of Jung and Ignatius—a common engagement in the most central and basic possibility of personal liberation and transformation. Exploring common ground and tensions in the Jung-Ignatius exchange on active imagination, Fogarty brings out the challenges each thinker poses to each other and their common engendering of a submission to the archetypal manifestations of the self within and for the collective. While considering Jung's wise call that we have *our* experiences rather than proceed *collectively*, a risk confronting us when guidance comes from a conversation with shared, inherited symbols rather than personally arising symbols, he cautions against ending up with *fool's gold* inasmuch as privileging such personally arising images may leave the collectively shared under-addressed.

Jung's attitude to Nature inspired several chapters about the perilous state of the planet, including "A Feeling of Kinship with All Things: Analytical Psychology, Deep Ecology, and Phenomenology" by **Teresa Arendell (Chapter 15)**. She follows Jung's quest to expand human consciousness through a phenomenological approach to Nature and Psyche through an attitude and narrative which weaves together forgotten and rejected aspects of the old, most especially the outer landscape—the spirits of the ancestral lands—and the inner landscape of the primordial in our psyches. An early theorist of deep ecology, historian and author Theodore Roszak, who developed the notion of an *ecological unconscious*, asserted that Jung's idea of the collective unconscious is the single most important concept in the creation of an ecological psychology.

Dennis L. Merritt (Chapter 16) vigorously outlines an approach he calls Jungian ecopsychology which he hopes can serve as a bridge between the various communities engaged with the realities of climate change. Knowing too well that effective work on climate change requires both dialogue on many levels and a means to contain the dialogue, Merritt proposes we draw on the large vision Jung offers.

John Davenport (Chapter 17) explores Jung's voluminous and important work on comparative symbolism, which includes the study of sacred myths of all cultures; comparisons of religious rituals, practices, and beliefs; analyses of symbols, motifs, and plot patterns of heroic legends, fairy tales, great epics, and related genres of modern literature; and the historical development of imagery in religious and secular art. Davenport traces and laments the historical loss of this engagement despite its tremendous importance and the failure of contemporary thought to address, let alone answer, the important questions raised by this tradition. Davenport calls for a renewal of attention to Jung's work and the venerable tradition of which it is a part. He details the potential benefits and contributions of a paradigm shift from deconstructive and post-modern thinking to the study of comparative mythology in contemporary humanities.

Gustavo Beck (Chapter 18) invites us, within our clinical work, to walk out into the streets and welcome into our sessions what is outside. Engaging the worlds of social media and political movements, he draws creatively on a session which unexpectedly occurred outside during a political march. How does a movement like YoSoy132, which arose in the context of the 2012 Mexican Presidential Race, interface with a Jungian approach? For Beck, it simply must and must do so more consciously.

In the realm of cultures, **Geoffrey Blowers (Chapter 19)** follows Jung's restless pursuit of non-Western symbol systems. He describes how Jung's interest in Eastern philosophies began in the early nineteen-twenties when he began experimenting with the *I Ching* [*Yijing*], then "referring the resulting oracles to one another in an interplay of questions and answers." His interest was sparked by two questions, the first dealing with the nature of the relationship between the random generation of physical patterns and *answers* contained in the text, and the second with the *amazing coincidences* obtained between the oracle and his own thoughts. Blowers cogently critiques how Jung's confrontation with the *Yijing* later spurred him to the development of key ideas in his theory of the psyche.

Conclusion and Acknowledgements

The breadth and depth of the papers and the discussions at the conference give us hope—hope that Jungian thought is alive in the Academy, where both will find enrichment; hope that the misunderstandings and old wounds within the depth of the psychological world may finally be healed; and hope for even more fruitful conversation among current scientific explorations, theological reflections, political concerns, and analytical psychology. Perhaps the 200th anniversary of Jung's Fordham lectures will celebrate treasures forged in the reconnection of Jung and the Academy.

Our thanks for both the conference and this book begin with Jungian analyst and Fordham alumnus Harry Fogarty, who brought the idea of a conference to Dean Nancy Busch of Fordham's Graduate School of Arts and Sciences. Dean Busch asked Mark Mattson, a Fordham psychology professor working on the history of psychology at Fordham, to work with Fogarty to plan the conference. Ultimately, the committee that selected the papers for the conference became the editors of this book: in addition to Fogarty and Mattson, Frederick Wertz, also of the Fordham Psychology Department; Beverley Zabriskie of the Philemon Foundation and the Jungian Psychoanalytic Association; and Margaret Klenck, also of the Jungian Psychoanalytic Association and of the Council of North American Societies of Jungian Analysts (CNASJA). CNASJA met in New York City and ended their conference by attending ours.

We are also thankful to Nancy Cater and Spring Journal Books for their enthusiasm and support which brings the proceedings of this conference to a wide audience.

Lastly, we wish to thank all those who presented papers and attended the conference. It was a lively, inspiring, and, we hope, catalyzing event as we foster conversation between Jung and the Academy.

Acknowledgements

The conference was sponsored by Fordham University and the Jungian Psychoanalytic Association. Fordham University also provided funds for indexing this book through an Arts and Sciences Deans' Internal Funding for Faculty Activities award to Mark Mattson.

Program Committee: Harry Fogarty, Margaret Klenck, Mark Mattson, Frederick Wertz, Beverley Zabriskie

Conference Committee: Nancy Busch, Lisa Cataldo, John Cecero, S.J., Anthony DeLuca, Ellen Fahey-Smith, Harry Fogarty, Anne Hoffman, Margaret Klenck, Mark Mattson, Harold Takooshian, Frederick Wertz, Beverley Zabriskie

Continuing Education: Harry Fogarty; Co-sponsored by the National Association for the Advancement of Psychoanalysis

Fordham University: Salvador Aceves, Denise Daniel-Mack, Charlene Dundie, Maureen Hanratty, Patrice Kane, Francis Katai, Ines Montero, Kevin Munnelly, Zachary Potts, Vivian Shen, plus Intercampus Transportation, SODEXO and Facilities

Council of North American Societies of Jungian Analysts (CNASJA): Margaret Klenck, Susan McKenzie

Spring Journal Books: Nancy Cater, JoAnne Barton, Erica Mattingly

NOTES

1. William McGuire, *The Freud/Jung Letters: The Correspondence between Sigmund Freud and C. G. Jung* (Princeton, NJ: Princeton University Press, 1974), p. 515.

Part I
Jung's Lectures at Fordham

CHAPTER ONE

JUNG'S BREAK WITH FREUD REVISITED
METHOD AND THE CHARACTER OF THEORY IN PSYCHOANALYSIS

Frederick J. Wertz

In this essay, I offer a reading of and commentary on the lectures Jung delivered at the Fordham University School of Medicine in 1912. These lectures are currently published in *Jung contra Freud: The 1912 New York Lectures on the Theory of Psychoanalysis*. Princeton University Press republished these lectures in 2012, with a new introduction by Sonu Shamdasani, to commemorate the 100-year anniversary of this historic event. This material was published originally in 1912, again in 1954, and by the Bollingen Foundation in 1961.[1] These Fordham lectures have been considered important in the history of psychoanalysis as "a critical piece in Jung's differentiation of his psychology from Freud's."[2] Reference to Jung's break from Freud is suggested by the title of the new volume, *Jung contra Freud*. The purpose of this chapter is to assess the relationship between the two men as framed in Jung's lectures and the extent to which these lectures are a harbinger of things to come.

The thesis of this essay is that Jung did not break with Freud in the Fordham lectures and that, moreover, Jung *never* broke with Freud in some of the most important respects, which are highlighted in these lectures. Nevertheless, the Fordham lectures were indeed an indication of things distinctly Jungian to come. Understanding the simultaneous convergence and divergence of Jung and Freud requires a nuanced grasp of their work, which Jung provides in the Fordham lectures. This understanding may be useful today as a general model of the divergences and unity among psychoanalysts.

The title that Jung gave these lectures, "The Theory of Psychoanalysis," is somewhat misleading. At the center of these lectures, the reader finds not *one* theory, but the exposition of a *new way of doing science*, a method of investigation that was unique in 1912 and remained deeply shared by Jung and Freud, notwithstanding the *break* that took place between the two pioneers shortly after Jung's visit to Fordham. This methodological bedrock, moreover, continues to form an implicit foundation underlying much that may be viewed as contentious and divisive through the history of psychoanalysis and among contemporary theoretical strands. What Jung and Freud shared, which Jung brilliantly articulated in the Fordham lectures, helps us appreciate principles that unify the variants of depth psychology, which, as a collective family, has enjoyed little understanding and hospitality in the larger field of academic psychology.

Psychoanalysts have more in common with each other than they have in common with the dominant traditions of academic psychology. The aversion and rejection of psychoanalysis in the field of psychology has a long and storied history that is beyond the scope of this essay. For evidence that the trend continues to this day, one need only look at the decreasing and now, in many areas, nonexistent coverage of psychoanalysis in psychology textbooks at every level and in every area. The reasons that academic psychologists and psychiatrists, along with their historians, have generally continued to reject Jung, Freud, and depth psychology is clear: psychoanalysis is not considered a science, whereas it remains of the utmost importance for psychology to define itself as a Science, Technology, Mathematics, and Engineering (STEM) discipline. In part an accurate reflection and in part an aspiration, psychology has defined itself as an *experimental science* based on the nineteenth-century model of Newtonian mechanics, an epistemology of positivistic reductionism that utilizes and considers the experimental research method to be the gold standard. This representation is at variance with the fundamental nature of psychology as a science in the views shared by Jung and Freud.

Jung's Warning to Freud:
Strong Critique and Original Divergence in Theory

In fall 1912, Jung openly informed Freud of the critical and original nature of his American lectures. Upon his return from Fordham, Jung wrote to Freud that he

> gave nine lectures at the Jesuit (!) university of Fordham in New York—a critical account of the development of the theory of psychoanalysis ... Naturally I made room for those of my views which deviate in places from the hitherto existing conceptions, particularly in regard to the libido theory.[3]

Jung's critiques and original views were no less than a rejection of Freud's concept of infantile sexuality, a dismissal of the sexual nature of the libido, a challenge to Freud's emphasis on the past in the etiology of neurosis and in mental life generally, and an introduction of collective mentality and spirituality as fundamental in mental life. In contrast to Freud, Jung asserted that sexuality does not appear in the developing child until what Freud called *latency*, where Jung claimed it emerges rather than goes underground as Freud supposed. Perhaps even more significant, Jung overthrew Freud's determinism and asserted the importance of the present and of teleology of mental life. Here we already find a bold expression, indeed a *tour de force*, of all the objections to Freud's theory for which Jung was to become so distinguished. One might be hard-pressed to identify more central tenets of Freudian theory than those Jung attacks in the Fordham lectures. Regarding his suggestion that sexual libido be considered pure desire/energy, Jung writes, "Give the concept of libido breathing space—remove it from the narrow confines of a sexual definition."[4] Further, Jung suggests that even regression serves a teleological function, which he does not hesitate to associate with human spirituality:

> It would, in general, be a great mistake to deny any teleological function to the apparently pathological fantasies of a neurotic. They are, as a matter of fact, the first beginnings of spiritualization, the first groping attempts to find new ways of adapting. His retreat to the infantile level does not mean only regression and stagnation, but also the possibility of discovering a new life plan. Regression is thus in very truth the basic condition for the act of creation.[5]

In these lectures, Jung emphasizes the prospective function of dreams. Such theoretical critiques and advances correspond to divergences from Freud in the arena of psychotherapeutic practice as well. Jung suggests movement from the mere interpretation of dreams to the facilitation of the patient's active use of dreams, viewed as a gateway to fuller participation in the world of fantasy and as a means of energizing forward movement in what Freud viewed as regressive.

Tension and Break between Jung and Freud

In early winter 1912, the communication between Jung and Freud broke down, and on January 3, 1913, Freud wrote Jung about ending their personal relationship. This correspondence provides a basis for the title, *Jung contra Freud*, along with the possibility that the Fordham lectures played a crucial role in the break between the two men. In summer 1913, Jung sent Freud a copy of the Fordham lectures, and Freud's trepidation is understandable given Jung's warning about his criticism of Freud's theories and unveiling of divergent views. Freud, however, wrote Ferenczi, "I have now read Jung's paper myself and find it good and innocuous beyond my expectation."[6] Although Freud disagreed with Jung and alluded to Jung's "mistakes" and even "stupidity," he considered even the most oppositional statements "congruent with psychoanalysis" and "the contradictions entirely on psychoanalysis's ground … much … even excellent. As a whole, I have very much overestimated the danger from a distance."[7]

How are we to understand Freud's response? How could Freud have at once disagreed with and still praised Jung, acknowledged contradictions and yet concluded a fundamental congruence? In his introduction to the Fordham lectures, Sonu Shamdasani offers clue from the pen of Jung in 1907:

> (H)ow much I have to thank the ingenious conceptions of Freud. … Freud could be refuted only by one who had applied the psychoanalytic method many times and who really investigates *as Freud investigates* … [unlike] those men of science who distained to look through Galileo's telescope.[8]

In other words, Jung held that he was following Freud even in his very criticism of Freudian theory!

Shared Epistemic Principles, Practices, and Values

In the foreword to the first edition of the lectures, Jung calls the work an attempt to "outline my attitude to the guiding principles which my honored teacher Sigmund Freud evolved from experience of many decades."[9] Jung maintains a positive attitude toward Freud's principles, which demand careful modifications of theory based on observation. "It has been wrongly suggested that my attitude signifies a 'split' in the psychoanalytic movement," he says. "Such schisms can only exist in matters of faith. But psychoanalysis is concerned with knowledge and its ever changing formulations."[10] Shamdasani rightly concludes that

> it would be a mistake to consider Jung's theoretical differences with Freud as leading to his break ... [R]ather, the collapse of their personal relationship and the political alliance they had formed led to a situation where, in the public domain, theoretical differences were presented as rationalized justifications.[11]

Even in 1955, Jung wrote in the foreword to the second edition,

> It is a milestone on the long road of scientific endeavor ... the constantly changing stages of the search in a newly discovered territory, whose boundaries are not marked out with any certainty even today ... [making it a] contribution to the story of an evolving science.[12]

Jung's central emphasis on psychoanalysis *as a science* is striking and begs for clarification.

For Jung, following Freud's lead, psychoanalysis is first and foremost based on experiences and observations of a very special sort—those made by practicing psychoanalysts. Jung remarked on the "vast distance" Freud had already traveled from contemporary psychology and how he had abstained from any criticism of Freud, avoiding the common pitfall of "unscientific chatter" that lacks "a proper knowledge of the facts."[13]

> [M]y criticism does not proceed from academic arguments but from experiences which have forced themselves on me during ten years of serious work in this field. I know that my own experience in no wise approaches Freud's quite extraordinary experience and insight, but nevertheless it does seem to me that

certain of my formulations do express the observed facts more suitably than Freud's version of them. ... I am far indeed from regarding a modest and temperate criticism as a "falling away" or a schism; on the contrary, I hope to thereby promote the continued flowering and fructification of the psychoanalytic movement and to open the way to the treasures of psychoanalytic knowledge for those who, lacking the experience or handicapped by certain theoretical preconceptions, have so far been unable to master the method.[14]

The problem Jung highlights repeatedly in the lectures is not between Freud and himself but between those within the psychoanalytic movement and those outside who fail to understand its scientific character.

Jung makes clear that psychoanalysis, as Freud practiced it and as he himself viewed it, is not a body of dogma but an ever-changing, complex set of formulations based on continuing observations. Jung draws from William James the notion that ideas are not solutions to problems but programs for further work, pragmatic tools for viewing and shaping reality. Theories are criticized and changed in accordance with factual observations. "Scientific theories are merely suggestions as to how things might be observed," and, therefore, psychoanalytic theory must be considered tentative and temporary, less important than the method that transforms it.[15] "Freud is anything other than a theorist," says Jung. "He is an empiricist, as anyone must admit who is willing to go at all deeply into Freud's writings and to try to see his cases as he sees them."[16] It cannot be overemphasized that for Jung, like Freud, the *cornerstone of psychoanalysis is observation*. Jung impels us to learn from "the nature of Freud's method" and avoid "the absurd conclusion that he is a theorist. ... Psychoanalysis is essentially empirical."[17] That method underlying psychoanalysis is not the postulation of brittle concepts; it is a unique scientific movement.

Jung's view of Freud is consistent with Freud's self-understanding, which emphasized the disposable and changing nature of theory subordinated to observation in the progress of science. Freud said of psychoanalytic theory, "For these ideas are not the foundation of science, upon which everything else rests: That foundation is observation alone. They are not the bottom but the top of the whole structure, and they can be replaced or discarded without damaging it."[18] For

Freud, neither specific theories nor therapy are to be considered the basic core or the most important contribution of psychoanalysis. That designation belongs to *the research method*. Jung's statement in the Fordham lectures that "the psychoanalytic method of investigation was and still is unknown" is true even today.[19] In 1926, Freud claimed that the future would show that psychoanalysis is most valuable as an instrument of research, and before his death, he acknowledged that the psychoanalyst's research practices, especially how observations are *worked over*, remained unaddressed.[20],[21] Even to this day, by far the most attention outside and inside psychoanalysis has been devoted to theories and therapy. What is this research method that takes priority over discrepant and changing theories and therapies and is instead their basis and, indeed, the scientific heart of the entire enterprise?

The Confluence of Divergences

Jung and Freud can be read for their revelatory statements concerning this research method, the character and status of theory, the relationship between theory and research, and even the nature of psychology and science itself. Here one finds whole-hearted, complete, and continuous agreement that is helpful in understanding the common ground of divergent theoretical developments. Diverse psychoanalysts are consistent with the perennial, general principles of science and contribute originally to psychological science in ways that are yet to be widely acknowledged.[22]

Attitude

This research method, the foundational scientificity of psychoanalysis, starts with a basic attitude of openness—the antithesis of a dogmatic stance. Psychoanalysis is profoundly and above all observational and aims at knowledge that is free from all prejudice. At the outset of this new science, Freud contrasted psychoanalysis with any form of knowledge that involves an imposition of previous ideas. This principle is reflected in clinical practice, which excludes suggestion, thereby enabling psychotherapy to be a prime laboratory for unbiased observations. Jung concurred that the practice of psychoanalysis involves the shedding of prejudices.[23] He too viewed clinical practice as intimately tied to science: "to give advise about dreams and to make direct attempts at interpretation is, in my opinion, absolutely wrong and scientifically inadmissible."[24] Psychoanalysts also set aside value judgments. While Freud emphasized the analyst's abstention from condemnation of anything in the psychological life of the analysand, Jung said of the analyst's emotionality, "[H]e must not shudder at dirty work."[25] The psychoanalytic stance is nonjudgmental, compassionate, and understanding, based on an engaged relationship of trust, humility, and an epistemic abstinence from any final certainty. In this form of engagement, the personal empathy of the analyst is crucial.[26] This attitude places priority on seeing (observing) over knowing, acting, and evaluating. Fresh discovery leads to understanding in a process that is openly acknowledged as corrigible, iterative, self-critical, self-correcting, and never-ending. As Jung says, "It is not our endeavor to put forward a paradoxical theory contradicting all previous theories but rather to introduce a new category of observations into science."[27]

Data

What are the new data that psychoanalysis introduced into science—this "firm empirical ground" upon which the entire enterprise rests?[28] Jung, still following Freud, notes that *special procedures* are needed to bring mental processes to consciousness.[29] No doubt he has in mind the extensive observations of human mental life he had enacted over the prior ten years that Freud had begun in a practical, therapeutic context, with all its unusual characteristics.[30] Freud saw each of his patients for an hour, six days a week, and gave them only one instruction—the fundamental rule of psychoanalysis: they must describe, as if observing the landscape out a train window, every momentary experience that occurred to them, no matter how seemingly irrelevant or shameful.[31] Freud's practice of *free association* and Jung's extension of amplification and active imagination (e.g., of dreams, as introduced in the Fordham lectures) are special data collection procedures that lead patients to extend their observations of mental life beyond what is initially reported. "It is only during psychoanalytic treatment that most patients learn to retain and observe (their) fugitive thoughts," Jung says.[32] In psychoanalysis, changing verbal reports are critically viewed; their veridicality and value are continually reassessed.

As the science emerged in this unique laboratory of continuous, uninhibited, and expansive self-disclosure, three intertwined sources of data evolved centrally: 1) prolonged, meticulous, and collaborative attention to others' psychological lives from first person report and dialogue (as a basis of other analysis); 2) a thoroughgoing, concrete, detailed, attentive exploration and gathering of the investigator's own experience of the patients and themselves (in part as a basis of self-analysis); and 3) a far-reaching focus on such individually and culturally expressive media as action, art, literature, history, religions, folklore, and language (as a basis of collective, cultural analysis supplementing individual analyses). Psychoanalytic observations came to span virtually every available form of human expression, rooted in an extended, intimate encounter with living human beings instructed to reveal their lives without any practical or moral limits. Jung expresses the unusual nature of this concrete exploration when he describes the transformation that takes place in therapy. Notably, although there is reference to changing mental life in his description, the precise nature of this change is the revelation of its innermost truth, which is therefore profoundly consistent with the enterprise of science:

> What psychoanalysis asks of the patient is the exact opposite of what the patient has always done. He is like a man who has unintentionally fallen into the water and sunk, whereas psychoanalysis wants him to act like a diver. It was no mere chance which led him to fall in just at that spot. There lies the sunken treasure, but only a diver can bring it to the surface.[33]

In Jung's characterization of the aim and outcome of psychoanalytic treatment, one can see a unique method of deepening exploration based in true knowledge of the analysand's life.

> Psychoanalysis stands outside traditional morality; for the present it should adhere to no general moral standard. It is and should be, only a means for giving the individual trends breathing-space, for developing them and bringing them into harmony with the rest of the personality. ... The best result for a person who undergoes an analysis is that he shall become in the end what he really is, in harmony with himself, neither good nor bad, just as he is in his natural state.[34]

> If this work is successful, the patient passes out of the treatment and out of the semi-infantile transference relationship into a life which has been carefully prepared within him, which he has chosen himself, and to which, after mature deliberation, he can declare himself committed.[35]

An error in patients' views of their ailments was naively adopted in early trauma theory, but Jung notes that the falsity was revealed by the psychoanalytic method of observation, and the theory was corrected accordingly.

> Besides the deeper insight into psychological determination, we owe to this "error" a method of inquiry of incalculable importance. It is for us to rejoice and be thankful that Freud had the courage to let himself be guided along this path. Not thus is the progress of science hindered, but rather by blind adherence to insights once gained, by the typical conservatism of authority, by the childish vanity of the savant and his fear of making mistakes.[36]

One of the great discoveries of psychoanalysis was to establish, apart from the actual environment, the importance of fantasy, which is itself part of the reality of mental life as observed and truly known. In the Fordham lectures, Jung repeatedly focuses on the special and extensive introduction of fantasy data within the full spectrum of psychological processes. He speaks about the parental *imagos*:

> Among the things that were of the utmost significance at the infantile period, the most influential are the personalities of the parents. Even when the parents have long been dead and have lost or should have lost all significance, the situation of the patient having perhaps completely changed since then, they are still somehow present and as important as if they were still alive. The patient's love, admiration, resistance, hatred, and rebelliousness still cling to their effigies, transfigured by affection or distorted by envy, and often bearing little resemblance to the erstwhile reality. It was this fact that compelled me to speak no longer of "father" and "mother" but to employ instead the term "imago." … The complex of the parental imagos, that is, the whole tissue of ideas relating to the parents, provides an important field of activity for the introverted libido.[37]

Empirical Analysis

Psychoanalytic method works over the data in an attempt to form concepts that describe psychological processes (expository) and interpret their meaning (explicative, hermeneutic) within far-reaching individual, historical, interpersonal/social, and cultural contexts. The analysis is meticulous, attending to every detail of the data, and comparative in that multiple observations of the same and different individuals are examined for similarities and differences of form, content, and motivation. With special attention to the relationship of particular moments to each other and to the whole of mental life, emphasizing recurrent themes, such comparisons yield commonalities and thereby generalizations in the analyst's search for principles and categories that can be observed in and across the lives of many individuals.[38]

The process involves rigorous absorption in concrete details and far-reaching comparative analysis.

> The principle of psychoanalytic elucidation is extraordinarily simple ... [We become] really absorbed in a dream ... and related reminiscences. ... We treat this material in accordance with a generally accepted scientific principle. If you have any experimental material to work up, you compare its individual parts and classify them according to their similarities. You proceed in exactly the same way with dream material. You look for common features, whether in form or content. In doing this one has to get rid of prejudices. I have observed that the beginner is always looking for some special feature and then tries to force his material to conform to his expectations ... to do violence to the material by their own preconceived opinions. Voluminous material must be compared—laborious.[39]

Analysis of a dreamer's entire life is necessary, and mistakes can creep in. Jung views the process as analogous to the historian's investigation of baptism, which extends its comparative examination to the rich world of myths.[40] Concrete data also compel psychoanalytic scientists to examine the realm of symbols whose origin, meaning, and purpose are obscure and cannot be grasped directly, as in the case of baptism in history and mythology.[41] One can easily observe the similarity between a patient's fantasies and mythological ideas, necessitating an acquaintance with mythology "that lies outside the ken of the medical man."[42]

> The analyst proceeds in the same way with a dream. He collects the historical parallels to every part of the dream, even the remotest, and tries to reconstruct the psychological history of the dream and its underlying meanings. Through this monographic elaboration we obtain, just as in the analysis of baptism, a profound insight into the marvelously delicate and meaningful network of unconscious determination—an insight that may legitimately be compared with the historical understanding of an act, which we had hitherto regarded in a very superficial and one-sided way.[43]

In the parallels between the patient's experience and mythology, Jung makes the observation that the "individual mind gradually develops out of the 'collective mind' of early childhood, thus giving rise to the old theory of a state of perfect knowledge before and after individual existence."[44] These mythological references found in children are also present in schizophrenia and in dreams, offering "a broad and fertile field of work for comparative psychological research."[45]

The broad reach of data gathering and the diverse kinds of data demanded by psychology, ranging through the spectrum of individual to cultural expressions, make psychoanalysis difficult for other scientists to understand as a science even though the comparative practices of rationality are shared with the other sciences. Jung agreed with Freud, who maintained throughout his career that the data of psychoanalysis would be unfamiliar and pose difficulties especially for those trained in the physical sciences and medical practice because of the particular requirements of method. Much misunderstanding and distortion comes from "training in natural science. It is difficult for medical men to get an intellectual grasp of the very subtle psychological method. ... The method I have described is the one that I adopt and the one to which I hold myself scientifically responsible."[46]

Conceptual Knowledge and Theory

As in all science, the theoretical postulations of psychoanalysis are bidirectional. On the one hand they are emergent, arising from contact with and comparative analysis of empirical observations, and on the other hand they are self-consciously creative, reflecting the investigator's stock of knowledge and imagination, which offers partly descriptive and partly speculative conceptual models that arise from the investigator's thinking and imagery as well as from sources as diverse as the physical sciences, art and literature, and religion. At all levels of conceptualization from the individual case study to the most general theory, there is an emphasis on parsimony—an effort to subsume large amounts of data from diverse sources under ideas that are elegant and relatively simple. This bidirectionality requires a balanced conceptual succinctness with the complexity and concrete details of the psychological subject matter. Analogies, metaphors, and imaginative constructions are adopted and adapted to retain a structurally revelatory and thereby descriptive relation to the subject matter, which exercises strict constraints on the building, evaluating, and modifying models that are better understood as evocative points of view than as mirrors of reality.

Psychoanalytic theory remains subordinate to empirically gathered observational data and analysis. Jung writes, "The decision as to what is the truth must be left to observation and research."[47] Abundant case material provides an evidentiary ground for validity.[48] In his essay "Analysis Terminable and Interminable," Freud calls metapsychological speculation and theory a "witch" and admits that he "almost said 'phantasizing.'" Well known is his statement in "New Introductory Lectures on Psychoanalysis": "The theory of instincts is so to say our mythology. Instincts are mythical entities magnificent in their indefiniteness."[49] Jung acknowledges that psychoanalytic concepts are "analogies" and insists that the question of whether they are suitable can be opened up at any time.[50] Psychoanalysis is about "freeing oneself from dogma" by means of "the abundant, perhaps all too abundant case material in the literature [that] offers enough and more than enough grounds [for changing theory]."[51]

> For us the unconscious is not an entity in this sense but a mere term, about whose metaphysical essence we do not permit ourselves to form any idea. ... In this we are unlike those arm-chair psychologists who are not only perfectly informed about the localization of the psyche in the brain and physiological correlates of mental processes, but can assert positively that beyond consciousness there are nothing but "physiological processes in the cortex."[52]

For Jung, it is important not to understand theoretical terms as literally depicting reality but to admit their relatively vague and changing character as part of a larger method that privileges observation.

Theory and Research

In psychoanalytic method, the relationship between the fresh collection of data and theory is a dialectical one. Careful attention to concrete observables is the cornerstone of progress as a fresh ground of ideation and as a court of appeal for truth and falsity of theories that can never be considered final or even completely clarified. As Jung emphasizes, concepts and theory generally are to be viewed pragmatically as valuable *heuristic principles* and tools, dialectically related to observations and the analytic procedures that work them over.[53] Jung calls the concept of *libido* "an extremely valuable heuristic principle" and feels free to rethink Freud's sexual definition in light of the infant's nutritive striving as he reconceives of the libido more generally as *energy*.[54] Indeed, as Freud emphasized in the *Interpretation of Dreams* that his notion of "the psychical apparatus" is "scaffolding" that should not be mistaken for the building, Jung viewed conceptual postulations not as literal representations of the psyche but as ways of summoning observations that inevitably outstrip and exceed them in the movement of science.[55] Theorizing and analysis function in mutually informative cycles wherein concepts are rigorously critiqued, qualified, and reformulated in the encounter with freshly collected data that theories bring into view. Theories are guides to, not replicas of, reality.

Science, therefore, includes room for more than one theory and for preferences among them—various positions being justified by reasoning with observational support and consistent critique by the larger scientific community that employs this method, as exemplified by Jung's critique of Freud that Freud found entirely consistent with the foundational practices of his own science. "I have endeavored to propound certain views which deviate from the hypotheses of Freud," said Jung, "not as contrary assertions but as illustrations of the organic development of the basic ideas Freud has introduced into science."[56] He continued by explaining that science is the

> slow progress of average experience by which ideas are evaluated. I hope my critics will not again accuse me of having contrived

> my hypotheses out of thin air. I would never venture to override the existing ones had not hundreds of experiences shown me that my views fully stand the test in practice.[57]

Complexity, Paradox, and Change in Psychoanalytic Theory

The central thrust of the Fordham lectures is to "make our peace with men of science. This will be my endeavor in attempting to sketch the further conceptual development of psychoanalysis."[58] In doing so, Jung portrays a subtle way in which relative truths are both confirmed and yet surpassed in the progress of science.

> Were Freud's observations true or not? That alone could be of importance to a truly scientific mind. I daresay his observations may seem improbable at first sight, but it is impossible to condemn them a priori as false. Whenever a really honest and thorough check has been carried out, the existence of the psychological connections established by Freud has been absolutely confirmed.[59]

Jung, however, demonstrates in these lectures numerous ways in which, starting with Freud himself, scientific concepts have proven only relatively true and were discarded or transformed on the basis of searching and thorough observations of real people's lives, and he provides additional case examples of this process in his own work. "The decision as to what is the truth must be left solely to observation and research."[60] For instance, Jung traces the movement from a neurological theory of neurosis to a literal theory postulating actual trauma to the breakthrough understanding of the role of fantasy and then the importance of intrapsychic conflict. Jung similarly offers insight into the changing concepts of psychological constitution and predisposition, which moved beyond initially rigid, physicalistic notions in the etiology of neurosis and became increasingly integrated with observations of experiential factors in a mutative process that Freud was to view as a "complemental series."[61] At each moment of these conceptual advances, prior notions were not simply discarded but were placed in a larger context and thereby modified. Jung demonstrates such conceptual advances with a case example, in which he beautifully details the patient's situation and adds understanding to it throughout the lectures—escorting his listeners from the old trauma-theory to a new, energetic standpoint. He presents this case in its natural setting and highlights how differently it "develops from what might have been expected on purely theoretical grounds."[62] Similarly, Jung shows, with observations, how obtaining pleasure is by no means exhausted in sexuality as it involves nutrition and how the present as well as the past has etiological significance for neurosis.[63]

As a defender of Freud, Jung insists that many criticisms are not of Freud's actual views, which are complex, ambiguous, musing, and suggestive of many directions, but of rigid hypostatizations that are incorrectly attributed to Freud. In contrast to common misunderstandings, Jung asserts that Freud's formulations are always multivalent, searching, and provisional. "[I]t would never occur to me to blame Freud personally for the innumerable misunderstandings. I know very well, that Freud, being an empiricist, always publishes only provisional formulations to which he does certainly not attribute any eternal value."[64] Freud's ideas are "fluid and flexible"; Freud's adversaries misunderstand the "vital creativity" of his ideas and "crystalize" certain "average conceptions" in his thought out of the sum total of Freud's more extensive work, "treat (them) far too dogmatically," and end up with "incorrect technical axioms, the existence of which cannot be postulated with any certainty in Freud's own work."[65] At times in these lectures, Jung attributes to Freud ideas that have since been attributed to Jung as supposed corrections of Freud! "If we agree with Freud that neurosis is an unsuccessful attempt at self cure, we must allow the fantasies too, a double character: on one hand a pathological tendency to resist, on the other a helpful and preparatory tendency."[66] Jung asserts that rather than blindly attributing the etiology of neurosis to the past (which Jung knew Freud did not), we must examine the present, when the neurosis arises perhaps in adulthood. The Freud depicted by Jung in these lectures understands the importance of the present and future purpose. Jung views himself as building on Freud's ideas, finding places for predisposition, past trauma, fantasy, conflict, and even future purpose—teleology at all phases.

This progressive process of science can even be seen in Jung's emphasis on spirituality. In the lectures, Jung offers evidence of what he later calls the transcendent function of psychological life as he grasps its inclusion not only of the past but also a present movement directed toward the future. In observing and conceptualizing the universal teleological character of psychological processes even in the apparently pathological, regressive fantasies of the neurotic, Jung brings to light not only progressive adaptation but a nascent spiritualization. As we see in the quotation cited on the fifth page of this chapter, Jung sees not ultimate stagnation in the phenomena of regression but a groping adaptation toward a new life plan, a spiritualization that truly is the basis for the act of creation.[67]

In this he is following Freud: "The analyst and observer ... must eschew formulas and let the living reality work upon him in all its lawless profusion."[68] "When will there be an end to the incessant squabbling about who is right? One has only to look at the history of science: How many have *been* right, and how few have *remained* right!"[69] Jung insisted that scientific principles and practices have norms that are ideal and are not always achieved. Jung hoped his audience "gained rather more confidence in the scientific character" of psychoanalysis despite deficiencies of particular instances.[70]

> I felt obliged to give you a very general account of the method and its position within the methodology of science. I do not doubt that there are superficial and improper applications of this method. But an intelligent critic should not allow this to detract from the method itself, any more than a bad surgeon should be used to discredit the value of surgery in general.[71]

Conclusion

The message from Jung in the Fordham lectures is clear: "Psychoanalysis is a general method of psychological research and heuristic principle of the first rank in the domain of the human sciences."[72] Above all else, the Fordham lectures highlight the scientific character of the psychoanalysis shared by Jung and Freud in anticipation of the entire movement of psychoanalysis through the twentieth century and into the current century. The fundamental principles of psychoanalysis are none other than the general principles of science itself—the wedding of rationality and observation, drawing specificity from the nature of observation uniquely demanded by psychological subject matter. Psychoanalysis expands the scientific enterprise by drawing on new forms of data collection and data, and, like the other sciences, it draws upon the full range of creativity of the scientist, whose ideas are never dogmatically held and change within an iterative process of expanding observation and comparative analysis. Many particular psychoanalytic theories have taken form and continue to be modified in this process of evolution, and, therefore, no one is to be identified with psychoanalysis. The Fordham lectures make it clear that there is no one psychoanalytic theory, Freud's or Jung's. Personalities, allegiances, fixed ideas, and theory without fruitful empirical reference have no place in this or in any science. In these lectures, Jung presents a method of investigation developed by Freud, and practiced and extended by himself as any genuine *follower* would use this method. His purpose is not to establish a theory that contradicts previous ones but to generate, criticize, and revise theories in the observational process of science. This method animates the entire psychoanalytic movement and, properly understood, protects it from dogma and dogmatizing. This method is not owned by any psychoanalyst exclusively. After all, Jung asserts, "Anyone who does not agree with us is at liberty to publish his own analysis of cases."[73] New data and analyses are the engine that drives the psychoanalytic movement forward in unity. To repeat the goal of the Fordham lectures, "True, we must give up trying to reach an understanding with those who blindly oppose us, which would be a waste of effort, but we do hope to make our peace with men of science. This will be our endeavor in attempting to sketch the further conceptual development of psychoanalysis."[74]

I would like to thank Margaret Klenck, Mary Beth Morrissey, Lisa Osbeck, and Mary Watkins for their wonderful help.

NOTES

1. In C. G. Jung, *Freud and Psychoanalysis*, vol. 4, *The Collected Works of C. G. Jung*, ed. and trans. Gerhard Adler and R. F. C. Hull (Princeton, NJ: Princeton University Press, 1970), pp. 83–226.

2. G. V. Hartman, "A Time Line of the History and Development of Jung's Works and Theories (1902–1935)," Nov. 26, 2003. Accessed Dec. 1, 2013, at http://www.cgjungpage.org/learn/articles/analytical-psychology/162-a-time-line-of-the-history-and-development-of-jungs-works-and-theories-1902-1935.

3. C. G. Jung, quoted by Sonu Shamdasani in the introduction to *Jung contra Freud: The 1912 New York Lectures on the Theory of Psychoanalysis* (Princeton, NJ: Princeton University Press, 2012), p. xviii.
4. Jung, *Jung contra Freud*, p. 36.
5. *Ibid.*, p. 98.
6. Sigmund Freud, quoted in Shamdasani, *Jung contra Freud*, p. xix.
7. *Ibid.*
8. Jung, quoted in Shamdasani, *Jung contra Freud*, pp. xi–xii.
9. Jung, *Jung contra Freud*, p. 3.
10. *Ibid.*, p. 4.
11. Shamdasani, in *Jung contra Freud*, p. xx.
12. Jung, *Jung contra Freud*, p. 5.
13. *Ibid.*, p. 4.
14. *Ibid.*
15. *Ibid.*, p. 25.
16. *Ibid.*, p. 60.
17. *Ibid.*, pp. 60–61.
18. Sigmund Freud, *On the History of the Psychoanalytic Movement* (1914), in *The Standard Edition of the Complete Psychological Works of Sigmund Freud*, vol. 14 (London: Hogarth Press, 1964), p. 77.
19. Jung, *Jung contra Freud*, p. 19.
20. Sigmund Freud, *The Question of Lay Analysis* (1926) (New York: Norton, 1978), p. 97.
21. Sigmund Freud, *Construction in Psychoanalysis* (1937), in *The Standard Edition of the Complete Psychological Works of Sigmund Freud*, vol. 23 (London: Hogarth Press, 1964), p. 275.
22. F. J. Wertz, "The Phenomenology of Sigmund Freud," *Journal of Phenomenological Psychology* 24 (2, 1993): 101–29; "Cognitive Psychology and the Understanding of Perception," *Journal of Phenomenological Psychology* 18 (2, 1987): 103–42; and "Common Methodological Fundaments of the Analytic Procedures in Phenomenological and Psychoanalytic Research," *Psychoanalysis and Contemporary Thought* 9 (4, 1987): 563–603.
23. Jung, *Jung contra Freud*, p. 63.
24. *Ibid.*, p. 65.

25. Sigmund Freud, *Therapy and Technique* (New York: Collier Books, 1912); Jung, *Jung contra Freud*, p. 105.
26. Jung, *Jung contra Freud*, p. 108.
27. *Ibid.*, p. 19.
28. *Ibid.*, p. 11.
29. *Ibid.*, p. 10.
30. See S. Kvale, "Psychoanalytic Therapy as Qualitative Research," in P. Ashworth, A. Giorgi, and A. De Koning, eds., *Qualitative Research in Psychology* (Pittsburgh, PA: Duquesne University Press, 1986); F. J. Wertz, K. Charmaz, L. McMullen, R. Josselson, R. Anderson, and E. McSpadden, *Five Ways of Doing Qualitative Analysis: Phenomenological Psychology, Grounded Theory, Discourse Analysis, Narrative Research, and Intuitive Inquiry* (New York: Guilford Press, 2011).
31. Freud, *Therapy and Technique*.
32. Jung, *Jung contra Freud*, p. 56.
33. *Ibid.*, p. 104.
34. *Ibid.*, p. 114.
35. *Ibid.*, p. 119.
36. *Ibid.*, p. 50.
37. *Ibid.*, p. 52.
38. *Ibid.*, p. 12.
39. *Ibid.*, pp. 62–63.
40. *Ibid.*, pp. 64–65.
41. *Ibid.*, p. 66.
42. *Ibid.*, p. 57.
43. *Ibid.*, p. 65.
44. *Ibid.*, p. 143.
45. *Ibid.*
46. *Ibid.*, p. 65.
47. *Ibid.*, p. 18.
48. *Ibid.*, p. 59.
49. Sigmund Freud, *New Introductory Lectures on Psychoanalysis* (1932), in *The Standard Edition of the Complete Psychological Works of Sigmund Freud*, vol. 22 (London: Hogarth Press, 1964), p. 95.
50. Jung, *Jung contra Freud*, p. 59.
51. *Ibid.*
52. *Ibid.*
53. *Ibid.*, p. 36.

54. *Ibid.*, p. 37.

55. Sigmund Freud, *The Interpretation of Dreams* (New York: Norton, 1900), p. 536.

56. Jung, *Jung contra Freud*, p. 143.

57. *Ibid.*, pp. 143–44.

58. *Ibid.*, p. 19.

59. *Ibid.*, p. 13.

60. *Ibid.*, p. 18.

61. Sigmund Freud, *Introductory Lectures on Psychoanalysis* (New York: Norton, 1916–1917).

62. Jung, *Jung contra Freud*, p. 122.

63. *Ibid.*, pp. 25, 84.

64. *Ibid.*, p. 85.

65. *Ibid.*

66. *Ibid.*, p. 98.

67. *Ibid.*

68. *Ibid.*, p. 122.

69. *Ibid.*, p. 51.

70. *Ibid.*, p. 69.

71. *Ibid.*, p. 65.

72. *Ibid.*, p. 120.

73. *Ibid.*, p. 20.

74. *Ibid.*, p. 19.

Chapter Two

Energy and Emotion
C. G. Jung's Fordham Declaration

Beverley Zabriskie

Introduction

In September 1912, the thirty-seven-year-old Swiss psychiatrist C. G. Jung presented nine lectures at Fordham University. He spoke of the matters on his mind, the emerging edge of his thoughts, and the on-going evolution of his theory. At Fordham, Jung crossed a theoretical, professional, and emotional threshold, announcing his essential difference from the founder of psychoanalysis, Sigmund Freud. In the course of presenting—and departing from—Freudian theory, Jung re-oriented his relation to the psychoanalytic enterprise and his engagement with the psyche itself. Jung's lectures, published as *The Theory of Psychoanalysis,* were both a declaration of independence after his six-year collaboration with Freud and a self-statement of his personal, clinical, and theoretical individuation.[1] They presented his unfolding understanding of psychic substance, dynamics, and the neutral nature of energy.

Jung was then known internationally as a psychiatrist for his studies of *dementia praecox* under Eugen Bleuler at Zürich's Burgholzli Clinic and for his research on emotionally charged complexes revealed in the word association experiment. He originally contacted Sigmund Freud in 1906 suggesting that his association test results were evidence of the existence of an unconscious. Freud, who had already procured a copy, agreed.

Many Mentors

Jung brought the Zürich school, then a leader in international psychiatry, into contact with Freud's psychoanalytic movement. As a Swiss psychiatrist, Jung came to be perceived as the Austrian neurologist's emissary to the psychiatric world beyond Vienna. By 1910, then thirty-five years old, Jung was appointed the first president of the International Psychoanalytic Association (IPA).

While Jung was viewed as Freud's heir apparent, Jung also counted multiple influences on his practice and theories, including Bleuler, Janet, and Charcot. Jung especially acknowledged that he was "tremendously impressed" by William James' explorations of the margins of psychology, his "bottom-up" primacy of emotion before understanding, and his perception of the complementary relationship between conscious and unconscious. The impact of the Jamesian model is revealed in Jung's privileging of emotion as a primal energetic force, his sense of psyche as an affect regulating system, his view of psyche as a dynamic of complementarities between conscious and unconscious, his emphasis on the complementary relation between psychology and physics, and his notions of analytic process as a field phenomenon. Jung posited that emotions determine our memories, charge our complexes, seek resolution through our dreams images, and create the immediate transferential fields between patient and analyst.

Jung's letters to Freud before his Fordham foray gave several clues about the directions of his thought. In his letter of March 3, 2012, Jung quoted yet another influence, Nietzsche's *Zarathustra*:

> I am ready at any time to adapt my opinions to the judgment of someone who knows better, and always have. I would never have sided with you in the first place had not heresy run in my blood. Since I have no professorial ambitions, I can afford to admit mistakes. Let Zarathustra speak for me:
>
> > *'One repays a teacher badly if one remains only a pupil.*
> > *And why, then, should you not pluck at my laurels?*
> > *You respect me: but how if one day your respect should tumble?*
> > *Take care that a falling statue does not strike you dead!*
> > *You had not yet sought yourselves when you found me.*
> > *Thus do all believers—.*
> > *Now I bid you lose me and find yourselves;*
> > *And only when you have denied me will I turn to you.*[2]

> This is what you have taught me through psychoanalysis. As one who is truly your follower, I must be stout-hearted, not least towards you.[3]

In several of his subsequent letters, one can nearly hear the statues toppling as Jung informs Freud of his evolving theories: the symbolic valence of incest motifs, the complex as the royal road to the immediacy of dreams, and most germane to Fordham, a broader theory of libido.

On March 22, 1912 Jung wrote Freud of his Fordham invitation and his hope that the dates of the IPA Munich Congress, scheduled for the autumn, could be changed. Two days later Freud encouraged Jung's decision to go to New York: "I think your trip provides excellent justification for skipping the Congress: everyone will admit that it serves the interests of psychoanalysis."[4] That July, Ernest Jones suggested, and Freud concurred, that they form a secret Committee, excluding Jung, with the aim of safeguarding Freud's theories.

Jung's writings had been veering toward the symbolic framing and mythic background of psychic imagery. Freud posited sexuality as the prime source of psychic determinants, of psychological history and relations, symptoms and conflicts. In his view, sexual energy was at the core, expressed directly, or indirectly, via the mechanics of suppression, repression, and sublimation.

At Fordham, Jung reveals the degree to which he was formulating a non-qualitative neutral psychic energy experienced through many instincts, appetites, needs, affects, emotions, desires, and conflicts emerging from various states of mind. In his evolving view, affect and emotion provide the basis for excitation for actions and expressive images. This neutral psychic energy can transform—energy can emerge from, manifest in, and mutate into various degrees of energic intensities. These are not disguises of the sexual, nor can they be attributed only to a sexual source.

The Influence of Physics

The newest news in Jung's Fordham lectures, although not then widely remarked, was the impact of contemporary physics on Jung's view of psychic energy. In January 1911, Jung had written to Freud of a dinner to which he had invited Bleuler: "we spent the whole evening talking with a physicist about … the electrical theory of light."[5] In later letters, Jung recounted having met this physicist, Albert Einstein, in the "very early days when he was developing his first theory of relativity ... his genius as a thinker ... exerted a lasting influence on my own intellectual work."[6]

In *The Origins of Consciousness in the Breakdown of the Bi-Cameral Mind,* Julian Jaynes argues that each epoch describes consciousness in the metaphors of its contemporary science.[7] In his Fordham discussion of psychic energy, Jung adopted the physics terminology of his era to psychological phenomena. Einstein measured light as a quantum. Jung ponders on "when one sees that a quantum of energy has disappeared, where this energy has re-emerged in the meantime."[8] Just as the theory of the conservation of energy deprived the various forces of their elementary character and made them manifestations of a single energy, so the theory of libido deprives the sexual components of their elementary significance as psychic *faculties* and gives them merely phenomenological value.[9]

For Jung, libido "is capable of the most varied application. ... This conceptual development is of greatest importance; it accomplishes for psychology the same advance that the concept of energy introduced into physics."[10] Jung later compared his offering of models of the psyche as similar to Niels Bohr's approach to the models of physics. Most central to his later explorations, his dialogue with the physicist Wolfgang Pauli resulted in their theory of synchronicity.

Transference as Teleology

Jung's move to expand the arena of psychic energy beyond Freud's sexual libido in clinical practice is most obvious when he described transference as teleological as well as historical, and hence potentially progressive more than regressive and oedipal. Whether because Fordham was a Roman Catholic setting, and/or because he felt himself a psychoanalytic heretic, Jung evoked quasi-religious terms as he articulated two stages in an analytic relationship. In the first stage of confession, "through the transference of his secret and all the unconscious fantasies underlying it, a moral bond is formed between the patient and his father confessor. We call this 'a transference relationship.'"[11] In the second stage, the analyst "must analyze the transference, a task left untouched by the priest"; due to the analyst's forbearance, the patient no longer hesitates to set the analyst among his family gods, i.e., to assimilate him to the infantile milieu. At the same time, the patient satisfies another need, that is, he achieves a relationship outside the family and thus fulfills a biological demand.[12]

In this context, psychoanalysis is "a biological method, whose aim is to combine the highest subjective well-being with the most valuable biological performance."[13] If we "purge" the patient's "social overtures" of "regressive components, their infantile sexualism," then "the transference becomes a most convenient instrument of adaptation."[14]

Jung termed the classical psychoanalytic transference "merely as a falsification, a sexualized caricature of the social bond which holds human society together and which also produces close ties between people of like mind."[15] He was en route to the notion of transference as stimulation toward growth. On this continuum, incest and regression are understood as a turning inward, rather than backwards, for the sake of going forward.

Jung also addressed counter-transference, possibly alluding not only to his practice but also to his tensions with Freud: "The only danger … is that the unacknowledged infantile demands of the analyst may identify themselves with the parallel demands of the patient."[16] Jung then recommends that an analyst must be analyzed. "The analyst can avoid this only by submitting to a rigorous analysis at the hands of another" so that he might "give up all isolationist tactics and autoerotic mystification if he wants to help his patients to become socially mature and independent personalities."[17] Through the analysis, the "tie to the analyst is cut, and the patient is set upon his own feet."[18]

The Cutting of Ties

Jung was indeed cutting his ties, both to Freud and his immediate circle in the psychoanalytic movement. On his return to Switzerland after delivering the Fordham lectures, Jung wrote to Freud that he had given nine English lectures to ninety eminent psychiatrists and neurologists, plus two-hour seminars each day for two weeks to eight professors. He offered to send Freud a copy, "in the hope that you will gradually come to accept certain innovations already hinted at in my libido paper."[19] Jung continues: "Naturally I also made room for those of my views which deviate in places from the hitherto existing conceptions, particularly in regard to the libido theory."[20] There was, however, no room within the IPA for this wider definition.

After Fordham, Jung continued to move toward a notion of the psyche as an emergent process, a linked body/mind subjective operation, and a personal equation within the collective. His 1912 statements forecast two significant 1935 lectures, one at London's Tavistock Clinic "On the Theory and Practice of Analytical Psychology"[21] and his 1935 address at Harvard, "The Psychological Factors Determining Human Behavior."[22]

At Tavistock nearly twenty-five years after Fordham, Jung framed themes relevant to current emotions research: a monistic view of the mind-body continuum, the interactivity of emotional states, and the tendency to express emotions in images and imagistic language. Jung's amplifications reveal his interest in symbolic expressions of states of mind. This curiosity was leading him into research of alchemical metaphors of the mind-matter interactions and convergences. He approached alchemical terminology to describe both material transmutations and intrapsychic transformations as precursors to what came to be called dual-function metaphors, by which human beings express their emotions in the sensate terminology of physics. At Tavistock (with Bion in the audience) Jung spoke of emotions as "not detachable like ideas or thoughts, because they are identical with certain physical conditions and are thus deeply rooted in the heavy matter of the body."[23] He noted that a strong value becomes an emotion "when it reaches such an intensity as to cause a physiological innervation."[24] Referring to the word association protocols, he remarked that "we have a pretty sensitive method by which to measure emotions, or the physiological part of them, and that is the psycho-galvanic effect. It is based on the fact that the electrical resistance of the skin decreases under the influence emotion."[25]

Anticipating modern views of inter-subjectivity and relational enactments, Jung noted that the "emotion of the projected contents always form a link, a sort of dynamic relationship between the subject and the object—and that is the transference."[26] Indeed, it is the doctor's "duty to accept the emotions of the patient and to mirror them."[27]

Embellishing his focus on emotional fields of analytic process, Jung declared that the psychotherapist may become "psychically infected and poisoned by the projections … it may even disturb his sympathetic system as the peculiar emotional condition of the patient does have a contagious effect ... (and) arouses similar vibrations in the nervous system of the analyst."[28] He reminded his professional audience that a patient's "emotions are most contagious. ... By sympathy your sympathetic system gets disturbed, and you will show the same signs after a while."[29]

When he spoke at Harvard, Jung had moved beyond any qualitative prescriptions: "we are dealing primarily with energy, with measures of intensity ... qualitative questions as to the nature of the libido—whether it be sexuality, power, hunger, or something else—recede into the background."[30] With this notion, different intensities of energy can move from one form of expression to another.

Jungian psychology, as an affective, therapeutic opus, is convergent with current research on emotion as the dynamic aspect between body and mind, between and among persons. In *The Mind Brain Reality*, Regina Pally writes,

> While most of psychoanalytic literature has focused on the unconscious symbolic meaning of non-verbal communication, neuroscience emphasizes the unconscious influence that one person's non-verbal communication has on another's biology, emotion, and verbal conversation ... {and} reveal[s] that non-verbal communication of emotion, as is well illustrated by attachment, regulates minds and bodies between individuals ... carr[ies] information about bio-emotional states between individuals, thus regulating the biological functioning of both people.[31]

Psychic Energy and Emotion

After centuries of Cartesian dualism and dismissal, emotion is again a focus in our psychodynamic and developmental schools, philosophies, and neurosciences. Research is confirming and amplifying the Jamesian/Jungian understanding of the physiological basis of emotions as ever-present sources of interactive communication and of those mutual registries that are experienced as synchronistic. Discovery of the human mirror neuron systems and neural coupling adds to our understanding of the sources of how we feel, experience, and interact. The definitions of psychic energy, kinship libido, the symbolic dynamics of incest themes, and the transferential field remained a constant focus and pre-occupation for Jung. He continued to link energic states to emotions and images.

For Jung, emotions are also the link, the rainbow arc between what he termed the infrared of instinct, on one hand, and the ultraviolet of images on the other. The need to express and share experience with others propels action, images, myths and narratives, and dreams. Emotional states and processes thus can be vectors toward imagination if emotion is channeled into imagery rather than discharged, into communication rather than physical reaction.

Jung also addressed the question of kinship emotion as the impelling force in the transference and in shaping the personality in relation to the world. In his 1945 essay, *The Psychology of the Transference,* transference phenomena are a context for the individual to negotiate interpersonal relations, intrapsychic patterns, as well as the greater surround and domain of the collective. Not just reductive and personalistic, considered and resolved transference relationships are

> without doubt one of the most important syndromes in the process of individuation. … By virtue of its collective contents and symbols it transcends the individual personality and extends into the social sphere … back … to the original and primitive order of primitive society and forward … to an inner order of the psyche.[32]

The neuroscientist Gerald Edelman expresses a similar view:

> We cannot individuate concepts and beliefs without reference to the environment. The brain and the nervous system cannot be considered in isolation from states of the world and social interactions. But such states, both environmental and social, are indeterminate and open-ended.[33]

In his late life biographical interviews, *Memories, Dreams, Reflections*, Jung looked back on the Fordham era, reflecting on his theoretical connections and divergences from Freud.

> In retrospect I can say that I alone logically pursued the two problems which most interested Freud: the problem of "archaic vestiges" and that of sexuality. It is a widespread error to imagine

> that I do not see the value of sexuality … it plays a large part in my psychology as an essential—though not the sole—expression of psychic wholeness.³⁴

Yet here again, we see a marked distance in perspective:

> I wished to investigate, over and above its personal significance and biological function, its spiritual aspect and its numinous meaning, and thus to explain what Freud was so fascinated by but was unable to grasp.³⁵

One can only imagine Freud's response to Jung's further remarks:

> Sexuality is of the greatest importance as the expression of the chthonic spirit. That spirit is the other face of God, the dark side of the God-image. The question of the chthonic spirit has occupied me. … Basically, this interest was awakened by the early conversation with Freud, when, mystified, I felt how deeply stirred he was by the phenomenon of sexuality.³⁶

Jung continuously expanded his sense of the matter-mind aspects of psychic energy that he signaled at Fordham, as

> a more or less quantitative concept, which therefore should not be defined in qualitative terms … to escape from the then prevailing concretism of the libido theory … in other words, I wished no longer to speak of the instincts of hunger, aggression, and sex, but to regard all these phenomena as expressions of psychic energy.³⁷

Jung's later formulations of psychic energy revealed the effects of contact with Einstein and the quantum physicist Wolfgang Pauli.

> In physics, too, we speak of energy and its various manifestations, such as electricity, light, heat, etc. Just as it would not occur to the modern physicist to derive all forces from, shall we say, heat alone, so the psychologist should beware of lumping all instincts under the concept of sexuality.³⁸

Psyche is an interactive process, intensities capable of transiting from a range of sources toward a variety of goals, the human psyche, emerging from a mind-body continuum, is thus capable of being *trans-formed*. Primal energy can emerge or be changed into various forms (sexual, creative, reflective, religious, etc.) rather than solely as sublimated expressions of sexuality and sexual libido. This formulation about the sources and vectors of psychic energy is essential to the Jungian template of the human psyche, its reality and its potential process.

And what of Albert Einstein? Was there a reciprocal effect between the psychiatrist and physicist? Perhaps so, as years after his evenings with Jung, Einstein wrote that imagination and emotion were essential to his theories:

> words or the language, as they are written or spoken, do not seem to play any role in my mechanism of thought. The psychical entities which seem to serve as elements in thought are certain signs and more or less clear images which can be 'voluntarily' reproduced and combined.[39]

Einstein described his scientific images as originally of the "visual and ... muscular type," admitting that

> the desire to arrive finally at logically connected concepts is the emotional basis of this rather vague play ... before there is any connection with logical construction in words or other kinds of signs which can be communicated to others.[40]

Concluding Thoughts

With his statements at Fordham, Jung moved further toward the exit from psychoanalysis' inner circle. His sense of the progressive nature of psyche, the prospective function of transference, and the neutral nature of psychic energy became tenets of his analytical psychology. His view of the symbolic aspect of incest motifs, of dream images as transparent rather than latent, and his contextualization of the personal psyche within the archetypal dimension of the collective unconscious gave a different cast to his psychology.

> The dream is a little hidden door in the innermost and most secret recesses of the psyche, opening into that cosmic night which was psyche long before there was any ego-consciousness, and which will remain psyche no matter how far our ego-consciousness may extend. ... All consciousness separates; but in dreams we put on the likeness of that more universal, truer, more eternal man dwelling in the darkness of primordial night. There he is still the

> whole, and the whole is in him, indistinguishable from nature and bare of all egohood. Out of these all uniting depths arises the dream, be it ever so childish, grotesque, and immoral.[41]

At the end of his life, Jung still acknowledged the contributions of Freud to depth psychology, recognized that the sexual was integral in psychic dynamics, and also insisted that their base was not only sexual. Hence, the myriad forms of human expression could not be seen as sublimations of the sexual, nor were dreams viewed as only repressed anxieties and wishes but rather as attempts at emotional resolution.

With his later notion of synchronicity, Jung placed the psyche in the world and the world in psyche on a mind-matter continuum. Today, this approach is termed dual-aspect monism. Years later, Jung offered this radical view of psyche's substance:

> The deeper layers of the psyche lose their individual uniqueness as they retreat farther and farther into darkness. Lower down, that is to say as they approach the autonomous functional systems, they become increasingly collective until they are universalized and extinguished in the body's materiality, i.e., in chemical substances. The body's carbon is simply carbon. Hence, at bottom, the psyche is simply the world.[42]

Jung and Freud were brought together through Jung's investigation of emotionally-toned complexes. A divergent view of the libido contributed to an emotional rupture between the two men and their colleagues which has lasted a century. Two years after the formation of the secret committee of the IPA around Freud, the Zürich Society withdrew from the IPA and was renamed the Association for Analytical Psychology.

Now, a century after Jung's Fordham lectures, conversations take place among all analytic schools, and also with neuroscientists, particularly those in emotions research. Jungian theory and practice, which began with the word association testing of emotionally-charged complexes, is convergent with the current research on emotions as the dynamic aspect between body and mind, between and among persons. Psychoanalysis itself has moved toward acknowledging the affective regulatory function of psyche and the field phenomena of analytic alliance and practice. One hundred years after Fordham, the empirical experience of many schools of analysts and psychotherapists, which accept, engage, and mirror the emotions of our patients within the intensified immediacies of transferential process, is creating consensus and moving toward a common ground.

NOTES

1. C. G. Jung, "The Theory of Psychoanalysis," in *The Collected Works of C. G. Jung*, vol. 4, ed. and trans. Gerhard Adler and R. F. C. Hull (London: Routledge and Kegan Paul, 1961) § 203–522.

2. Friedrich Nietzche, *Thus Spake Zarathustra*, trans. R.J. Hollingdale (New York: Penguin Books, 1960), p.103.

3. William McGuire, ed., *The Freud-Jung Letters: The Correspondence between Sigmund Freud and C. G. Jung*, trans. R. F. C. Hull and Ralph Manheim (Princeton, NJ: Princeton University Press, 1974), pp. 491–492.

4. *Ibid.*, p. 497.

5. *Ibid.*, p. 384.

6. Gerhard Adler, ed., *C. G. Jung Letters, vol. 2: 1951–1961* (Princeton, NJ: Princeton University Press, 1975), p. 109.

7. Julian Jaynes, *The Origin of Consciousness in the Breakdown of the Bicameral Mind* (Boston, MA: Houghton Mifflin Company, 1990), p. 7.

8. Jung, CW 4, § 253.

9. *Ibid.*

10. *Ibid.*, § 254.

11. *Ibid.*, § 433.

12. *Ibid.*, § 438–439.

13. *Ibid.*, § 448.

14. *Ibid.*

15. *Ibid.*

16. *Ibid.*, § 449.

17. *Ibid.*

18. *Ibid.*, § 435.

19. McGuire, *Freud-Jung Letters*, p. 515.

20. Jung, CW 4, § 448.

21. Jung, "The Tavistock Lectures," in *The Collected Works of C. G. Jung*, vol. 18, ed. and trans. Gerhard Adler and R. F. C. Hull (London: Routledge and Kegan Paul, 1968).

22. C. G. Jung, "Psychological Factors Affecting Human Behavior," in *The Collected Works of C. G. Jung*, vol. 8, ed. and trans. Gerhard Adler and R. F. C. Hull (Princeton, NJ: Princeton University Press, 1960).

23. Jung, CW 18, § 317.

24. *Ibid.*, § 48.

25. *Ibid.*

26. *Ibid.*, § 317.

27. *Ibid.*, § 319.

28. *Ibid.*, § 356.

29. *Ibid.*, § 318.

30. *Ibid.*, § 234.

31. Regina Pally, *The Mind-Brain Reality* (London: Karnac Books, 2000), p. 95.

32. C. G. Jung, "The Psychology of the Transference" (1946), in *The Collected Works of C. G. Jung*, vol. 16, ed. and trans. Gerhard Adler and R. F. C. Hull (London: Routledge and Kegan Paul, 1966), § 539.

33. Gerald Edelman, *Bright Air, Brilliant Fire, On the Matter of the Mind* (New York: Basic Books, 1992), p. 224.

34. C. G. Jung, *Memories, Dreams, Reflections* (New York: Pantheon Books, Random House, 1961), p. 224.

35. *Ibid.*

36. *Ibid.*

37. *Ibid.*, pp. 208–209.

38. *Ibid.*

39. Jacques Hadamard, *The Psychology of Invention in Mathematical Field* (Princeton, NJ: Princeton University Press, 1945), p. 142.

40. *Ibid.*

41. C. G. Jung, "Civilization in Transition," in *The Collected Works of C. G. Jung*, vol. 10, ed. and trans. Gerhard Adler and R. F. C. Hull (Princeton, NJ: Princeton University Press, 1960), § 304.

42. C. G. Jung, "The Archetypes and the Collective Unconscious," in *The Collected Works of C. G. Jung*, vol. 9, ed. and trans. Gerhard Adler and R. F. C. Hull (London: Routledge and Kegan Paul, 1966), § 291.

Chapter Three

The 1912 International Extension Course in Medical and Nervous Diseases
The Instructors and the Fordham Context

Mark E. Mattson

Carl G. Jung's lectures at Fordham University have long been a matter of legend at Fordham. These lectures were part of the International Extension Course in Medical and Nervous Diseases offered by the School of Medicine, September 9–28, 1912. The idea was to present in three weeks a complete overview of cutting-edge work by international and national experts in one medical specialty—disorders of brain and behavior—for an audience of practicing physicians. The goal of this paper is to identify the Extension Course instructors and, in the process, to connect the course to its Fordham context as well as to larger contexts.

The main artifact that we have from the International Extension Course in Medical and Nervous Diseases is a group photo, preserved in the Fordham Archives.[1] The photo was taken on the steps of Collins Hall at Fordham's Rose Hill campus in the Bronx, which has a large auditorium that was probably used for the lectures, since there were

Table 1. Honorary Degree Recipients and Non-Fordham Instructors

Photo Number	Name and Affiliation in 1912	Presentation topics	Sources
	Honorary Degree Recipients		
4	Nicolás Achúcarro, M.D. Spanish University, Madrid	Histology 1-5, Pathology 6-10	NYT 9/8&12&13/12, FM
6	Henry Head Fellow of the Royal College of Physicians, London	Sensibility in Nerve & Nerve Root, Spinal Cord, Brain-Stem, Thalamic & Cortical Lesions 1-12	NYT 9/8&12&13/12, NYT obit 10/10/1940, FM, Wiki
8	Gordon Morgan Holmes University of London	Topographical Diagnosis Spinal Cord, Brain Stem, Mid and Fore-brain Lesions 1-10	NYT 9/8&12&13/12, FM, Wiki
not in photo	Carl Gustav Jung, M.D. University of Zurich	not on schedule: probably Psychoanalysis 1-2 (no name listed)	NYT 9/8&12&13/12, NYT obit 6/7/1961, FM, Wiki
not in photo	Horatio Robinson Storer, M.D. Boston MA & Newport RI	not on schedule	NYT 9/8&12&13/12, 11/9/1912, NYT obit 9/19/1922, FM, AMS 1906, 1921, Wiki
	Other Non-Fordham Instructors		
3	Alvyn Knauer, M.D. Psychitrische Klinik of Munich	not on schedule but in later reports as instructor	NYT 9/8/12, FM
5	William Alanson White, M.D. Superintendent of Government Hospital, Washington DC	not on schedule but in later reports as instructor	NYT 9/8&12&13/12, NYT obit 3/8/1937, FM, AMS 1921, 1927, Wiki
9	Colin Kerr Russel, M.D. McGill University & Victoria Hospital, Montreal	Peripheral Neuritis, Tabes, Hereditary Ataxias 1-5,	NYT 9/8&13/12, FM, obits McNaughton (1957), Penfield (1957)
not in photo	Henry Herbert Goddard, Ph.D. New Jersey School for Feeble-Minded Children	Neurological Clinic: Tabes Backward Children 1-2	NYT 9/8&13/12, NYT obit 6/22/1957, AMS 1927, FM, Wiki
not in photo	Carl Lucas Alsberg, M.D., Ph.D. Washington DC	Chemistry 1-5	NYT 9/8&13/12, NYT obit 11/2/1940, AMS 1927, FM
not in photo	James Vance May, M.D. President of Commission in Lunacy, New York State	Criminal Responsibility 1-2	NYT 9/8&13/12, FM, AMS 1927, Wiki, obit Trapp (1948)

NYT = *New York Times*; obit = *obituary*; AMS = *American Men of Science*; FM = *Fordham Monthly, Nov. 1912*; Wiki = *Wikipedia article*

Figure 1 (opposite page). International Extension Course in Medical and Nervous Diseases, Fordham University, New York, Sep. 9 to 18, 1912 (http://digital.library.fordham.edu/cdm/ref/collection/PHOTO/id/7). By permission: Archives & Special Collections, Fordham University Library, Bronx, New York

1912 International Extension Course

eighty to ninety enrollees.² The ninety-eight participants numbered in the photo include course instructors as well as enrollees, and their first initials and last names were recorded. The instructors can be categorized into three groups: the select group that was awarded honorary degrees by Fordham, the non-Fordham instructors, and the Fordham Medical School faculty who participated. Table 1 lists the full names, affiliations, presentation topics, and biographical sources for the first two groups, and Table 2 lists the same for the Fordham faculty.³ If they appear in the photo, their number is included in each table. The presentation topics come from the Fordham Medical School Bulletin for 1912–1913, in which a preliminary description and schedule for the Course was published before September 1912.

Honorary Degree Recipients: International Superstars

Five doctors were presented with honorary degrees on the third night of the course, Wednesday, September 11, 1912.⁴ Two were awarded Doctor of Laws in absentia: Jung was on his way to New York, and **Dr. Horatio Storer (1830–1922)** was unable to leave his home in Rhode Island due to an injury.⁵ Storer introduced American doctors to the use of chloroform as an anesthetic, helped found the specialty of gynecology and post-graduate training in medicine, and campaigned against abortion.⁶ Jung and Storer do not appear in the photo, suggesting that it may have been taken in the first week of the course. Jung presented nine lectures to the full group and a two-hour seminar for a small group each day for the last two weeks of the course.⁷ Jung is not listed on the preliminary schedule in the Medical School Bulletin, suggesting that his participation had not been confirmed when the Bulletin went to press and that the schedule as published was not as it was executed. There were two sessions on Psychoanalysis scheduled for the last week, along with two special lectures, and Smith Ely Jelliffe (discussed later) was scheduled for more sessions than any other person, so it could be that Jung lectured in some of these time slots.

Dr. Henry Head (1861–1940) received the Doctor of Laws. According to the Bulletin, he was scheduled to lecture on how sensation is affected by lesions of nerves, nerve roots, the spinal cord, brain stem, thalamus, and cortex, following the sensory pathways from beginning to end. This was a natural topic for the English neurologist, who was well-known for being his own subject in sensory lesion studies: "He had an incision made in his own arm six and a half inches long, the radial nerve was divided ... and a small portion was excised. The external cutaneous nerve was also divided, and then, with the problem of sensation simplified, observations were begun."[8] At the time of the Extension Course, he was the youngest Fellow of the Royal Society and the editor of *Brain*; in 1927 he was knighted.[9]

Dr. Gordon Holmes (1876–1965) had recently begun collaborating with Head; he received the Doctor of Science. Holmes was an Irish neurologist who specialized in the visual system and the cerebellum. The Bulletin lists him as scheduled to lecture on topographical diagnosis, dealing with identification of areas of damage in lesions of the spinal cord, brain stem, and brain. He later became a Fellow of the Royal Society (1933) and was knighted (1951).[10]

Dr. Nicolás Achúcarro (1880–1918) also received the Doctor of Science. He offered lectures on histology (microscopic observation) and pathology, along with Saturday lab sessions. He was trained in Europe, and then served as histologist at the Government Hospital for the Insane in Washington, DC. On his return to Spain and at the time of the Extension Course, he served as 1906 Nobel laureate Santiago Ramón y Cajal's assistant. Today the Achucarro Basque Center for Neuroscience is named for him.[11]

Other Non-Fordham Instructors: "Picked Men in the East"

Degree recipients Jung, Head, Holmes, and Achúcarro were the international superstar instructors for the Extension Course. **Dr. Alvyn Knauer**, assistant to Emil Kraepelin of Munich's Psychiatric Clinic, also offered lectures, though he was also not listed in the Bulletin schedule.[12] Then there were those instructors referred to by Dean Walsh of Fordham as "the picked men in the East here in America": May, Alsberg, Russell, White, and Goddard.[13] **Dr. James V. May (1873–1947)** was then President of the New York State Commission in Lunacy and presented two lectures on criminal responsibility.

Dr. Carl L. Alsberg (1877–1940) was an American biological chemist who offered lectures on chemistry of the central nervous system the first week of the Extension Course. He served as Chief of the Bureau of Chemistry from 1912 to 1921, which later became the Food and Drug Administration.[14]

Dr. Colin K. Russel (1876–1956) was "a pioneer of Canadian neurology."[15] Along with Wilder Penfield, he was a founder of the Montreal Neurological Institute in 1934.[16] At Fordham, he offered lectures on nerve inflammation, hereditary motor coordination disorders, and tabes dorsalis (i.e., sensory degeneration due to syphilis), as well as a clinic on tabes.

Dr. William Alanson White (1870–1937) was the Superintendent of the Government Hospital for the Insane in Washington, DC, where Achúcarro had served as histologist. The William Alanson White Institute of Psychiatry, Psychoanalysis & Psychology, named for him, is near Fordham's Lincoln Center campus in New York City.[17] As this eponym suggests, White was an important figure in psychiatry—serving as President of the American Psychiatric Association in 1924–1925— as well as psychoanalysis—serving as President of the American Psychoanalytic Society in 1928.[18] White and Jelliffe (1913) edited the two-volume *Modern Treatment of Nervous and Mental Diseases* and collaborated on *Diseases of the Nervous System.*[19] The former included contributions from White, Jelliffe, Holmes, May, and Goddard, as well as Havelock Ellis, Ernest Jones, Adolf Meyer, E. W. Scripture, and several other Extension Course instructors from Fordham Medical School.

The one psychologist in this group of M.D.s was Dr. Henry H. Goddard (1866–1957), who earned his Ph.D. at Clark University in 1899. He was the psychologist at the New Jersey School for Feeble-Minded Children in Vineland, New Jersey, was the first to translate Binet's new intelligence test into English, and introduced the term *moron*. Goddard had also attended the 1909 Clark University conference that featured Freud and Jung. The year of the Extension Course was the year that he published his best-known book: *The Kallikak Family: A Study in the Heredity of Feeble-mindedness.*[20] He presented two lectures on backward children the last week of the course. Goddard was a eugenicist and the subject of Zenderland's (1998) *Measuring Minds: Henry Herbert Goddard and the Origins of American Intelligence Testing.*

Fordham University Medical School Faculty: The Home Team

The third group of instructors was the home team: Fordham Medical School faculty, led by **Dean James J. Walsh (1865–1942)**, also Professor of Nervous Diseases and the History of Medicine. Walsh

Table 2. Fordham Medical School Faculty

Photo Number	Name and Affiliation in 1912	Presentation Topics	Sources (*all listed in Fordham Bulletin 1912-13*)
7	James Joseph Walsh, M.D. Fordham, Dean of Medical School	History of Nervous Diseases, Psychotherapy, Hypnotism, Suggestion, Auto-suggestion, Psycho-Therapeutic Treatment 1-6	NYT 9/12&13/1912, 11/9&10/1912, 1/20/1913, NYT obit 3/1/1942, AMS 1921, 1927, 1938, FM, Wiki
1	Victor Edgar Sorapure, M.B. Fordham, Pro-Dean of Medical School	Nervous Phenomena of Visceral Diseases, Disorders of Ductless Glands 1-3	NYT 11/9&10/1912, 1/20/1913
2	Thomas F. Reilly, M.D. Fordham, Prof of Applied Therapeutics	Chemotherapy 1	
10	Louis Faugeres Bishop, M.D. Fordham, Prof of Heart & Circulatory Diseases	Cardiac Symptoms of Nervous Origin 1-3	AMS 1921, 1927
11	Smith Ely Jelliffe, M.D. Fordham, Clinical Prof of Nervous Diseases	Psychiatry Clinics: Exhaustion & Infectious Psychoses, Alcoholic & Allied Psychoses, Syphilitic Psychoses, Dementia Praecox, Manic Depressive Psychoses 1-15	NYT obit 9/26/1945, AMS 1921, 1927, FM, Wiki
12	William Joseph Marie Alois Maloney, M.D., Ch.B., F.R.S., Fordham, Prof of Neurology	Anatomy 1-3, Cranial Nerve Palsies 5, Neurological Clinics: Lower & Upper Neuron Lesions, Tabes, Cerebro-spinal Syphilis & Allied States	NYT 9/13/1912, 11/9&10/1912, 1/20/1913, NYT obit 9/5/1952, FM, obit Annan (1953)
13	Charles Zeh Garside, M.D. Fordham, Prof of Bacteriology	Reaction 1-2, Cytological Diagnosis Cerebrospinal Fluid 3, Vaccine Therapy 4	NYT obit 6/3/1916
14	Roy H. Nicholl, M.D. Fordham, Prof of Physiology & Biochemistry	not on schedule	
not in photo	Isadore Abrahamson, B.S., M.D. Fordham, Clinical Prof of Neurology Attending Neurologist: Montefiore Home Associate, Neurologist: Mt Sinai	Case Taking, Reflexes, Electrodiagnosis, Aphasia, Alexia & Apraxia, Co-ordination & Tremor 1-6, Neurological Clinics: Lower & Upper Neuron Lesions, Tabes, Cerebro-spinal Syphilis & Allied States	NYT 11/9/1912, NYT obit 7/19/1933
not in photo	Thomas Darlington, M.D. Fordham, Prof of Sanitary Science	Occupational Neuroses 1	NYT obit 8/24/1945, AMS 1921, 1927
not in photo	T. Joseph Dunn, A.M., M.D. Fordham, Prof of Materia Medica & Clinical Prof Medicine	Clinical Lecture 1	NYT 9/13/12
not in photo	Charles Albert Elsberg, A.B., M.D. Fordham, Prof of Neurological Surgery	Surgical Anatomy of Brain & Cord 1-4, Operative Indications & Contraindications 5-6, After-treatment of Operations 7	AMS 1921, 1927, NYT 11/9/1912, NYT obit 3/19/1948, Society of Neurological Surgeons website
not in photo	Albert C. Geyser, M.D. Fordham, Prof of Physical Therapeutics	Electro Diagnosis in Visceral Diseases 1-2, Electrotherapy 3-4	
not in photo	William S. Gottheil, M.D. Fordham, Prof of Dermatology	Tropho-neurosis, Anglo-neurosis 1-2	
not in photo	Charles Graef, M.C.P.S., M.D. Fordham, Prof of Ophthalmology	The Pupil, Visual Acuity & Visual Fields, Optic Neuritis, Retinitis & Optic Atrophy 1-4	NYT obit 2/28/1944
not in photo	Robert Holmes Green, A.B., A.M., M.D. Fordham, Prof of Genito-Urinary Surgery	Genito-Urinary Symptoms in Nervous Disease 1	
not in photo	John B. Huber, A.M., M.D. Fordham, Prof of Pulmonary Diseases	Pulmonary Symptoms 1	
not in photo	Carl Keppler, M.D. Fordham, Prof of Orthopedics	Orthopedics 1, Mechano-therapy 2-4	NYT obit 12/28/1939
not in photo	Frances J. Quinlan, Ph.D., M.D., LL.D. Fordham, Prof of Laryngology	Laryngoscopic Examination 1	AMS 1921, 1927, NYT obit 1/20/1951
not in photo	William T. Shanahan, M.D. Fordham, Special Lecturer on Epilepsy	Epilepsy 1-2	NYT 11/9/1912, NYT obit 2/19/1946
not in photo	Siegfried Wachsmann, M.D. Fordham, Clinical Prof of Medicine Medical Director: Montefiore Home	Frenkel's Exercises & Motor Reeducation, Hydrotherapy, Equipment & Construction of Neurological Hospital, Mental Changes in Chronic Diseases 1-4, Neurological Clinics: Lower & Upper Neuron Lesions, Tabes, Cerebro-spinal Syphilis & Allied States	
29	Jacob Diner, Ph.G. Fordham M.D. 1913 & founder School of Pharmacy		AMS 1927, NYT obit 7/27/1937, FU Archives

NYT = New York Times; obit = obituary; AMS = American Men of Science; FM = Fordham Monthly, Nov. 1912; Wiki = Wikipedia article opened the Extension Course with a lecture on the history of nervous disorders—he wrote extensively on medical history—and was scheduled for lectures on hypnotism and psychotherapy the final week of the course. He earned his undergraduate degree at Fordham and his M.D. at Penn State. Walsh taught the first non-philosophical psychology course at Fordham: Physiological Psychology. He founded the Fordham Press and authored over forty books, including *Psychotherapy*, one of the first texts in this area, published the same year as the Extension Course. He became Acting Dean of the Medical School in 1906, just after its founding in 1905, and then a regular Dean later. Walsh eventually became affiliated with the graduate School of Sociology and Social Service established in 1916.[21]

Dr. Victor Edgar Sorapure (1874–1933) was the Pro-Dean and Professor of Pathology. He was born in the British West Indies and studied at Edinburgh. He returned to the U.K. during World War I, and edited *The Oxford Index of Therapeutics* (1921).[22] Sorapure was scheduled to lecture on nervous phenomena in visceral diseases and in disorders of ductless glands.

Dr. William J. M. A. Maloney (1882–1952) was Professor of Neurology and one of the organizers of the Extension Course. Maloney was scheduled to lecture on anatomy and on neurological examination, and he participated in several neurological clinics with other instructors in the late afternoons. He was born, educated, and later died in Edinburgh.[23]

Dr. Smith Ely Jelliffe (1866–1945) was the other organizer of the Extension Course and was Clinical Professor of Mental Diseases. Jelliffe and Maloney invited Jung, and Jelliffe had a long-term collaboration with White, as previously mentioned. White and Jelliffe founded the journal *Psychoanalytic Review* in 1913, which was where Jung's Fordham lectures were first published. Jelliffe's biography and his correspondence with both Freud and Jung share a volume.[24] He was a psychoanalyst who was open to both Freud and Jung.

Also in the photo are **Dr. Charles Zeh Garside** and **Dr. Roy H. Nicholl**, who along with Walsh, Sorapure, and Maloney formed the Committee on Examinations for the Medical School. The larger Medical Council included, in addition to Walsh, Sorapure, and Maloney, course instructors **Drs. T. Joseph Dunn, Frances J. Quinlan, Charles**

Graef, Carl Keppler, **Charles Albert Elsberg (1871–1948)**, and the next Dean of the Medical School, Dr. William P. Healy, who apparently did not participate in the Extension Course. Elsberg was called the "father of spinal cord surgery."[25] **Dr. Thomas Darlington (1858–1945)** served as New York City Commissioner of Health from 1904–1910, and later he was the Grand Sachem of Tammany Hall, the Democratic political organization.[26]

The Fordham Context

Dean Walsh looks unhappy in the photo. Less than two months after the course, at the beginning of November, Walsh, Sorapure, Maloney, and about ten others resigned from the Medical School, as reported in a series of articles in the New York Times.[27] Their resignation did not end the Fordham Medical School, but the reason they resigned foreshadowed the reason it would eventually close in 1921.

The 1910 Flexner Report reshaped medical education in the United States. Flexner visited every medical school in North America and evaluated each on five criteria, with many schools receiving scathing reviews. He advocated higher standards and fewer medical schools and students. For example, he called for closing or combining medical programs so there would be no more than one in a city, which would serve the surrounding region. This report led directly to the closing of at least twelve of the 168 schools he evaluated.[28] While he did not single out Fordham's Medical School for closing, reducing the many schools in New York City to one would necessarily mean "universities of limited means [could] retire without loss of prestige."[29] The Flexner Report pointed out that Fordham had seventy-two professors for forty-two students—too many part-timers and not enough full-time professors— and that its expenses over tuition had to be met by the university. The lack of endowment was discussed at the dinner held to honor the honorary degree recipients September 12 at the Hotel Astor.[30]

In the wake of this report, Walsh, Sorapure, and Maloney negotiated an agreement with the accreditors at the American Medical Association (AMA). In exchange for a commitment of resources from Fordham of a minimum of six full-time faculty, opening a clinic, and $20,000 a year beyond tuition for teaching expenses, the medical school would receive the highest rating of A from the AMA.[31] When

Fordham President McCluskey, S.J., decided on a different approach, they each resigned, followed by ten or more other faculty including Abrahamson, Wachsmann, Elsberg, and honoree Horatio Storer, who was a consultant.[32] The new Dean, Dr. William P. Healy, M.D., was Clinical Professor of Surgery and attending surgeon at Fordham Hospital, where it was argued students could get their clinical experience instead of a university clinic. The AMA responded by lowering Fordham's rating to B.[33]

The Fordham Medical School soon (1914) regained its A rating and maintained it up to its closing in 1921. The number of students and faculty grew to a peak in 1914, but the underlying issue of the cost of a medical school exceeding the tuition revenue was not resolved and became acute during World War I, when other programs shrank. Repeated attempts to create an endowment to pay for the additional costs failed, and in May 1919 it was announced that the school would close with the class of 1921.[34]

Conclusions

The International Extension Course in Medical and Nervous Diseases can be seen as the swan song of Dean Walsh and his supporters in the Medical School. Despite the apparent success of the Extension Course, this was the only one offered at Fordham. The Medical School closed in 1921 because the cost of running a medical school was too great for a tuition-driven institution with a small endowment, as was the case for almost all Catholic institutions in North America.[35] Even today, Fordham's endowment is much smaller than that of comparable research universities.

The Extension Course offered an early example of international continuing education for physicians, and medical continuing education had been championed by honorary degree recipient Storer. The international superstars and "picked men of the East" were an eminent group of instructors able to present the state of the art in theory, research, diagnosis, and treatment of disorders of the brain and behavior. One indication of their collective eminence is that a century later, seven of the eleven non-Fordham instructors have their own Wikipedia entry. The presentation topics show the range of areas under study in 1912. Most topics are quite similar to what would be covered today, though today there is probably less emphasis on the neurological consequences of syphilis, for example, as a result of advances in treating this disease that occurred after 1912.

Jung and Jelliffe brought the then-new psychoanalytic approach to the Extension Course. Jung's continued fame as the most influential of Freud's "errant" disciples and the impact of these particular lectures as the point when his theoretical differences with Freud became public enhanced the legendary status of the Extension Course at Fordham. Thanks to this conference and book, we now know much more about this Extension Course and Jung's impact, and what we know only enhances the legend.

NOTES

1. My thanks to Patrice Kane, Head of Archives and Special Collections, for this photo and other help. The photo is reproduced in this volume and is available at this link to Fordham University's Digital Collection: http://digital.library.fordham.edu/cdm/ref/collection/PHOTO/id/7.

2. "Medical Leaders in Fordham Course," *New York Times*, Sept. 8, 1912, p. 5; and Freud/Jung letters, cited in Sonu Shamdasani, introduction to *Jung contra Freud: The 1912 New York Lectures on the Theory of Psychoanalysis* (Princeton, NJ: Princeton University Press, 2012).

3. Sources for the tables include the *New York Times*; J. M. Cattell and D. R. Brimhall, eds., *American Men of Science* (Garrison, NY: Science Press, 1921); J. M. Cattell and J. Cattell, eds., *American Men of Science* (Garrison, NY: Science Press, 1927); "The International Extension Course in Medicine," *Fordham Monthly*, Nov. 1912; and Wikipedia, various articles. Accessed Mar. 2013, at http://www.wikipedia.org/.

4. R. I. Gannon, *Up to the Present: The Story of Fordham* (Garden City, NY: Doubleday, 1967); and "Famous Doctors Get Fordham Degrees," *New York Times*, Sept. 12, 1912, p. 6.

5. Jung was not on his way home, as reported by Shamdasani, introduction to *Jung contra Freud*.

6. "Famous Doctors Get Fordham Degrees," *New York Times*, p. 6; Wikipedia, "Horatio Storer." Accessed Mar. 17, 2013, at http://en.wikipedia.org/wiki/Horatio_Storer; and Storer's website. Accessed Mar. 17, 2013, at http://horatiostorer.net/.

7. Freud/Jung letters, cited in Shamdasani, introduction to *Jung contra Freud*.

8. Fordham University, "The International Extension Course in Medicine," *Fordham Monthly* 31 (November 1912): 2.

9. Wikipedia, "Henry Head." Accessed Mar. 17, 2013, at http://en.wikipedia.org/wiki/Henry_Head.

10. Wikipedia, "Gordon Morgan Holmes." Accessed Mar. 17, 2013, at http://en.wikipedia.org/wiki/Gordon_Morgan_Holmes.

11. Achucarro Basque Center for Neuroscience, "About Nicolás Achúcarro." Accessed Mar. 17, 2013, at http://www.achucarro.org/about-nicolas-achucarro.

12. "Medical Leaders in Fordham Course," *New York Times*, p. 5; and "International Extension Course in Medicine," *Fordham Monthly* 31.

13. "Only Brain and Grit behind New Clinic," *New York Times*, Sept. 13, 1912, p. 6.

14. U.S. Food and Drug Administration, "Carl L. Alsberg, M.D." Accessed Mar. 17, 2013, at http://www.fda.gov/AboutFDA/CommissionersPage/ucm113675.htm.

15. F. L. McNaughton, "Colin Russel, a Pioneer of Canadian Neurology," *Canadian Medical Association Journal* 77 (1957): 719–23.

16. W. Penfield, "A Tribute to Colin Russel," *Canadian Medical Association Journal* 77 (1957): 715–16.

17. William Alanson White Institute of Psychiatry, Psychoanalysis and Psychology. Accessed Mar. 17, 2013, at http://www.wawhite.org.

18. Wikipedia, "William Alanson White." Accessed Mar. 17, 2013, at http://en.wikipedia.org/wiki/William_Alanson_White.

19. W. A. White and S. E. Jelliffe, eds., *Modern Treatment of Nervous and Mental Diseases, Volumes 1 & 2* (Philadelphia, PA: Lee & Febiger, 1913); and S. E. Jelliffe and W. A. White, *Diseases of the Nervous System* (Philadelphia, PA: Lee & Febiger, 1915).

20. H. H. Goddard, *The Kallikak Family: A Study in the Heredity of Feeble-mindedness* (New York: Macmillan, 1912).

21. R. A. Schroth, *Fordham: A History and Memoir* (Chicago, IL: Loyola Press, 2002).

22. "Dr. Victor Edgar Sorapure," *British Medical Journal* 3764 (1, 1933): 348.

23. "William J. M. A. Maloney, M.D.," *Bulletin of the Medical Library Association* 41 (1, 1953): 100–101.

24. J. C. Burnham, "Jelliffe: American Psychoanalyst and Physician," in W. McGuire, ed., *Jelliffe: American Psychoanalyst and Physician and His Correspondence with Sigmund Freud and C. G. Jung* (Chicago, IL: University of Chicago Press, 1983).

25. E. Alexander, "Charles Albert Elsberg, M.D. (1871–1948): Father of Spinal Cord Surgery," *Neurosurgery* 20 (1987): 811–14.

26. "Darlington Dead; Health Crusader," *New York Times,* Sept. 24, 1945, p. 19.

27. "Fordham Teachers Quit Medical School," *New York Times,* Nov. 9, 1912, p. 1; "Blame Dissenters for Fordham Split," *New York Times,* Nov. 10, 1912, p. 10; "Fordham's Medical School Rated Low," *New York Times,* Jan. 20, 1913, p. 6; See also Gannon, *Up to the Present,* pp. 134–160; and R. A. Schroth, *Fordham,* pp. 123–128.

28. M. D. Hiatt and C. G. Stockton, "The Impact of the Flexner Report on the Fate of Medical Schools in North America after 1909," *Journal of American Physicians and Surgeons* 8 (2003): 37–40; (see also the extended version online at http://www.jpands.org/vol8no2/hiattext.pdf).

29. A. Flexner, *Medical Education in the United States and Canada: A Report to the Carnegie Foundation for the Advancement of Teaching* (New York: Carnegie Foundation for the Advancement of Teaching, 1910).

30. "Only Brain and Grit behind New Clinic," *New York Times,* p. 6.

31. Schroth, *Fordham,* p. 127.

32. "Fordham Teachers Quit Medical School," *New York Times,* p. 1.

33. "Fordham's Medical School Rated Low," *New York Times,* p. 6.

34. "Closes Medical School," *New York Times,* May 30, 1919, p. 3.

35. E. J. Power, *Catholic Higher Education in America: A History* (New York: Appleton-Century-Crofts, 1972).

CHAPTER FOUR

CARL JUNG, BEATRICE HINKLE, AND CHARLOTTE TELLER, THE NEW YORK TIMES REPORTER

Jay Sherry

Jung's lectures at Fordham in 1912 were part of its International Extension Course in Medicine that was devoted to "affectations of the mind and nervous system."[1] In them he made his divergence from orthodox psychoanalytic theory public by presenting his case for a non-sexualized definition of libido and for the therapeutic importance of focusing on current life problems rather than childhood memories. Besides his nine lectures, Jung's busy schedule also included seminars and clinical demonstrations at local hospitals. In New York to meet Edith Rockefeller McCormick, he spent an afternoon with her father John D. Rockefeller at Kykuit, his country estate in Tarrytown, north of the city. Jung also gave a lengthy interview to the New York Times that appeared in its Sunday magazine on September 29 and which can be found in *C. G. Jung Speaking* where the interviewer is identified as being "anonymous." I have determined that her name was Charlotte Teller and will present what I have learned about her life, their relationship, and the role that Beatrice Hinkle, America's first Jungian psychoanalyst, had in promoting Jung's new psychology to the Greenwich Village avant-garde.

Teller (1876–1953) was the daughter of an attorney and the niece of a senator from Colorado. There was a strong streak of independence in the family; her uncle switched his political loyalties from the Republican to the Democratic Party and her father took up the cause of copper miners. She graduated from the University of Chicago and was briefly married to Frank Minitree Johnson, a civil engineer in Washington, D.C. An aspiring writer, she moved to New York with her grandmother and took up residence at the A Club, a cooperative apartment building filled with young radicals. It apparently got its name when somebody said that they were forming *a* club, someone else quipped that it should be called the "A" Club. Later, a local wag suggested that the *A* really stood for *Anarchist*. They made headlines by hosting the Russian revolutionary writer Maxim Gorky and his common-law wife after local hotels refused to rent them a room because his divorce was not finalized. Teller befriended Mark Twain who lived nearby and would stop in to enjoy some lively conversation and a cigar. A close friend of Kahlil Gibran who drew several pencil portraits of her, she was also romantically involved with Ameen Rihani, one of his friends.

Her interest in social reform led to her involvement in the Public Forum started by Percy Stickney Grant, the rector of the nearby Episcopal Church of the Ascension. Its Sunday night meetings were devoted to discussions of such controversial topics as labor unions, divorce laws, the suffrage movement, and what was then euphemistically called the "Negro Question." As time went on, she helped it merge with the Liberal Club, among whose members were prominent social reformers who started the NAACP; in her letters Teller wrote about trying to arrange a meeting between Jung and W. E. B. Du Bois.

Two older members who sided with the Club's contingent of young radicals were fellow Californians Beatrice Hinkle and the muck-raking journalist Lincoln Steffens.[2] A San Francisco native with a medical degree, Hinkle was appointed city medical officer, the first woman in the U.S. to hold that position. In 1905 she moved to New York where she joined the staff of Charles L. Dana, America's leading neurologist, at Cornell Medical College where she helped him establish one of the first psychotherapy clinics in the country. To stay abreast of developments in the field she went to Europe for two years, meeting Freud and Jung with whom she traveled to the 1911

Weimar Psychoanalytic Congress. After returning to New York she began a private analytical practice. When Jung came for the Fordham lectures he visited Hinkle at her Gramercy Park apartment where he was introduced to Teller who was working as a freelance journalist. She had gotten the assignment to do an interview with him for the New York Times and was also planning an article entitled "Jung—Psycho-Analyst" for the popular magazine *Metropolitan* that never appeared.

In the interview Jung discussed the role of race in the American psyche and although he did employ such stereotypes as the necessity of mastering the "savage races," he did make some perceptive observations as well. For example,

> You today, are influenced by the Negro race, which not so long ago had to call you master. ... In the South I find what they call sentiment and chivalry and romance to be the covering of cruelty ... they treat the Negro as they would treat their own unconscious.[3]

He had observed Southern race relations first-hand two years before while in Chattanooga, Tennessee to treat a patient, Medill McCormick. This experience later figured in a dream Jung had while on his 1925 trip to East Africa in which the Negro barber he had in America tries to make him "go black" by kinking his hair with a curling iron.[4] The emotionally charged duality of Southern brutality and sentimentality was portrayed on the silver screen just a few years later in D. W. Griffith's film *The Birth of a Nation*, the racist epic that was instrumental in helping to revive the Ku Klux Klan.[5]

Jung devoted much of the interview to discussing gender relations, in particular how American men had invested so much of their libido in business that they had little left for their wives. All in all, though, he did admire the pioneer spirit that had propelled the country to the pinnacle of power and economic success but warned about the dangers in such a one-sided enterprise.

> [The American] has to express himself in big buildings, in trusts, in systems, of which we in Europe have as yet only the beginnings. We envy you. We have not learned to think in such great abstractions—and we are not in as great a danger as you Americans.[6]

Just one example of that drive was the soon-to-be-completed Woolworth Building, the "cathedral of commerce," which became the world's tallest skyscraper and the icon of Modern New York City until it was surpassed by the Empire State Building.

Teller wrote several letters to a friend that give an intimate view of her personal encounter with Jung. On September 24 she wrote,

> Dr. Jung has been here a week and I have given all my time getting an interview for the 'Sunday Times.' ... I met him on Wednesday, the day he arrived—at Dr. Hinkle's. He had a quick sense of humor and good English at his command. We walked up Fifth Avenue afterwards and he spoke of a prophetic dream about me. The next time I saw him he began his remarks (so startling from so stalwart and sturdy [a] Swiss) by saying 'You have a poison in you which affects men terribly, what is it? You kept me awake all night. ... You are dangerous ... I tell you this because you are already a terrible temptation to me although I know nothing about you—I did not even get your name.' ... He asked me to go to the West Indies and back to Zürich with him.

Ten days later she continued:

> He came over last Friday afternoon ... and then he told me that he loved me with passion ... that he had a fearful struggle within himself until in true Mithraic fashion—the words were his—he had decided to sacrifice the bull to me—in order that I might at last be free. [He said] 'you can only be freed by one who never touches you' ... [he said that] he was not a woman's man—his wife and one other woman being the only ones in his 'Unconscious.' ... He reminds me constantly that his work is the study of mankind and his desire, their freedom.[7]

This infatuation complicated her relationship to her fiancé Gilbert Hirsch but they weathered the storm, got married a few weeks later, and went to Europe where they met other expatriates like Ezra Pound, Gertrude Stein, and the painter Marsden Hartley. It is probably Teller who was the "occultist" who told Hartley in Paris that his pictures were full of Kabbalistic signs and symbols. Although Hartley disagreed with her, they clearly did reflect motifs adopted from the mystical writings of Jacob Boehme that he was reading at the time.[8]

There are two points about the letters that I would like to make here: the first is to note just how seductive Jung's behavior toward Teller was. In the interview he discussed how American women, with husbands married to their jobs, were frequently attracted to "dangerous" European men. Consider that this scenario would also have included Jung himself whose "polygamous components" were constellated once again as he turned on the charm when meeting Teller. With his talk of sacrificing the bull, however, there is an important reversal as he decides to control his erotic impulses. Secondly, this letter contains one of the first formulations of his as-yet unnamed concept of the animus. Teller writes,

> [Jung] said that until I admitted my 'male-ness' and took life consciously as a man—I could not conclude my undertakings. He told me that the feminine, in me, however ignored, would live of itself—but that the man I had always searched for as companion was within me. ... I told him one of my very recent dreams and he pointed out that I always carried the male symbol—which was not merely a sex-symbol—but the symbol of creative-ness.[9]

Jung's return visit the next spring gave Hinkle the opportunity to introduce him to other members of her downtown Greenwich Village circle. They attended a dinner party hosted by members of the Heterodoxy Club, America's first feminist organization; the party was remembered the following way:

> Guests ranged from university professors and writers to distinguished labor administrators ... Patchin still talked about a visit by the famous analyst, Carl G. Jung. The atmosphere had been rather stiff and formal until Jung broke the ice by addressing a pet dog who was misbehaving with his leg: 'Come, come, be reasonable, I'm not a female.'[10]

Hinkle also introduced Jung to Gibran who drew his pencil portrait, most likely at his studio on West 10th Street, just a block from Patchin Place. The two men would almost certainly have discussed William Blake and perhaps the American visionary artist Albert Pinkham Ryder with whom Gibran became acquainted. They hit it off so well that Jung ended up inviting Gibran to visit him in Zürich.

Capitalizing on Jung's celebrity status, Hinkle had arranged an invitation for him to speak about dreams to the Liberal Club. Although no copy of Jung's talk seems to exist, it would have expressed views similar to those he presented shortly afterward in a lecture.

> But any one keenly interested in the dream problem cannot have failed to observe that a dream has also a *progressive* continuity ... since dreams occasionally exert a remarkable influence upon the conscious mental life ... [it is] usually seen in a more or less distinct change in the dreamer's frame of mind.[11]

With new emphasis on the creative potential of the unconscious Jung was aligning his psychology with such popular concepts as the *stream of consciousness* of William James and Henri Bergson's *creative evolution*. It was a moment of great optimism and cultural ferment both in America and in Europe. Bergson had just given lectures at Columbia University to standing-room-only crowds, and Hinkle wrote an article showing how similar his idea of *elan vital* was to Jung's new conceptualization of the libido. In a Bergsonian-flavored passage deleted from later editions of *Wandlungen und Symbole der Libido* Jung wrote that

> Man as an individual is a suspicious phenomenon, the right of whose existence from a natural biological stand-point could be seriously contested, because, from this point of view, the individual is only a race atom, and has a significance only as a mass constituent.[12]

Belief in humanity's capacity for change was also evident in the political situation of the country at that time. The Democrat Woodrow Wilson was inaugurated as the country's new president shortly before Jung's arrival. The election of 1912 represented the high tide of political reformism: besides Wilson, Teddy Roosevelt ran on the Progressive Party ticket and the Socialist candidate Eugene Debs won the largest number of votes in the party's history.

Hinkle was *the* key figure in promoting Jung's new approach to psychology in America through her network of analysands and her translation of *Wandlungen und Symbole der Libido* as *Psychology of the Unconscious*. It was one of the publishing sensations of 1916 and closely read by such talents as Jack London, Eugene O'Neill, and Alfred Stieglitz. O'Neill said, "The book that interested me the most of the Freudian school is Jung's *Psychology of the Unconscious*. ... If I have been influenced unconsciously, it must have been by this book more than any other."[13] London said that after reading it he was "standing on the edge of a world so new, so terrible, so wonderful that I am almost afraid to look into it."¹⁴ Stieglitz's copy of the book shows that he underlined many passages in Hinkle's introduction.¹⁵ This occurred at the time he was introducing Georgia O'Keeffe to the New York art world and, for now, we can only speculate on the influence that the book had on his ideas about creativity and the feminine.

A moment in American cultural history that is usually seen through a Freudian lens had, in fact, a remarkably Jungian character. The Greenwich Village avant-garde got to meet Jung and talk with him. The Montessori-trained women who were in the process of opening New York's first progressive schools adopted his ideas about child development in their curriculums. They promoted the emotional development of their students through social activities that emphasized creative self-expression and play. Remember, though, that influence flows in two directions. I would suggest that his playing with stones by the lake soon after his return to Zürich might have been prompted in part by the discussions he had in New York. Also, talking to Gibran and visiting the historic Armory Show would have given Jung major exposure to modern art, an experience that certainly factored into the active imaginations that he would begin that fall.

In conclusion, might we not imagine Hinkle as the Beatrice to Jung's Dante, the woman who helped point him down the path to the interior journey he was about to begin?

NOTES

1. "A New Medical Enterprise," *New York Sun*, Sept. 17, 1912.

2. Steffens was an uncle of Jane Hollister who, along with her husband Joe Wheelwright, became a Jungian analyst.

3. C. G. Jung, *C. G. Jung Speaking*, eds. William McGuire and R. F. C. Hull (Princeton, NJ: Princeton University Press, 1977), p. 16; See also his "Report on America" in *The Collected Works of C. G. Jung*, vol. 18, ed. and trans. Gerhard and R. F. C. Hull (Princeton, NJ: Princeton University Press, 1980), § 1284; and footnote 6 in William McGuire, ed., *The Freud/Jung Letters: The Correspondence between Sigmund Freud and C. G. Jung*, trans. Ralph Manheim and R. F. C. Hull (Princeton, NJ: Princeton University Press, 1974), p. 377.

4. C. G. Jung, *Memories, Dreams, Reflections* (New York: Vintage, [1961] 1989), pp. 273–274; and for a contemporary Jungian perspective, see Michael Vannoy Adams, *The Multicultural Imagination* (London and New York: Routledge, 1996). I want to thank Dave Sedgwick for confirming Jung's visit to Chattanooga with his photo copy of the ship's manifest from 1912 listing that city.

5. For the most complete history of the film see Melvyn Stokes, *D. W. Griffith's The Birth of a Nation: A History of "The Most Controversial Motion Picture of All Time."* (Oxford and New York: Oxford University Press, 2007).

6. Jung, *Jung Speaking*, pp. 17–18.

7. Charlotte Teller, letter to Mary Haskell, file 159, box 24, Minis Family Papers, 1739–1948 (Collection #2725), Southern Historical Collection, Wilson Library, The University of North Carolina at Chapel Hill; for Jung's analysis of the Mithraic sacrifice see *The Collected Works of C. G. Jung*, Vol. 5 (Princeton, NJ: Princeton University Press, 1970), § 396–398; and see also his letter of June 26, 1910 to Freud in McGuire, *The Freud/Jung Letters*, pp. 335–337.

8. See Barbara Haskell, *Marsden Hartley* (New York: Whitney Museum/New York University Press, 1980), pp. 29, 93; also Bruce Robertson, *Marsden Hartley* (New York: Harry N. Abrams, 1995), p. 45. Hartley said that the couple were "people who know me and who have just come over to Berlin again from N.Y. Two Americans Mr. and Mrs. Gilbert Hirsch—good friends—who know my personality rather well—I knew them in Paris" in James Timothy Voorhies, ed., *My Dear Stieglitz: Letters of Marsden Hartley and Alfred Stieglitz 1912–1915* (Columbia, SC: University of South Carolina Press, 2002), p. 200.

9. Minis Family Papers.

10. Carl Zigrosser, *My Own Shall Come to Me: A Personal Memoir and Picture Chronicle* (Haarlem, Netherlands: Joh. Enschede en zonen, 1971), pp. 100–101. "Patchin" refers to #1 Patchin Place, the address in Greenwich Village where a group of the women lived.

11. C. G. Jung, "The Psychology of Dreams" in *Collected Papers on Analytical Psychology, 2nd ed.*, ed. Constance Long (London: Baillière, Tindall, and Cox, 1922), p. 299. It later became the opening section of "General Aspects of Dream Psychology" in *The Collected Works of C. G. Jung*, vol. 8 (Princeton, NJ: Princeton University Press, 1972), §§ 443–476.

12. C. G. Jung, *Psychology of the Unconscious*, trans. Beatrice Hinkle (New York: Dodd, Mead, & Co., [1916] 1946), p. 199.

13. Quoted in Louis Sheaffer, *O'Neill: Son and Artist* (Boston, MA: Little Brown, 1973), p. 245.

14. Quoted in Charmian London, *The Book of Jack London, Volume 2* (New York: The Century Co., 1921), p. 323.

15. See Kathleen Pyne, *Modernism and the Feminine Voice: O'Keeffe and the Women of the Stieglitz Circle* (Berkeley and Los Angeles, CA: University of California Press, 2007), p. 175.

Part II
Jung: Science and the Academy

CHAPTER FIVE

JUNG, SCIENCE, GERMAN ROMANTICISM
A CONTEMPORARY PERSPECTIVE

Joseph Cambray

In March 1912 C. G. Jung received an invitation from the American physician Smith Ely Jelliffe (1866–1945), a medical editor and pioneer psychoanalyst who was a clinical professor at Fordham Medical College. The offer was to present a series of lectures for the International Extension Course in Medicine in September 1912 along with a number of other medical experts from around the world. At this date Jung and Freud were still on friendly terms, though this was to be a year of significant difficulties between the two, and barely a year and half before their termination of relations. By the end of April 1912 Jung had sent off part two of *Wandlungen und Symbole der Libido* (later translated as *The Psychology of the Unconscious*) to his publisher without first getting Freud's input. Then, in May, Freud visited the ailing Binswanger in Kreuzlingen without contacting Jung, for which he felt snubbed—the so-called "Kreuzlingen gesture"—a symptom of the growing alienation between the two men. In September Jung gave nine lectures at the medical school of Fordham University under the title "The Theory of Psychoanalysis." A number of points differentiating himself from Freud were made in these lectures, especially Jung's views on the libido theory. Jung's nine lectures were published initially in the inaugural volumes of the *Psychoanalytic Review* (in the first five issues of Volumes 1 and 2, from 1913 to 1915) co-edited by Jelliffe and William Alanson White, who had also been an instructor in the same course.

The invitation to Jung was based on his scientific contributions, especially to the emerging field of psychoanalysis, and, in particular, the word association experiments and his studies on *dementia praecox*. While he was in transit to Fordham University, Jung was conferred an honorary doctorate of law (on September 11 by Fordham University)—his second, as he had received his first honorary doctorate from Clark University in 1909; the American scientific and medical communities clearly valued his research efforts. Soon after arrival (September 18) he was interviewed by the New York Times and a long article was published in the magazine section on Sunday, September 29, including a photo-portrait. The text was reprinted in *C. G. Jung Speaking*.[1] This must have seemed a new height of success for the then thirty-seven-year-old Jung.

The audience of his lectures consisted of eighty-eight psychiatrists and neurologists—American physicians who were especially interested in learning about his clinical approach and analytic techniques. In addition to these lectures Jung also held a number of individual consultations, small discussion groups, and larger clinical demonstrations. He also lectured at Bellevue Hospital, the New York Psychiatric Institute, and gave a presentation to the New York Academy of Medicine, all within the space of a ten day stay in New York, a whirlwind tour.[2]

I will not go through the content of Jung's lectures as other contributors to this volume will be exploring them. The full text can be found in volume four of his *Collected Works*, recently released as a paperback monograph in the Philemon Series with a valuable introduction by Sonu Shamdasani. My focus instead will be on the type of scientific writing Jung was involved with here and going forward for the remainder of his career in the context of various traditions of science writing available. Jung's biographer Deirdre Bair rightly notes the following about these lectures:

> The nine lectures employ the same writing pattern and exhibit the same scientific precision as the writings on word association and dementia praecox that established his international

reputation. They are more "Freudian" than "Jungian" in style, for each begins with a thesis, develops it with logical consistency, and ends with a convincing summation. They are classical in the Freudian sense, with none of the Jungian circularity that pervades most of his other writing.[3]

The *circularity* to which Bair refers, however, could more accurately be read as *non-linear* and reflect an aspect of Jung's new approach which needs to be reappraised.

The Fordham lectures should be seen as the acme of Jung's writing style based on the idea of scientific objectivity that held sway in the intellectual culture of the time. The foundations of the certainty (in the world, and in Jung himself) that still prevailed in 1912, however, had already begun to crack and crumble: quantum theory and relativity were emerging to reshape scientific thought, though they were still nascent; the first theory of continental drift in earth sciences was proposed by Alfred Wegner but was ridiculed; technologically, the grandiose and iconic Titanic sinks (on April 15) while *The White Star Line* claimed it was "designed to be unsinkable"; and the world order itself was also about to be severely challenged, as in less than two years the outbreak of "The Great War" (WWI) would alter the fate of nations.

The First Phase of Scientific Writing in Jung's Career

As I have written elsewhere, the nineteen-year-old Jung had two similar dreams which he felt were crucial in deciding on a career in the sciences.[4] These dreams are recorded in *Memories, Dreams, and Reflections* (*MDR*). In both he enters some woods and makes a remarkable discovery: in the first, the bones of prehistoric animals and in the second, "a circular pool with the strangest and most wonderful creature, a *round animal, shimmering in opalescent hues … It was a giant radiolarian* … [which] aroused in me an intense desire for knowledge, so that I awoke with a beating heart."

Jung goes on to say: "These two dreams decided me overwhelmingly in favor of science, and removed all my doubts."[5] The lure of archeology, paleontology, zoology, and biology is evident in his framing of the dreams. As a young man he was reading these fields as potential career choices rather than as explicit metaphors for exploration of psychological depth; later they would become significant expressions for archaic and core aspects of the psyche. For the adolescent Jung the visionary inner world and the scientific were already intertwined and mutually interacting.

Soon after the dreams, Jung entered the medical school of Basel University in April 1895. He quickly joined the Basel section of the Swiss student fraternity, *Zofingiaverein*, and gave his very first lecture to this group in November 1896; it was entitled "The Border Zones of Exact Science."[6] Jung's eclectic tendencies were already in evidence in this first lecture as he ranges over topics in physics (gravitation, ether, conservation of energy, the newly discovered X-rays), chemistry (atomic and molecular theory), biology (Darwinism, mechanistic versus vitalistic theories, origin of life), and even a dash of psychology by the end (the entry of hypnotism into German science). His final plea was "to allow the immaterial to retain its immaterial properties."[7] The scientific content was of student quality, many of the exciting developments of the previous several decades were not included, yet his intuitions were strong; he was searching for important questions and revealing the limits of the science he had been taught.

Upon completion of his medical studies, Jung secured a position at the University Psychiatric Hospital and Clinic of Zürich, the Burghölzli Hospital, under its director Dr. med. Eugen Bleuler at the end of 1900. The hospital at this time was focused on humane patient care, likely the first milieu model in-patient psychiatric facility in the world. In contradistinction to Emil Kraepelin's strictly biological view of *dementia praecox*, Bleuler held to a view combining biological and hermeneutic elements in the etiology of these conditions—at the time the only major European psychiatrist to do so.[8] By 1908 Bleuler coined the term *schizophrenia* and then proceeded to expand Kraeplin's *dementia praecox* into a class of illnesses, the "group of schizophrenias."[9] The Burghölzli under Bleuler is, of course, where Jung conducted the research that won him international acclaim.

In 1905 Jung qualified as a lecturer (*Privatdozent*) in psychiatry at the University of Zürich. As an instructor he injected lively cultural and historical dimensions into his material and developed a large following. His research interests predominated and students came to observe and some to study at the Burghölzli from around the world, including many of those who would go on to become prominent psychoanalysts (Karl Abraham, Ludwig Binswanger, Sandor Ferenczi,

Ernest Jones, A. A. Brill, etc.). In this period, Jung was operating within the standard scientific paradigm of the times, with a strong focus on objective observations with precise measurements; the subjective aspects of the research was almost wholly focused on internal dynamics in the mental world of the patients to be described in clinically objective terms.

Jung retained his university position until April 1914, at which time he voluntarily resigned it. The internal changes behind this decision were already brewing in 1912 but did not openly appear in his Fordham lectures. Those lectures should be seen as an expression of his dedication to scientific objectivity written in the idiom prevalent amongst his medical and scientific colleagues; however, in his writing of part two of the *Psychology of the Unconscious*, an alteration in writing style had become evident. Deirdre Bair observes Jung's discomfort noting,

> he said it "embarrassed" him because it went against his grain, referring to all his medical training and previous writings that his peers considered models of scientific objectivity. But he had no choice and was compelled to write it down as he heard it spoken inside himself.[10]

Since having access to Jung's *Red Book*, we can now understand this was just the prelude to a much more profound change he was about to undergo based on his internal experiences. Before turning to that transformation, I would like to say a bit more about the state of science in 1912.

Science Around 1912: A Selection

The need for a new theory of matter and energy had already been apparent from the turn of the century, starting with Max Planck's work on black body radiation, which showed light was quantized. Attempts, however, to describe the atom remained stymied in classical, mechanistic accounts. In 1897 J. J. Thompson had shown that the supposed smallest particle of matter, the atom, was, in fact, comprised of components when he discovered the electron in his work on cathode rays. He proposed the "plum pudding" model of the atom (negatively charged electrons embedded in a uniform sea of positive material). His former student Ernst Rutherford disproved this model, showing the positively charged portion of the atom was indeed quite small; by 1912 he had advanced the miniature solar system model of the atom. The new image was still wholly classical, however, this same year Rutherford had a young visiting scientist in his laboratory, Niels Bohr. The next year, 1913, Bohr was to radicalize our views of matter by bringing quantum physics into the vision of the atom. The full articulation of a quantum theory of matter required almost fifteen more years of intensive research but in retrospect 1912–1913 can be seen as a major turning point.

Similarly, the theory of relativity, the cornerstone of modern cosmology, was not fully articulated at this time. Einstein had proposed the special theory of relativity in 1905 and was working towards the inclusion of gravitation. By 1911–12 Einstein had revived a prediction about the deflection of light rays by massive objects such as the sun and described the curvature of space-time. His calculations were not complete until he was in possession of the full general theory in 1915; the predictions were spectacularly verified by observations made during a solar eclipse in 1919 by Arthur Eddington, making front page news around the world.

In 1911 the Olduvai Gorge in the Great Rift Valley of Tanzania was discovered along with an abundance of fossils, which, beginning in 1913, would eventually lead to a much richer view of hominid evolution than was currently held. Franz Boas published *The Mind of Primitive Man* (1911), in which he cogently argues for cultural plurality, showing the interdependence of biological, linguistic, and cultural traits of any people result from their historical developments, which includes environmental as well as cultural forces. Boas here echoes one of his heroes, Alexander von Humboldt, and similarly brings a strong humanistic, anti-racist perspective to cultural anthropology. Boas had, of course, been at the Clark University festivities in 1909 along with Jung, Freud, William James, and a host of others; Shamdasani has devoted several pages to Boas' influence and its limits on Jung.[11] In 1912 Émile Durkheim published *The Elementary Forms of the Religious Life* which further explored religious phenomena from the perspective of sociology, speaking of a collective consciousness and discussing totemism. Jung later drew on two of Durkheim's students, Hubert and Mauss, in discussing his formulation of archetypes, acknowledging the two had formulated the idea of *categories of the imagination* from their ethnographic work.[12] Jung's notion of the collective unconscious also seems to have been formed partially in counterpoint to Durkheim's collective consciousness.[13] Jung first used the term in a 1916 lecture "on the unconscious and its contents."[14] In brief, at the time of Jung's Fordham lectures, the fundamental, scientific view of the world was undergoing radical transformations and this majorly affected his own conceptualizations.

The next year was one of personal trauma and exploration for Jung. As we now know in some detail, following within a month of his severance of ties with Freud in October 1913, Jung underwent a series of inner experiences that were to make him into the figure we largely know today. With the publication in 2009 of his *Red Book*, we can now see the evidence of this transformation.

The Red Book and a New View of Science

The processes already underway in the writing of part two of the *Psychology of the Unconscious* burst forth in a much more powerful way in October–November 1913. As we know, Jung experienced waking visions in which he saw "a terrible flood that covered all of the northern and low-lying lands between the North Sea and the Alps … yellow waves, swimming rubble, and the death of countless thousands"; once it was a sea of blood.[15] Although he feared for his psychological stability, he intentionally entered into and recorded this material along with other fantasies and dreams during the period from November 1913 through April 1914. This came to form the basis for his method of "active imagination," the deliberate engagement with the unconscious through direct exploration of internal image and affect, a forerunner of the contemporary use of analytic reveries in assessing activations in the interactive field.

Realizing the importance of this archaic material for his own psychological development, Jung wrote down the fantasies and dreams along with his reflections. Reworking drafts, elaborating and refining commentaries, he gradually produced a calligraphic volume bound in red leather in the fashion of a medieval, illuminated manuscript, *Liber Novus*.

By the end of April 1914 he had resigned as president of the International Psychoanalytic Association and from his position on the medical faculty of Zürich University. Clearly he was facing a crisis in his life; much of what he had embraced no longer sustained him.

Although he had a series of dreams from April into June 1914 that he ultimately found healing, it was not until August 1, 1914 that he felt released from the feeling of being endangered by "an overcompensated psychosis."[16] The onset of World War I gave him the conviction that his experiences were not wholly personal but had an objective dimension to them. This, however, placed him on the horns of a seeming impossible dilemma: was this madness or prophecy? His struggle to work through this and other conundrums posed by his internal experience was formative; it is what made Jung *Jung*. By 1916 he was able to write his essay on "The Transcendent Function" in which he detailed his innovative approach to the unconscious, especially as accessed through active imagination.

In Jung's grappling to fully enter the inner dialogues, emergent phenomena became evident in the deep background of his thought. While descriptions of complex systems were unavailable to Jung, a qualitative appreciation of phenomena of this type could be found in the biological literature of the time that he was reading, as evident in his examples of archetypal analogies from instincts found in nature. The logic of emergence can be readily found in *The Red Book*, e.g., "if you marry the ordered to the chaos you produce the divine child, the supreme meaning beyond meaning and meaninglessness."[17] Jung wrestled to stay poised on this edge of order and chaos as he descended into depths of imagination.

In the epilogue to *The Red Book* Jung writes,

> My acquaintance with alchemy in 1930 took me away from it. The beginning of the end came in 1928, when Wilhelm sent me the text of the 'Golden flower,' an alchemical treatise. There the contents of this book found their way into actuality and I could no longer continue working on it.[18]

In *MDR* Jung also identifies a deeply meaningful synchronistic occurrence at this moment: his painting "a mandala with a golden castle in the center" having a curiously Chinese feeling about it just prior to receipt of a Taoist manuscript from Richard Wilhelm who had translated it while in China.[19] The text eventually was published as *The Secret of the Golden Flower* with a commentary by Jung accompanying Wilhelm's German translation, subsequently translated into English by Cary F. Baynes, and found in Jung's *Collected Works*, volume 13.[20] The corresponding castle painting is found on page 163 of *The Red Book*, marking where Jung was in his composition of *The Red Book* when this definitive event occurred.

As his confrontation with the unconscious drew to a close, the confrontation with the world began. Shamdasani comments,

> In retrospect he described the *Red Book* as an attempt to formulate things in terms of revelation. He had hope that this would free him, but found that it didn't. He then realized that he had to return to the human side and to science. He had to draw conclusions from the insights.[21]

The timing of Jung's original formulation of the concept of synchronicity is highly significant here. The term first emerged in Jung's dream seminars in 1928 (near the time he received the *Golden Flower* text) where meaningfully coincident clusters of dreams and images were also being discussed. I have suggested it was Jung's formulation of this new idea, which became a redemptive *third* position beyond his prophecy-madness dilemma that was the real exit from *The Red Book*.[22] By taking the synchronistic exit, Jung was attempting a transformation in culture from a theological to a psychological ground. In contemporary parlance, synchronicity became a conceptual means for discussing emergent phenomena, and as George Bright has commented is the basis for the Jungian analytic attitude.[23]

My thesis is that the experiences involved in producing *The Red Book* fundamentally altered Jung, including his vision of science and scientific writing. In this vein at the encouragement of his friend, Professor Fierz, Jung wrote to the president of the ETH in May 1933 to resume his public lectures but now wanted to speak about "the general subject of modern psychology, so this could not be within the medical faculty;" his request was granted and he began in October 1933.[24]

In the years following his exit from *The Red Book* project he developed a relationship with Wolfgang Pauli, one of the star physicists who gave birth to modern quantum theory. They had a long correspondence, available in English as *Atom and Archetype* in large part due to Beverley Zabriskie. Together they authored *The Interpretation of Nature and the Psyche*, a book containing Jung's essay on synchronicity, though this was much later, in 1952. Pauli's critique of Jung's use of science in his understanding of objectivity in quantum theory is important. As science historian Suzanne Gieser notes, Pauli

> compared Jung's way of describing the unconscious with the classical field concepts of physics. ... Jung still used a mode of description which did not take the new epistemological situation revealed by quantum physics satisfactorily into account ... he still had a tendency to treat the unconscious as a field that may be observed without considering the influence of the observation.[25]

I believe Jung vacillated on this point as he was trying to meld subjective experience into objective observation, though he was seeking to bring a form of objectivity to seemingly subjective experiences, rather than solely trying to include subjective factors in objective observation. In this project he was unconsciously drawing on an older, discarded scientific tradition, e.g., from German Romanticism, that he could not let himself directly claim.

German Romanticism and Science

In response to the French and English domination in science during the seventeenth and eighteenth centuries, which was increasingly aligned with governmental agendas, German scientists developed a more individual, less nationally-oriented form of science in the latter half of the eighteenth century. In contradistinction to the analytic, reductive methods of the Enlightenment, the German scientists retained an older, holistic perspective, which also was congruent with the emerging Romantic Movement.

Closer to Jung's education and cultural affinity, the scientific aspects of German Romanticism have generally not been considered in his works beyond philosophical implications. The scientific contributions themselves have largely been ignored, or demeaned until recently. A small but growing scholarly interest in the German Romantics has been developing over the last several decades. The intertwining of science and art in ways that generate intuitive knowledge about systems of nature is regaining attention and providing an alternative vision with an interest in the science of wholes. Andrew Cunningham and Nicholas Jardine note the following in their introduction to their edited volume on *Romanticism and the sciences*:

> the stereotype of the Romantic sciences as speculative, fantastic, mystical and ill-disciplined, and their alleged defeat by the empirical natural sciences, are polemical constructs rather than the fruits of unbiased historical research.[26]

The collection of essays they offer provides a useful, broad introduction to the range of accomplishments of the Romantic scientists. For the purpose of this essay, I will skip over the obvious and well-known figure of Goethe and, instead, will use the life and work of Alexander von Humboldt (1769–1859) as an example I have explored elsewhere.[27]

Alexander, a traveler and scientist, and his brother Wilhelm, a renowned linguist and humanist, are both memorialized by Humboldt University in Berlin. Alexander developed personal friendships with numerous scientists and philosophers, including Goethe, who was twenty years his senior. When Alexander was twenty years old and studying at Göttingen, he met Georg Forster, who was by that time a best-selling author with his 1777 travelogue and scientific narrative, *A Voyage Round the World*, based on sailing with James Cook on his second Pacific voyage. Forster brought the young Humboldt along with him on a trip across Europe to London, where they met with the great British naturalist, Sir Joseph Banks. This trip was life-altering for Humboldt and a prelude to his great adventures in Latin America.[28]

Before turning to his trek in South America, it should be noted that although Humboldt is only mentioned once in Jung's *Collected Works* volume 5 (originally in part II of the *Psychology of the Unconscious*, Hinkle p. 352) where Jung makes reference to a South American Indian libido symbol that he found in Humboldt's final work *Cosmos*, there is good reason to consider deeper influence.[29] Alexander von Humboldt is the person responsible for the Jung family living in Switzerland. Briefly, Karl Gustav Jung-Frey (C. G. Jung's grandfather), a native of Mannheim Germany, arrived in Basel via Paris in 1822 to take up a professorship in medicine at the university there, becoming Swiss in the process due to a letter from Humboldt to the Burgermeister of Basel recommending him for the post.[30] Andreas Jung, C. G. Jung's grandson, has provided a detailed account of how this occurred: as a young man Karl Jung was involved in German unification politics and was unjustly imprisoned, then exiled without trial; he went to Paris where he found Humboldt who "wanted to make up for what his government did to me in a series of injustices. The unforgotten, gracious man kept his word!" which was to help Karl Jung obtain the professorship.[31] With such a family story directly tied to his namesake, it is not much of a leap to imagine Humboldt's life and works may have held attractions for Jung in unreported ways. One path by which this may have occurred is through Humboldt's scientific travel narrative, itself a clear work of German Romantic science.

Before traveling to Latin America, Humboldt had already established himself as a plant geographer with his first significant publication in 1793 which was based on his work in the mines around Freiberg. Even at this early date he argues "plants should not be studied in isolation but as an integral part of the environment in which they are found."[32] His holistic-environmental views were later adopted by Ernst Haeckel when he coined the term ecology—Haeckel's artistic renditions of marine creatures was also to unconsciously affect the imagery of Jung's *Red Book*.[33] The empiricism Humboldt learned from Forster was deliberately "combined with enthusiastic recording of emotional responses and subjective impressions" as when studying the morphology of landscape.[34] Humboldt was a well accomplished, respected scientist in Europe before setting off on his travels.

Humboldt, together with the botanist Aimé Bonpland, obtained permission and royal support from the Spanish Crown for a scientific expedition to Spanish America. In 1799 they left on a voyage that took them to Venezuela and from there inland by canoe to explore the Orinoco River. Collecting specimens, discovering many new species of plants, insects, and animals, they also demonstrated the existence of the Casiquiare Canal: a unique, natural link between the Orinoco and Amazon River systems. They made astronomical observations and took data on geomagnetism; however, as Humboldt details in his travel memoirs, they also suffered many (mis)adventures, such as experimenting on themselves with electric eels (being severely shocked in the process), having their pet Mastiff eaten by jaguars, nearly drowning in capsizes, becoming violently ill, and enduring seemingly limitless torture of biting insects in the rainforest. At times there is an inferno-like quality to the narrative, so intense that the reader feels the emotions of the travelers.

After a trip to Cuba to recover their health and to explore that island, the next phase of their travels took them through New Granada (including modern day Colombia and Ecuador) and Peru. In addition to river travel and rainforests they also trekked through the Andes Mountains with tremendous ascents at the limits of human capacities—they set the world record at the time for height, 19,286 feet, unaided by artificial sources of oxygen. This gave them the opportunity to study the diversity of life, especially plant life, at differing altitudes and climates as they ascended from rainforest to snow-capped mountain. In an important essay that came from these observations Humboldt sought to link plant geography, as he termed it, to cultural forms:

> the man who is sensitive to the beauties of nature will ... find there the explanation of <u>the influence exerted by the appearance of vegetation over Man's taste and imagination</u>. He will take pleasure in examining what is constituted by the "character" of the vegetation and the variety of sensation it produces in the soul of the person who contemplates it. These considerations are all the more significant because they are closely linked to the means by which the imitative arts and descriptive poetry succeed in acting upon us. ... What a marked contrast between forests in temperate zones and those of the Equator, where the bare slender trunks of the palms soar above the flowered mahogany trees and create majestical portico arches in the sky. ... How does this ... appearance of nature, rich and pleasant to a greater or lesser degree, affect the customs and above all the sensibility of the people?[35]

Historian of science, Margarita Bowen, incorporating a quote from Humboldt, remarks "'the apparently impossible gulf between thought and being, the relationship between the knowing mind and perceived object' was seen by Humboldt as the locus of the sciences. Science is mind applied to nature."[36] Hence, sciences in Humboldt's definition would make central what Jung termed the psychoid.

Humboldt's scientific travelogue, his multi-volume *Personal Narratives* (1819–1829), was a source of inspiration to numerous scientists including the father of Geology, Charles Lyell, as well as Charles Darwin. For a young Darwin, Humboldt was a hero; he brought volumes of the *Personal Narratives* aboard the Beagle (and Captain Fitzroy also had a full set). In a letter to his closest friend, the botanist and explorer Sir Joseph Dalton Hooker, Darwin wrote "I believe that you are fully right in calling Humboldt the greatest scientific traveler who ever lived" (Darwin, 1887, 6 August 1881). In his *Beagle* diary Darwin wrote: "I am at present fit only to read Humboldt; he like another Sun illumines everything I behold."[37]

The nearly solitary journey into the unknown, at great personal risk and expense, for the purpose of seeking knowledge of the interior, can be viewed as a highly informative precursor to some of Jung's own responses to the experiences that he crafted into *The Red Book*. From this vantage, *The Red Book* can be viewed as a scientific contribution in line with the travel narrative reports of a romantic scientist such as Humboldt, the unknown territory moving from the external physical world to the interior, psychological one, similar to the way that some of the Romantics moved back and forth between inner and outer worlds.

Humboldt's last great project was his five volume *Cosmos: A sketch of a physical description of the universe* (1866). When he started to formulate the idea of writing a comprehensive treatise on the physical description of the entire universe, a lifetime's passion that began from a young man, it took his travels, a series of sixty-one lectures at Berlin University on the whole of the physical sciences, and then almost two decades of writing to produce the first several volumes.[38] As scholar Laura Dassow Walls remarks: "Historians credit Humboldt's lectures with jump-starting German science, which went on to surpass even the French in brilliance … in its power to raise and educate the many."[39] In its scope *Cosmos* was perhaps the last work of its kind, with one scientist attempting a total description of the world, displaying his essential vision that nature is a single, unifying force in which "everything is related" which Gerhard Müller notes emphasizes interrelationship or interrelatedness, making Humboldt's perspective the direct background to environmental sciences and a forerunner to Jung's field theory with its intensely relational quality as well as the relational paradigm in psychoanalysis.[40,41,42]

The initial volumes of *Cosmos* were immensely popular and influenced generations of scientists. In the first volume, published in German in 1845, Humboldt focuses on the outer world, an "objective journey through the external world of the senses."[43] The second volume, also in German, published in 1847, shifts to a focus on "an inner or 'subjective' journey through mind, 'the inner, reflected intellectual world.'"[44] As Walls observes, for Humboldt this shift to the subjective is not what we would normally understand as a psychological exploration:

> but something more Wordsworthian, the emergence and growth of mind-in-nature, 'the reflection of the image impressed by the senses upon the inner man, that is, upon his ideas and feelings.' The second volume thus journeys through time—historical time, from the earliest civilizations.[45]

The first section of volume II is entitled "Incitements to the Study of Nature," referring to "the image reflected by the external world on the imagination"; it offers an ecologically-based archeology of civilization and mind as formed in response to the natural environment with the life-forms, especially plants, present. The second section of this volume is titled: "History of the Physical Contemplation of the Universe: Principal Causes of the Gradual Development and Extension of the Idea of the Cosmos as a Natural Whole."[46] Robert Richards sees Humboldt's explicit intention, in its attempts at a poetics of nature, as arguing: "the natural historian had the duty to re-create in the reader—through the use of artful language—aesthetic experiences of the sort the naturalist had himself undergone in his immediate encounter with nature."[47] When examined carefully, I believe this volume can be seen as holding a worldview which Jung will reformulate in terms of an objective psyche and the collective unconscious. Humboldt's views even more closely anticipate ideas to be found in the work of Jungian analyst James Hillman with his "poetic basis of mind" and his attention to the *anima mundi* (the soul of the world).[48]

Humboldt's project in creating a vision of *Cosmos* involved marrying scientific measurement and precision to artistic, aesthetic experience. He states,

> It is by a separation and classification of phenomena, by an intuitive insight into the play of obscure forces, and by animated expressions, in which the perceptible spectacle is reflected with vivid truthfulness, that we may hope to comprehend and describe the *universal all* (τὸ πάν) in a manner worthy of the dignity of the word *Cosmos* in its signification of *universe, order of the world,* and *adornment* of this universal order.[49]

In the grand vision of *Cosmos*, Humboldt seeks to weave a coherent unity of nature, self, and nation, or *race*. (In his study of human differences, Humboldt is one of the first Western scientists to challenge the notion of difference in human groups being due to inherent traits; his views are remarkably democratic for his age and this is part of what won him Boas' admiration.) According to Walls this synthesis "is a necessary part of the *Bildung*, or growth and integration of the self in the world. ... One could call what he was after *grounded imagination*."[50]

The cosmological vision Humboldt is seeking through his study of the physical universe in fact bears resemblance to Jung's late life cosmological musing. As I have written about elsewhere, Jung's goal in his synchronicity monograph—to supplement the triad of classical physics (space, time, and causality) with a fourth principle, synchronicity—is founded on a cosmogonic insight.[51] In response to the articulation of the Big Bang model of the universe of the astrophysicists of his day, Jung sought to locate a pattern-forming tendency emerging from an originary singularity that he identified as synchronicity. At that time, there was no complexity theory available. Starting from Jung's intuitions I suggest his work on synchronicity deserves reconsideration and some modification in terms of modern theory. Thus the phase transitions proposed in the immediate wake of the Big Bang which are the ultimate source of all of known physics are now understood in terms of symmetry-breaking that leads to increasing complexity.[52] Patterns of increasing complexity emerged as the early universe cooled and evolved; much later in cosmic time this same propensity leads to the origins of life and to the psyche. All of these key events occur through phase transitions that are associated with self-organizing systems that yield new, higher level/emergent properties. Therefore, through this late argument, Jung, at his most far-reaching, places the origins of the psyche in the same milieu as belongs to the origins of the physical universe; mind, and even the imagination, are thereby most fundamentally grounded in nature. In making this link, it should be noted that Jung is hardly a consistent writer: he draws on many sources, and over the course of his long life, his views alter as his understandings change. As I have argued elsewhere, his views on topics such as symmetry-breaking vacillate; my interest is pursuing the edges of his thought, which is where influences outside consciousness often enter, rather than his definitive, unconflicted statements.[53]

As you also may recall, while working on *The Red Book* Jung reported an internal struggle around defining what he was doing, seeing it as neither art nor science; his conscious conclusion was that it was *nature*.[54] His mistrust of the aesthetic dimension to his work is captured by his irritable dismissal of the inner voice that was insisting he was doing art—"I recognized it as the voice of a patient, a talented psychopath who had a strong transference to me"—together with his fear of his vulnerability to her suggestions.[55] This struggle peaked following receipt of a letter from this woman who stressed "the fantasies arising from my unconscious had artistic value and should be considered art."[56] Jung's subsequent emotional distress provoked a rupture in the mandala he was working on: "part of the periphery had burst open and the symmetry was destroyed."[57] As mentioned, such symmetry-breaking is essential to emergence, and Jung was both fascinated and repelled by such breaks—making, then backing away from them.[58] In *The Red Book* the broken mandala can be seen to reflect the inauguration of a transformative process stemming from an activation of the unconscious and taking him to ground that is analogous to that of the scientist of the German Romantic tradition.[59]

Reemergence of Holistic Studies in Contemporary Science

With the advent of high-speed computers and the capacity for advanced simulation of systems that had been considered beyond scientific modeling, new possibilities have opened up in the last two decades. In particular, exploration of non-linear dynamical systems has become a topic of accelerating interest. Such systems exhibit complex spatial and temporal evolution. The accuracy of the simulations performed on many of these systems has opened up the field of complexity studies. Some of the most intriguing examples come from what is termed *complex adaptive systems*, as they exhibit the capacity for self-organization with emergent properties (irreducible to properties of the component parts). These studies necessarily form an interdisciplinary branch of science drawing on multiple disciplines. The results have proven useful at multiple levels, e.g., they tend to be *scale-free* and even include human activities, such as understanding traffic patterns, fluctuations in stock-markets, and so forth. This has helped to spark a renewed interest in holistic perspectives thereby rekindling a major concern of the German Romantic scientists, now with enhanced scientific rigor.

One set of applications is geared towards understanding the mind-body relationship. Cognitive and neuro-scientists have begun to generate more integrated views of the role of emotions, images, and imagination in the formation of the mind, as in the writings of Antonio Damasio among many others.[60] Similarly, there has been a turn towards revaluing the importance of aesthetics in the emergence of the mind, e.g., in the work of the visual neurologist V. S. Ramachandran and the new field of neuroesthetics.[61] The return to scientific research of topics at the heart of German Romanticism such as subjectivity, affect, and imagination suggests the possibility for reevaluation of this older tradition as holding some necessary perspective if a paradigm shift towards scientific holism is to be accomplished. Perhaps, as a part of this reconsideration, the tendency for oscillations between reductionism and holism may decrease in a manner that allows both approaches to be held in tension in any ongoing discourse.

In another paper, I offer a further example from the ecological perspective that emerged out of the work of the German Romantic scientists: epigenetics.[62] The concept itself is derived from the much older term *epigenesis* which referred to a developmental theory whereby "an individual is developed by successive differentiation of an unstructured egg rather than by a simple enlarging of a preformed entity."[63] The self-organizing tendencies felt to be in response to environmental pressures inherent in the theory of epigenesis caught the imagination of the Romantic scientists, and, as historian of science Stefan Willer comments, "[t]his is why *generation* in an epigenetic view could become closely linked to *genius* and furnish a leading model for philosophical and poetical productivity."[64]

The concept went in and out of fashion over the course of the nineteenth century, but was largely dismissed as genetics came to dominate, especially through the work of August Weismann. Weismann persuasively argued that once an egg was fertilized nothing essential was added; he linked this with Darwinian evolution (but now in the service of genetics), severing development from heredity.

This view was not significantly modified in the scientific community until the work of C. H. Waddington who coined the term *epigenetics* in 1940. Nevertheless, this new field, despite greatly reduced modest claims—no longer an entire theory of inheritance but just a description of the way environmental effects act on and modify an individual's genetic program of development—was often met with scorn.

It has not been until the current century, with the completion of the human genome project, that the limits of a genetic approach alone for understanding organisms have become widely recognized in the scientific community. A key element in the theory of epigenetics is that there are classes of heritable modifications which are not involved in alterations of DNA bases or their sequences. Within a decade of this resurgence there has been an explosion of interest and applications of epigenetic research, which can be seen for various disease and ageing processes such as the origins of different cancers, for example.[65] Similarly, some psychological issues, especially multigenerational trauma, have been recognized to have epigenetic components. The reintroduction of the impact of the environment on hereditary processes does herald a return to the importance of ecology in discussions of evolutionary biology in line with German Romantic scientific concerns with *organic memory*.

A host of recent studies have begun to document epigenetic influences on biological transmission of traumatic memory. For example, writer Nessa Carey recently published a book with numerous accounts of empirical research verifying epigenetic mechanism at work in various human situations.[66] A particularly poignant example she cites is on the victims of the Dutch Hunger Winter (November 1944 until May 1945), when the German authorities halted food supplies in the portion of the Netherlands that they occupied at this late stage of the Second World War. This tragic situation gives a clearly delineated time frame for this famine. Epidemiologists have been able to study the impact on pregnant mothers and their newborns as detailed records survive due to the excellent healthcare system in place at the time. The findings have been quite surprising:

> If a mother was well-fed around the time of conception and malnourished only for the last few months of the pregnancy, her baby was likely to be born small. If, on the other hand, the mother

suffered malnutrition for the first three months of the pregnancy only ... but then was well-fed, she was likely to have a baby with normal body weight. ... The babies who were born small stayed small all their lives, with lower obesity rates than the general population [despite availability of ample food] ... the children whose mothers had been malnourished only early in pregnancy, had higher obesity rates than normal. Recent reports have shown a greater incidence of other health problems as well, including certain tests of mental activity. ... Even more extraordinarily, some of these effects seem to be present in the children of this group, i.e., in the grandchildren of the women who were malnourished during the first three months of their pregnancy.[67]

In this case, researchers have begun to identify specific epigenetic biochemical markers not found with same-sex siblings who were not exposed to the famine. Furthermore, the researchers acknowledge

[a]n additional contribution of other stressors, such as cold and emotional stress, cannot be ruled out, however. Our study provides the first evidence that transient environmental conditions early in human gestation can be recorded as persistent changes in epigenetic information.[68]

Although these results are primarily concerned with biological mechanism of transmission of environmentally-generated trauma, they do open the possibility of serious consideration of the impact of the psychological environment on unconscious memory transmission. With this, Jung's notion of a collective unconscious deserves a careful reexamination. More generally, Jung's writing in the aftermath of his *Red Book* experience when contextualized against the background of Romantic science offers a way to return to a vision that has largely been lost in the Academy outside literature.

NOTES

1. C. G. Jung, *C. G. Jung Speaking: Interviews and Encounter*, eds. William McGuire and R. F. C. Hull (Princeton, NJ: Princeton University Press, 1977), pp. 11–24; and see chapter by Sherry in this volume.

2. Deirdre Bair, *Jung: A Biography* (Boston, New York, London: Little, Brown and Co., 2003), pp. 229–230.

3. Bair, *Jung: A Biography*, p. 230.

4. Joseph Cambray, "Jung, Science, and His Legacy," *International Journal of Jungian Studies* 3 (2, 2011): 110–124.

5. C. G. Jung, *Memories, Dreams, Reflections* (New York: Pantheon Books, 1961), p. 85.

6. C. G. Jung, "The Border Zone of Exact Science," in *The Collected Works of C. G. Jung: Supplementary Volume A, The Zofingia Lectures*, ed. William McGuire (Princeton, NJ: Princeton University Press, 1983).

7. Jung, *Zofinga*, p. 19.

8. Paul Hoff, Private lecture on the history of the Burghölzli Hospital, 2011.

9. Eugen Bleuler, *Dementia praecox oder Gruppe der Schizophrenien*. in G. von Aschaffenburg, ed., *Handbuch der Psychiatrie* (Leipzig, Vienna: Deutike,1911); published in English as *Dementia Praecox or the Group of Schizophrenias*, trans. J. Zinkin (New York: International Universities Press, 1950).

10. Bair, *Jung: A Biography*, p 224–225.

11. Sonu Shamdasani, *Jung and the Making of Modern Psychology* (Cambridge: Cambridge University Press, 2003), pp. 276–78.

12. C. G. Jung, *The Archetypes and the Collective Unconscious*, vol. 9, *The Collected Works of C. G. Jung*, ed. and trans. Gerhard Adler and R. F. C. Hull (Princeton, NJ: Princeton University Press, 1940), § 153.

13. Susan F. Greenwood, "Émile Durkheim and C. G. Jung: Structuring a Transpersonal Sociology of Religion," *Journal for the Scientific Study of Religion* 29 (4, 1990): 482–495.

14. David Tresan, "Collective Unconscious," in the *International Dictionary of Psychoanalysis*, ed. Alain de Mijolla (New York: Thomson Gale, 2005).

15. C. G. Jung, *The Red Book: Liber Novus*, ed. Sonu Shamdasani (New York, London: W. W. Norton & Co., 2009) p. 231.

16. C. G. Jung, *C. G. Jung Analytical Psychology: Notes of the Seminar Given in 1925 by C. G. Jung*, ed. William McGuire (Princeton, NJ: Princeton University Press, 1989), p. 44.

17. Jung, *The Red Book*, p. 235.

18. *Ibid.*, p. 360.

19. Jung, *Memories, Dreams, Reflections*, p. 197.

20. C. G. Jung, "Commentary on 'The Secret of the Golden Flower,'" in *The Collected Works of C. G. Jung*, vol. 13, ed. and trans. Gerhard Adler and R. F. C. Hull (Princeton, NJ: Princeton University Press, 1967), pp. 1–56.

21. Jung, *The Red Book*, p. 219.

22. Joseph Cambray, "*The Red Book*: Entrances and Exits," in *The Red Book: Reflections on C. G. Jung's Liber Novus*, eds. T. Kirsch and G. Hogenson (New York & London: Routledge, 2013), pp. 36–53.

23. George Bright, "Synchronicity as a Basis of Analytic Attitude," *Journal of Analytical Psychology* 42 (4, 1997): 613–635.

24. Angela Graf-Nold, "C. G. Jung's Position at the 'Eidgenössische Technische Hochschule Zürich' (ETH Zürich) —the 'Swiss Federal Institute of Technology Zürich,'" *Jung History* 2 (2, 2007):12–15.

25. Susan Gieser, *The Innermost Kernel* (Berlin, Heidelberg, New York: Springer, 2005), p. 245.

26. Andrew Cunningham and Nicholas Jardine, eds., *Romanticism and the Sciences* (Cambridge: Cambridge University Press, 1990), p. 7–8.

27. Joseph Cambray, "Romanticism and Revolution in Jung's Science," in *Jung & Science*, ed. Raya Jones (Hove and New York: Routledge, 2014).

28. Gerard Helferich, *Humboldt's Cosmos* (New York: Gotham Books, Penguin Group Inc., 2004), pp. 10–11.

29. C. G. Jung, *Symbols of Transformation*, vol. 5, in *The Collected Works of C. G. Jung*, ed. and trans. Gerhard Adler and R. F. C. Hull (Princeton, NJ: Princeton University Press, 1956), § 481 & n.

30. Bair, *Jung: A Biography*, p. 10.

31. Andreas Jung, "The Grandfather," *Journal of Analytical Psychology* 56 (5, 2011): 653–673, p. 661.

32. Helferich, *Humboldt's Cosmos*, p. 343.

33. Cambray, *The Red Book: Reflections on C. G. Jung's Liber Novus*, pp. 36–53.

34. Malcolm Nicholson, "Alexander von Humboldt and Vegetation," in *Romanticism and the Sciences*, eds. Cunningham and Jardine (Cambridge: Cambridge University Press, 1990), p. 171.

35. Nicolson, *Romanticism and the sciences*, p. 172.

36. Margarita Bowen, *Empiricism and Geographical Thought: From Francis Bacon to Alexander von Humboldt* (Cambridge: Cambridge University Press, 1981), p. 257.

37. Robert J. Richards, *The Romantic Conception of Life: Science and Philosophy in the Age of Goethe* (Chicago and London: University of Chicago Press, 2002), p. 514.

38. Helferich, *Humboldt's Cosmos*, p. 320–323.

39. Laura Dassow Walls, *The Passage to Cosmos: Alexander von Humboldt and the Shaping of America* (Chicago and London: The University of Chicago Press, 2011), p. 216; also see her note 11.

40. Helferich, *Humboldt's Cosmos*, p. 323.

41. Gerhard H. Müller, "*Wechselwirkung* in the Life and Other Sciences: A Word, New Claims and a Concept around 1800 ... and Much Later," *Romanticism in Science: Science in Europe, 1790–1840*, eds. S. Poggi and M. Bossi (Dordrecht, Boston, London: Kluwer Academic Publishers, 1994), p. 1 and n. 1 & 2.

42. Joseph Cambray, *Synchronicity: Nature and Psyche in an Interconnected Universe*, Fay Lecture Series (College Station, TX: Texas A & M University Press, 2009), chap. 2.

43. Walls, *Passage to Cosmos*, p. 221.

44. *Ibid*.

45. *Ibid*.

46. Alexander von Humboldt, *Cosmos: A Sketch of a Physical Description of the Universe,* 5 vols., trans. E. C. Otté (and B. H. Paul for vol. 4; and W. S. Dallas for vol. 5) (New York: Harper and Brothers Printing, 1866). All the volumes available online by the Biodiversity Heritage Library at, http://www.biodiversitylibrary.org/bibliography/32462.

47. Richards, *Romantic Conception of Life*, p. 521.

48. James Hillman, *Re-Visioning Psychology* (New York: Harper and Row Publishers, 1975), p. xi.

49. Humboldt, *Cosmos*, vol. 1, p. 79.

50. Walls, *Passage to Cosmos*, p. 223.

51. Joseph Cambray, "Cosmos and Culture in the Play of Synchronicity," in *The Playful Psyche Entering Chaos, Coincidence, Creation, Jungian Odyssey Series, Vol. IV*, eds. Stacy Wirth, Isabelle Meier, and John Hill with Consulting Editor Nancy Cater (New Orleans, LA: Spring Journal Books, 2012), pp. 133–147.

52. Klaus Mainzer, *Symmetry and Complexity: The Spirit and Beauty of Nonlinear Science* (Hackensack, NJ: World Scientific Publishing Co., 2005), pp.147–158.

53. Cambray, *Synchronicity*, pp. 57–67.
54. Jung, *Memories, Dreams, Reflections,* p. 186.
55. *Ibid.,* p. 185.
56. *Ibid.,* p. 195.
57. *Ibid.*
58. Cambray, *Synchronicity*, chap. 3.
59. Cambray, *The Red Book: Reflections on C. G. Jung's Liber Novus*, pp. 44–45.
60. Antonio Damasio, *The Feeling of What Happens* (New York: Harcourt, Inc., 1999); *Looking for Spinoza: Joy, Sorrow, and the Feeling Brain* (New York: Harcourt, Inc., 2003); and *Self Comes to Mind* (New York: Pantheon Books, 2010).
61. V. S. Ramachandran, *The Tell-Tale Brain* (New York: W. W. Norton & Co., 2011).
62. Cambray, *Jung and Science.*
63. The American Heritage® Medical Dictionary Copyright © 2007, 2004 by Houghton Mifflin Company.
64. Stefan Willer, "'Epigenesis' in Epigenetics: Scientific Knowledge, Concepts, and Words," in *The Hereditary Hourglass, Genetics and Epigenetics, 1868–2000,* eds. Ana Barahona, Edna Suarez-Diaz, and Hans-Jörg Rheinberger (Berlin: Max Planck Institute for the History of Science [pre-print 392], 2010), p. 17.
65. Scott F. Gilbert and David Epel, *Ecological Developmental Biology: Integrating Epigenetics, Medicine, and Evolution* (Sunderland, MA: Sinauer Associates, Inc., 2009).
66. Nessa Carey, *The Epigenetics Revolution* (New York and Chichester: Columbia University Press, 2012).
67. Carey, *Epigenetics Revolution*, pp. 2–3.
68. Bastiaan T. Heijmans, Elmar W. Tobi, Aryeh D. Stein, Hein Putter, Gerard J. Blauw, Ezra S. Susser, P. Eline Slagboom, and L. H. Lumey, "Persistent Epigenetic Differences Associated with Prenatal Exposure to Famine in Humans," *PNAS* 105 (44, 2008): 17046–17048.

CHAPTER SIX

JUNG—ROMANTIC, MODERNIST, AND POST-MODERNIST
DISCUSSION OF DR. CAMBRAY'S CHAPTER

Martin A. Schulman

I would like, for personal as well as professional reasons, to thank both Fordham University and the Jungian Psychoanalytic Association of New York for inviting me to this celebratory conference. On a personal note, Rose Hill is near where I was born and spent what Quentin Crisp calls one's "deformative years," so it's good to be home again.[1] Jung in his Fordham lectures posited an infantile presexual stage.[2] He obviously never treated a Bronxite. In spite of my wife's saying I shouldn't mention this blemish on my pristine reputation, Rose Hill was the site, in 1959, of my first political arrest. There was a TV show called *Hootenanny*, which tried to capitalize on the folk music boom. They filmed on college campuses and refused to hire blacklisted artists such as the Weavers, Pete Seeger, etc., replacing them with more commercial-sanitized performers. A group of us led by the folk singer and composer Dave Van Ronk picketed the show when it broadcast from this campus and we were arrested for trespassing. The charges were dropped; however, I believe Jung would appreciate our action since he too was blacklisted—in his case, from the psychoanalytic movement and replaced by more conventional, less creative thinkers. Therefore, if the invitation to this weekend's conference was meant as an apology by Fordham University for my being branded a criminal, *I accept.* All is forgiven.

On a professional level, some of you might wonder, to paraphrase Admiral Stockdale, "who is he and why is he here?" Jung's Fordham lectures, as Dr. Cambray mentioned, were published in volume 1, issues #1–4 and volume 2, issue #1 of the newly founded *Psychoanalytic Review.* This led Ernest Jones to label the *Review* as a *journal of malcontents.*[3] I prefer to see the *Review* in its initial volume and throughout its history as a journal of discontents rather than malcontents: Discontent with rigidity, sectarianism, and orthodoxy, having instead a commitment to open inquiry. I am convinced that while the Fordham lectures highlighted distinct differences between Freud and Jung as to etiology of disorders, role of infantile sexuality, aims of treatment, the nature of libido, etc., and by then the tension between these two giants was at the threshold of rupture, I agree with Paskauskas that it was Jones who goaded Freud to finalize the break and have Jung excommunicated, as he later did with others that might interfere with his *second-in-command* status.[4] This is evidenced by his pushing for the establishing of the *secret committee* to destroy the reputation of dissidents, and even modifiers to use Bergmann's term, as well as keeping the theory pure.[5] I refer specifically to his maligning of Ferenczi after Ferenczi's death and the banishment of David Eder, the first British psychoanalyst, for being sympathetic to Jung's view of libido. This ostracism of Eder, who was the male witness for Jones at his tragically brief first marriage, led Jones to lay claim to being the first *legitimate* British analyst. But that's another paper!

During my sixteen-year tenure as Editor of the *Review* one of my more innovative ventures was volume 83, issue #4 (1996) in which I gave over to my friend Andrew Samuels to edit a symposium informing our readership of contemporary post-Jungian thinking and clinical work. The issue included contributions by Samuels, Beebe, Kirsch, Taylor, Kast, Sidoli, and Brooke, representing a sampling of the different tendencies within contemporary post-Jungian scholarship. The reaction to this issue was curious. The troglodytic heirs to Jones condemned me as a heretic, labeled me a fifth columnist, and suggested the stockades. Most, however, found this exposure to contemporary Jungian thought to be informative and interesting. While not glossing over the differences between Freud and Jung, my feeling, both then as Editor and now as a mere humble practitioner, is that the systems are more alike than the Freudian model is to many of the contemporary tendencies within psychoanalysis; those that downplay or disregard unconscious dynamics, disregard childhood development, ignore sexuality, askew symbolization, and see analysis as exclusively bound to the clinical domain are thus disregarding the cultural impact of psychodynamic thinking. Mills states the following:

> Psychoanalysis today is largely a psychology of consciousness: post- and neo-Freudians form a marginalized community within North America in comparison to contemporary relational and intersubjective theorists who emphasize the phenomenology of lived conscious experience, affective attunement, social construction, and interpersonal recognition over the role of insight and interpretation.[6]

Paradoxically within the current craze of neuroscience and imaging/stimulation technologies, there is one thing that is agreed upon: much goes on outside of conscious awareness, something both Freudians and Jungians have known all along.

Freud said in *The Question of Lay Analysis* that he was apprehensive that psychoanalysis would end up in psychiatry textbooks as just another method of treatment, believing its real power was beyond the clinical realm, serving as the foundation for a general understanding of human behavior.[7] Thus, history, literature, the arts, and the social sciences are encompassed within its realm. This is how the *Review* has historically envisioned psychoanalysis, and I think the Jungians would concur with this broader sentiment. In fact, one of my reasons for publishing the Jung symposium was to try to close the chasm between the two systems, seeing them both as variations of depth psychology and within the same family—with family unification a necessity at this time in our history since we are under attack from psychopharmacology, from behaviorally oriented modalities, and certainly from insurance companies and HMOs.

I would like to extend Dr. Cambray's paper and posit that Freudian psychoanalysis is grounded solidly in modernism, while Jungian psychoanalysis is more extensive: it has elements of modernism, pre-modernism or romanticism, and the roots for present-day post-modernism. In the 1930s those Americans who fought against fascism in Spain were labeled premature anti-fascists. I believe that, without too great a stretch, we can see in elements of Jung's writings, particularly those on therapy, a premature post-modernism.

Modernism

First, for Modernism, there is still no terse accepted definition. What seems inherent, however, to the various definitions of modernism is the attempt to demystify, clarify, and reveal. The advocacy of reason, rationality, universal moral truths, and linear historical progress all culminating in the ideals of emancipation and enlightenment are integral to this perspective. This is counterposed to irrationality and superstition, the forces in opposition to which modernism arose. Jameson also posits that *depth* is an ingredient of modernist thinking and can be seen in dichotomous categories or binary opposites such as true and false consciousness as witnessed in the writings of the Marxists; essence and appearance (Hegel); good and bad faith (the existentialist paradigm); true and false selves a la Winnicott, but for historical accuracy, originating in Jung, although not often credited to him; and latent and manifest content and primary and secondary process as developed by Freud.[8] As Rustin says,

> at all events, the advance of human understanding required the probing of unknown depths, whose secrets were protected, implicitly or explicitly by forces of conservatism which could not afford to see the world rendered transparent to understanding and thereby opened to choice.[9]

Within this frame, Freudian psychoanalysis can be seen as representative of modernism in regard to its understanding that reason needs to struggle with the resistance to understanding and emancipation, both clinically as well as societally. Freudian psychoanalysis can also be viewed as the attempt to apply the domain of reason to emotions and those aspects of irrationality, which Rustin posits, "were not readily comprehensible within rationalistic categories."[10] Indeed, as Fenichel in *his* red books points out, "the subject matter, not the method of psychoanalysis is irrational."[11]

Understanding through insight, not just cognitive, but having the attached affect, and rendered via interpretations, follows from this as does the need to differentiate psychoanalysis from its historical, irrational antecedent: suggestion. Freud's famous aphorism "where id was, there shall ego be" highlights this striving for the triumph without any expectation of success or rationality.[12] This same "where id was, there shall ego be," or "*wo es war, zoll ich sein*" can also be translated as "where it was, I shall become," a translation in line with Jung's concept of individuation and the synthesis of disowned and contradictory aspects of the psyche. Thus, for Freud and for contemporary Freudian-based psychoanalysis, the triumph of rationality, along with the belief that the irrational can be understood rationally, leads to the belief that the technique of psychoanalysis is a scientific endeavor, and this belief has been a hallmark of psychoanalysis' historical development. As Freud stated,

> Our best hope for the future is that intellect—the scientific spirit, reason—may in the process of time establish a dictatorship in the mental life of man. The nature of reason is a guarantee that afterwards it will not fail to give man's emotional impulses and what is determined by them the position they deserve. But the common compulsion exercised by such a dominance of reason will prove to be the strongest uniting bond among men and will lead the way to further unions. Whatever, like religion's prohibitions against thought, opposes such a development is a danger for the future of mankind.[13]

There are indeed elements of Jung's writings that fit squarely within this modernist frame and, in fact, anticipate developments in contemporary mainstream psychoanalysis:

1. While Freud's theory is Oedipally-oriented, with Jung we find, even predating Klein, the emergence of the importance of pre-Oedipal life and more importantly of the mother, whether as an archetype or as a primal self a la Fordham.[14] Thus, we move from phallocentrism to a convergence with object-relations theorists, like Winnicott, and Bowlby with his attachment theory.[15]

2. Even if we leave aside Grubrich-Simitis and the Hofers' publishing of Freud's phylogenetic writings and Lacan's view of the unconscious as structured like language, we find in contemporary psychoanalysis the acceptance that the unconscious has a structure to it that goes beyond individual history, almost a Piagetian schema that allows the dynamics to be internalized and unfold.[16,17] Is this terribly different from the impersonal collective tier Jung posits and the

archetypes around which experience crystallizes? Neither the unconscious nor psychoanalysts are pure empiricists. There is always a structured *anlage* to which input is assimilated.

3. Beginning with Sharpe's and Noy's writings on primary process and Winnicott's on play, contemporary Freudians see the dynamic unconscious as not just a repository of the unacceptable but also a source of inspiration and creativity.[18,19,20] As I used to tell my students, when one dreams, one is not just reducing tension but creating a drama where one is the actors, the director, the producer, the camera person, and I imagine the *goffer*, if I knew what that was. As for creativity and imagination rooted in unconscious processes, just looking at twentieth-century art and literature it is difficult to *not* see this.

4. There has been a distinct shift from transference as the exclusive source of information about the patient to seeing countertransference in its totalistic vein as also operative. We find Jung emphasizing that countertransference is an important organ of information. Many contemporary analysts indeed define psychoanalysis as the study of the transference/counter-transference dynamic.

5. The self, while still poorly defined even by Kohut, is no longer viewed as simply a representation in the system *ego* as posited by Hartmann.[21] It is now seen by many as a superordinate structure encompassing the full individual: soma and psyche. Along with this, we have accepted the concept of the *false self* or as I prefer the *defended against self*, a concept not too different from Jung's stating that contemporary neurosis are due to modern man having lost himself in his persona, if he believes that that is the totality of who he is. Thus, there is a movement in psychoanalysis to strive for authenticity and not just the lifting of repressions and intrapsychic structural change.

6. Freudian psychoanalysis has moved beyond ego psychology and become a psychology of the full person, as Jung advocated, and not just reified structures in conflict. Even Brenner, during the last decade of his life, moved away from the structural model he espoused for much of his productive career.[22]

7. By positing the process of individuation and a true self, Jung is envisioning an end state to psychological development—an ultimate state of completeness—a modernist view as we see in other modernists such as Freud, Marx, and Sartre. If we conceive of the self as a psychic

wholeness, i.e., the totality of conscious and unconscious, then this development of a self becomes a goal of both treatment and life.

8. In line with the modernist tendency for dichotomy, we find in Jung the arranging of psychic configurations in a dichotomous mode, e.g., persona-shadow, anima-animus, introversion-extroversion, thinking-feeling, sensing-intuiting, etc.

9. While this might seem to contradict the position I will later take in discussing Jung as a precursor of post-modernism in the development of a contextualized psychoanalysis, we also find universals in Jung. For example, the archetypes show the commonality of all humanity at the deepest possible level.

Does this imply that Jung was prescient in regard to the direction psychoanalysis will take? Not necessarily. It simply means that an open system rather than a closed, finalized one has many contributors who along with Jung were ostracized (e.g., Ferenczi and Sullivan) and whose work, rather than being incorporated in a total theory as espoused by Rangell, had to be rediscovered.[23] It also points out the ironic ahistoricity of many younger analysts who believe psychoanalysis began in the 1980s with Greenberg and Mitchell's tome.[24] I often have students read Fenichel's little red book (not Jung's or Chairman Mao's) to realize that those controversies that seem so novel and original have indeed been debated for decades.

Post-Modernism

In regard to the post-modern trend in psychoanalysis, definitions are even vaguer. I see the following factors as integral to the postmodern perspective: the outright rejection of the concepts of objectivity, historical reality, truth, analytic neutrality, and biological underpinnings of psychic elaboration, essentialism, and universalism. Clinically, the stance includes the dicta that both patient and analyst create an interactive system that affects both of them; along with this, meaning is co-created and not absolute, each analytic dyad is unique and therefore absolute technique cannot exist, and the analytic experience is an interaction of the subjective worlds of the participants. The differences can be delineated as following the gradients of transference replaced by countertransference as the main source of psychic data; countertransference as feeling replaced by countertransference as enactment; and countertransference in turn replaced by co-creation as the dynamic within the consulting room. Thus, a two-person psychology replacing a so-called one person model; objectivity and neutrality replaced by subjectivity; the interpersonal or the intersubjective replacing the intrapsychic; the here and now replacing the past; insight replaced by intersubjectivity; truth and distortion replaced by perspectivism; interpretive content replaced by process; and what has all too often been overlooked, cognition being replaced or superseded by affectivity. This in many ways has become the modal model, at least in the United States. Why do I see Jung as a precursor of this mode of conceptualization? Simply, it fits so well with his writings. In general, his valorization of subjective experience, as Dr. Cambray points out, and the irrational as a legitimate epistemology contrast with the modernist view which privileges rationality.

1. Along with Ferenczi's mutual analysis, Jung created a two-person psychology long before the relational school developed the idea as an emendation of Sullivan's participant-observer model.[25,26] We find Jung positing as early as the late 1920s that one cannot exert an influence if one is not also subject to influence. We also find him, from the alchemical perspective, noting that two personalities sharing a common space, as in treatment, is like the contact of two chemical substances: if there is any reaction, both are transformed. Thus, treatment is a process of mutual interaction and influence, where the analyst is anything but the objective neutral ideal of the Freudian model, yet operates in line with postmodern thinking. I need not, nor am presumptuous enough, to tell this audience that I am simply pointing out parallels.

2. Post-modern psychoanalysis posits multiple contextualized selves. Bromberg holds that the unitary self is a myth: "What exists instead are multiple selves, determined by language, culture, society and relationships."[27] Does Jung's concept of affectively centered complexes fit with this? I think so. Jung, after all, did view the complexes as autonomous sub-personalities. I also think that when an archetypical imagery overwhelms the psyche we have further evidence of multiple selves.

3. Unlike Freud's modernist view where the mind can be conceptualized as a vertical model with deeper layers determining the nature of the more surface layers, for Jung we find a horizontal model. Here we find multiple selves in reciprocal relationships.

4. Jung also shows similarities with the postmodern psychoanalysts in his emphasis on the centrality of affect. Unlike for Freud and modernism where cognition and rationality are prized, for Jung and post-modern analysts the affective domain becomes salient. As Moore and Fine state in regard to the Freudian view: "although Freud thought that some affective structures in the Ucs. might become conscious, he believed that there were no unconscious affects comparable to unconscious ideas."[28]

5. While I find Jung's views on gender and women archaic at best, as I do Freud's, and his views on race reprehensible, I agree with Samuels, that stripped of the content of his beliefs, differences (race, gender, nationality, and I would add, class) lead to the introduction of a cultural dimension to psychoanalysis.[29] There is a decentering of the European phallocentric model; it no longer is the only one, nor the ideal. Indeed the emphasis on gender, race, and class define the post-modern tendency. (Add rock-and-roll and the picture is complete.) Here too, Jung can be seen as a precursor to this school of thought, developing a non-essentialist, non-universalist, contextualized psychoanalysis with an emphasis on the uniqueness of each therapeutic dyadic interaction.

6. There is indeed in Jungian analysis, as with post-modern analysis, the emphasis on intersubjectivity and the dyad.

While many of the post-modern psychoanalysts, particularly the relationalists, are willing to rightfully resurrect Sullivan from his splendid isolation from mainstream analytic thought, the shame is that they have continued the Freudian tendency to make Jung a nonperson. Whether this is due to Jung's political statements during the period of the Third Reich, his editorship of the *Zentralblatt,* the fear of being seen as non-scientific, the acceptance of the historic psychoanalytic banishment of Jung and his pioneering work, or for other reasons, has yet to be determined. One would have expected with the negation of Freud by post-modern thinkers that Jung would be reconsidered or at least read, but, alas, this doesn't seem to be the case, leading to a continued skewed history of the field.

Pre-Modern Romanticism

We now come to the pre-modern, or romantic, aspect of Jung, a state with which I am sure you are more familiar than I am. This encompasses the mystical (a term Jung seemed to dislike), the mysterious, the occult, and the non-rational spiritual aspects of his theory that go beyond the limits of conventional scientific standards (or perhaps *scientism* would be a preferable term). On the one hand, we have the Jung of *The Red Book* and his own personal journey with its mystical underpinnings, while, on the other, we find Jung the scientist interested in that aspect of the human psyche that is self-evident. He states the following in *Modern Man in Search of a Soul*:

> I do not, however, hold myself responsible for the fact that man has, everywhere and always, spontaneously developed religious forms of expression, and that the human psyche from time immemorial has been shot through with religious feelings and ideas. Whoever cannot see this aspect of the human psyche is blind.[30]

Getting up close and personal, I am neither a religious nor a spiritual person. That oceanic feeling Freud never understood is also alien to me.[31] After working with ultra-religious patients for the last decade, however, I have come to see religion as not simply a *universal neurosis* but serving psychological functions of self-cohesion, growth, and connectedness to overcome the anomie so prevalent in our society. This same position within mainstream psychoanalysis is evidenced in the writings of Meissner, Spezzano, and Gargiulo, amongst others.[32,33] I have also come to appreciate that mystical experiences (many of these patients were immersed in the Kabbalah) add a dimension that is not attainable by scientific procedures and thinking. This dimension and the concomitant information coming from it are neither pathological nor reducible to rational categories. What I'm saying, perhaps poorly, is that I no longer see the non-rational as necessarily primitive or indicative of pathology, but simply another dimension of the human experience. This becomes manifest even in non-religious patients where what is consciously experienced as hope, not of necessity grounded in life experiences, is the motivator and feeling that keeps one going in the face of life's inevitable adversities. While the twenty-first century scientific community will continue to look askance at this dimension of the human condition and what it tells us about the boundless nature of the psyche, clinicians, whether Freudian, Jungian, or otherwise, have to adopt an attitude of neutrality to the material presented to fully understand the totality of their patients' psychological beings. I see Jung's phenomenological perspective operating here, where experiencing outweighs understanding and certainly interpreting. This perspective, parenthetically, is what is necessary in working with psychotic patients, as R. D. Laing demonstrated.[34] It is also operative for anyone whose psychological *language* differs from the consensually validated one. This is manifested also in the understanding of art and symbolism. Where a Freudian might look for the personal equation or a reduction to some life event of the artist or some repressed element, Jung would give credence to the visionary experience, the attempt to create something *real but unknown*. In the illustrative use of psychosis, art, and religion, there is naturally no intention to equate the categories.

As for the personal journey of Jung, here I am totally unqualified to comment, and, for once, I won't revert to the Bronx in me (that part that has a definitive opinion about everything). The question as to why Jung has been less influential in academia than is called for needs to be briefly addressed. If one gives any credence to my thesis that Jung straddles three different *Weltanschauungs* and recognizes that academics love to categorize and compartmentalize (some would say pigeonhole) theorists and theories, then the answer becomes obvious. For those of us that are clinicians, ambiguity—not knowing the shifting of boundaries—and indeterminacy are daily occurrences. For academics, these are discomforts that need to be resolved in one direction or the other. Thus, Jung, more than Freud, presents a challenge.

I'd like to finish by stating, particularly to the theoretically committed amongst you, that I do not envision psychoanalysis as a *Platonic Republic* where an elite group of initiates possess absolute and eternal truths and there is no need for change, for opposition, or for doubt, and where perfection is permanent and any change must be for the worse. So on this 100th anniversary of Jung's Fordham lectures let the dialogue between family members be reopened, and let our science and craft benefit from the exchange.

NOTES

1. Quentin Crisp, *The Naked Civil Servant* (New York: Plume Publishing, 1983), p. 14.

2. C. G. Jung, "The Theory of Psychoanalysis," in *The Collected Works of C. G. Jung*, vol. 4, ed. and trans. Gerhard Adler and R. F. C. Hull (Princeton, NJ: Princeton University Press, 1966), p. 117.

3. Sigmund Freud and Ernest Jones, *The Complete Correspondence of Sigmund Freud and Ernest Jones 1908–1939* (Honolulu, HI: Belknap Press, 1995), p. 361.

4. Andrew Paskauskas, "Introduction to the Freud/Jung Letters," in *The Correspondence of Sigmund Freud and C. G. Jung* (Cambridge, MA: Harvard University Press, 1988).

5. Martin S. Bergmann, "Reflections on the History of Psychoanalysis," *Journal of the American Psychoanalytic Association* 41 (1993): 929–955.

6. Jon Mills, ed., introduction to *Relational and Intersubjective Perspectives in Psychoanalysis: A Critique* (Lanham: Jason Aronson, 2005), p. ix.

7. Sigmund Freud, "The Question of Lay Analysis" (1930), in *The Standard Edition of the Complete Psychological Works of Sigmund Freud*, vol. 20 (London: Hogarth Press, 1961), pp. 179–258.

8. Frederic Jameson, *Postmodernism; or, the Cultural Logic of Late Capitalism* (London: Verso, 1991).

9. Michael Rustin, *Reason and Unreason: Psychoanalysis, Science and Politics* (Middletown, CT: Wesleyan University Press, 2001), p. 16.

10. *Ibid.*, p. 56.

11. Otto Fenichel, *Problems of Psychoanalytic Technique*, trans. Mark Brunswik (New York: Psychoanalytic Quarterly Inc., 1941), p. 12–13.

12. Sigmund Freud, *New Introductory Lectures on Psychoanalysis* (1933), in *The Standard Edition of the Complete Psychological Works of Sigmund Freud* (London: Hogarth Press, 1964), p. 112.

13. *Ibid.*, pp. 172–173.

14. Michael Fordham, *The Self and Autism* (London: Heinemann, 1976).

15. John Bowlby, *Separation: Anxiety and Anger,* vol. 2, Attachment and Loss (New York: Basic Books, 1973).

16. Sigmund Freud, *A Phylogenetic Fantasy: Overview of the Transference Neuroses,* ed. Ilse Grubrich-Simitis, trans. Axel Hoffer and Peter Hoffer (Honolulu, HI: Belknap, 1987).

17. Jacques Lacan, "The Function and Field of Speech in Language and Psychoanalysis," in *Ecrits* (New York: W. W. Norton & Co., 2004), pp. 31–107.

18. Ella Sharpe, "Psycho-physical Problems Revealed in Language: An Examination of Metaphor," *International Journal of Psycho-Analysis* 21 (1940): 201.

19. Pinchus Noy, "A Theory of Art and Aesthetic Experience," *Psychoanalytic Review* 55 (4, 1968): 623–645.

20. D. W. Winnicott, *Playing and Reality* (Harmondsworth: Penguin Books, 1974).

21. Heinz Hartmann, *Ego Psychology and the Problem of Adaptation* (New York: International Universities Press, 1958), p. 122.

22. Charles Brenner, "Conflict, Compromise Formation and Structural Theory," *Psychoanalytic Quarterly* 71 (3, 2002): 397–417.

23. Leo Rangell, *My Life in Theory* (New York: Other Press, 2004).

24. Harvey Greenberg and Stephen A. Mitchell, *Object Relations in Psychoanalytic Theory* (Cambridge, MA: Harvard University Press, 1983).

25. Sandor Ferenczi, *The Clinical Diary of Sandor Ferenczi,* ed. Judith Dupont, trans. Michael Balint and Nicola Zarday Jackson (Cambridge, MA: Harvard University Press, 1988).

26. H. S. Sullivan, *The Interpersonal Theory of Psychiatry* (New York: Norton, 1953).

27. Phillip Bromberg, *Standing in the Spaces: Essays on Clinical Process, Trauma, and Dissociation* (Hillsdale, NJ: Analytic Press, 1998), p. 34.

28. Burness Moore and Bernard Fine, *Psychoanalytic Terms and Concepts* (New Haven, CT: Yale University Press, 1990), p. 202.

29. Andrew Samuels, "Introduction to Contemporary Jungian Thought," *Psychoanalytic Review* 83 (4, 1996).

30. Carl G. Jung, *Modern Man in Search of a Soul* (New York: Harcourt Brace & Company, 1969), p. 123.

31. Sigmund Freud, *Civilization and its Discontents* (1927–31), in *The Standard Edition of the Complete Psychological Works of Sigmund Freud*, vol. 21 (London: Hogarth Press, 1961), pp. 11–12.

32. W. W. Meissner, *Psychoanalysis and Religious Experience* (New Haven, CT: Yale University Press, 1984).

33. Charles Spezzano and Gerald J. Garguilo, eds., *Soul on the Couch: Spirituality, Religion, and Morality in Contemporary Psychoanalysis (London and New York: Routledge, 1997).*

34. R. D. Laing, *The Divided Self* (London: Tavistock, 1960).

CHAPTER SEVEN

THE FADING OF C. G. JUNG IN THE ACADEMY

Frances M. Parks

My background and experience influence my perspectives on the topic "The Fading of C. G. Jung in the Academy." My training in clinical psychology was in traditional Boulder model programs with an emphasis on the scientist-practitioner model. Later I completed analytic training at the C. G. Jung Institute, Zürich. Most of the forty-plus years of my professional life have been almost equally divided between teaching and training in clinical psychology and an analytic practice. These two perspectives, academic clinical psychology and Jungian practice, give me two, but certainly not all, perspectives on the current situation.

This chapter will address two points: The first is the issue of evidence-based practice and its influence on the world of mental health training and practice. The second, not-unrelated issue is how we, as Jungian analysts, might respond and even benefit from the requirement for evidence-based practice and how we might contribute to the now rich dialogue surrounding this issue. Examining the interface of traditional research in psychology and psychiatry and the Jungian practice of psychotherapy has been a focus and challenge to me for several years.[1]

Two incidents illustrate some current issues. Recently, I attended a convention of the Washington State Psychological Association. The majority of presentations were consistent with the training model of the University of Washington and the American Psychological Association (APA) emphasis on evidence-based practice. Presentations included models for the treatment of anxiety disorders, eating disorders, etc. In a presentation by two persons who have worked for several years with suicidal people in a state inpatient psychiatric facility, I listened to statements about respecting the person's point of view and about understanding the suicidal experience in an emerging process. Later, I said to one presenter, "I thought I heard the voice of James Hillman in some of your thinking. Is that accurate?" He replied that the presenters had talked with Hillman sometime before his death, as they had found his work of great value in developing their perspectives. This is only one example of how Jungian thought is incorporated in a work where it may not be referenced in a specific way. The next day, a psychologist who writes on spirituality and psychotherapy presented some of the research being conducted at his institution, making reference to concepts of C. G. Jung. He mentioned a new handbook on psychotherapy and spirituality to be published by the APA. After his presentation, I mentioned that I appreciated his reference to Jung and was looking forward to his book. He said that one book chapter was being written by a Jungian analyst, adding that he had insisted on inclusion of this chapter in spite of resistance by other collaborators. He said he did this in part because he valued the work of this analyst, and because he did not wish to see Jung *marginalized* to a greater extent than is already so. This exchange highlighted for me a situation I have experienced before—where therapists value the Jungian perspective but are clear that it is not in the mainstream of the work deemed appropriate for publication (or training) by the APA.

During my time in the academic side of psychology, I have seen a major change in the environment of the Academy. It is not unusual that students entering training to become clinical psychologists have disdain for Freud and psychoanalysis (though they have actually had little exposure to the concepts), and they have never heard of C. G. Jung. So I would like to begin with the first of my topics, a major factor that has led to the fading of Jung in the Academy—the issue of evidence-based practice.

Evidence-Based Practice

The requirement for evidence-based practice is tied closely to cost-containment in the health field. While we will see changes, the mandate is here to stay. I would suggest there are ethical reasons to support this. Jungians with analytic practices have largely ignored this change, but I here suggest there are at least two reasons that this attitude is problematic.

First, let us take a glance back to the 1990s. The origin of this movement toward evidence-based practice was in the United Kingdom with the adoption of a model called *Evidence-Based Medicine* (EBM).[2] Influenced by the British model, it was adopted in the U.S. by the medical and mental health fields. In the earlier literature, you see the term *Empirically Validated Treatments* (EVT). In 1995 the APA, Division 12, Society of Clinical Psychology, published a very short list of *Empirically Supported Treatments* (EST). In 2005, the APA endorsed the term *Evidence-Based Practice in Psychology* (referred to as EBPP or EBP).[3] This is the term you are most likely to see today.

The Division 12 list has been expanded over the years and currently lists some seventy-seven such treatments on the APA Division 12 website. Reviewing the current list, I found only two treatments that appeared to have some connection to dynamically-oriented treatment: Transference-Focused Therapy for Borderline Personality Disorder and Psychoanalytic Therapy for Panic Disorder.

We are becoming increasingly aware of the requirement for evidence-based practice in our work. Those not currently in an academic setting may be less aware of how this requirement is affecting training in the fields of psychology and psychiatry. In the field of clinical psychology, for a training program to be accredited by the APA, it must demonstrate the inclusion of evidence-based practices in all applied training. In order to give APA-approved continuing education credit for a lecture or workshop, the question "How does this presentation build on doctoral level training?" must be answered. Hence, the structure becomes tighter. Materials in textbooks reflect this policy. I have started reviewing material on C. G. Jung in current introductory psychology and personality theory texts. In the typical introductory text, I am finding about three to four short paragraphs mentioning Jung's concept of archetypes and the collective unconscious with illustrations from *Star Wars* or *Batman*. I rarely find Jungian theory included in any graduate text. If there is little to no exposure to Jungian concepts in the education system or in the training of mental health professionals, this does and will affect choices of people who want training beyond graduate school and it will influence choices people make regarding the type of psychotherapy or analysis they seek.

The Common Factors Tradition

Another line of research, considerably older than the evidence-based model, is relevant to our concern. This is the tradition of common factors research which is likely familiar. This tradition is seen as beginning with the Saul Rosenzweig's 1936 (reprinted in 2002) classic paper which he opened with a quote from *Alice in Wonderland*: "At last the Dodo said, 'Everybody has won, and *all* must have prizes.'"[4] The Dodo bird reference, which provides the metaphor for the common factors approach, suggests the common traits that predict successful treatment have more to do with relationship and other human factors than with the theoretical approach or method. Common factors research has continued over the seventy-six years since Rosenzweig wrote about and researchers continue to speak of the Dodo bird effect. The research of Carl Rogers, Lester Luborsky, and currently Michael Lambert is in this tradition.

Where Do We Go from Here?

The response of analysts to the research and treatment trends described above is the second focus of this paper. It is critical that Jungian analysts become more aware of what has and is being done in the areas of efficacy of traditional psychoanalytic and Jungian treatment. It is gratifying to see in recent years the growth in sharing and collaborating between our two traditions. Both schools benefit by working together on this issue. Research is emerging that demonstrates superiority of psychoanalytic treatment for some kinds of disorders, especially when outcomes are measured over a span of years rather than weeks or months. A landmark paper by Leichsenring & Rabung documenting evidence for the value of psychoanalytic treatment was printed in the *Journal of the American Medical Association* in 2008.[5] The work of Jonathan Shedler and colleagues at the University of Colorado also presents evidence for the efficacy of psychodynamic psychotherapy and much more. We need studies similar to the one Seth Rubin worked on for several years at the C. G. Jung Institute of San Francisco.[6] His challenges in this work suggest some of the problems Jungians face in these efforts.

Pragmatic Case Studies in Psychotherapy (PCSP), is an online peer-reviewed journal from Rutgers edited by Daniel B. Fishman, Ph.D. with Stanley B. Messer, Ph.D., and others.[7] This journal emerged out of the common factors tradition. It presents a model for evidence-based research differing from that of statistical comparisons. The journal requires that papers follow a format in presenting case studies that is not unlike that learned in our training.[8] The premise is by having a consistent format used for presentations representing varying theoretical approaches, findings of therapeutic efficacy will emerge. PCSP journals represent almost every approach except the Jungian one. The editors have suggested they would be very pleased to have an edition, or more, with a Jungian focus.

It is my wish to see one training institute adopt the format for case presentations used by PCSP. I have suggested to graduate students that they use this format for oral and written presentations, and they have found it most useful. If one or more institutes generated such presentations and perhaps collaborated on the submission to PCSP, we could easily start to contribute to evidence-based research.

The above suggestion is one of many approaches we might take to thwart the fading of Jung in the Academy. Without the influence of Jung's theory and the rich work that has followed from it, education of students in the area of psychology is limited, and the training of therapists is diminished. I also suggest that we have an ethical obligation to evaluate the efficacy of our work. If analysts engage this endeavor, beneficiaries will include both ourselves and those whom we serve.

NOTES

1. F. Parks, "Bridging the Domains of Jungian Practice and Evidence-Based Research," *Proceedings of the 18th Congress of the International Association of Analytical Psychology*, ed. P. Bennett (Einsiedeln: Daimon Verlag, 2012).

2. G. Castelnuove, E. Faccio, E. Molinari, G. Nardone, and A. Salvini, "A Critical Review of Empirically Supported Treatments (ESTs) and Common Factors Perspective in Psychotherapy" (2004), *Brief Strategic and Systemic Therapy European Review.* Accessed May 31, 2008, at http://www.terapiabreve.it/journal%20english%201/Articoli_Inglese/castelnuovo.pdf.

3. APA Presidential Task Force on Evidence-Based Practice, "Evidence-Based Practice in Psychology," *American Psychologist* 61 (4, 2006): 271–285. doi: 10: 1037/0003-066X61.4.271.

4. S. Rosenzweig, "Some Implicit Common Factors in Diverse Methods of Psychotherapy," *Journal of Psychotherapy Integration* 12 (2002): 5; Reprint of the classic 1936 article.

5. F. Leichsenring and S. Rabung, "Effectiveness of Long-term Psychodynamic Psychotherapy: A Meta-analysis," *Journal of the American Medical Association* 300 (13, 2008): 1551.

6. S. I. Rubin and N. Powers, "Analyzing the San Francisco Psychotherapy Research Project," 2005. http://www.sirseth.net/doc/SFresearch.pdf.

7. D. B. Fishman, "Editor's Introduction to PCSP—from Single Case to Database: A New Method for Enhancing Psychotherapy Practice," *Pragmatic Case Studies in Psychotherapy* 1 (2005): 1.

8. Instructions for Authors, *Pragmatic Case Studies in Psychotherapy.* Accessed May 28, 2008 at, http://pcsp.libraries.rutgers.edu/index.php/pcsp/about/pcspAuthorInstructions.

Chapter Eight

A Tale of Two Institutes
Research-led Teaching and Teaching-led Research in a Jungian/Archetypal Studies Doctoral Program

Jennifer Leigh Selig and Susan Rowland

The conference from which this paper arose raised the question, where is Jung in the Academy today? In this paper, we offer *one place* where Jung is in the Academy, a place where we practice Jung's call for the study of *complex psychology*, and we additionally explore an example of how *teaching Jung* became indivisible from *researching Jung*. This place is Pacifica Graduate Institute, an institute dedicated to carrying out the mission of the C. G. Jung Institute, especially in its early incarnation as the Institute for Complex Psychology. The two institutes are places of Jungian scholarship where collaboration with the deep psyche in teaching cannot be wholly separated from the consequent emergence of new perspectives.

A Tale of Two Institutes
by Jennifer Leigh Selig

This is the tale of two institutes separated by historical time and place but united in the spirit of their missions. I offer them as comparative case studies: one to describe a place where Jung *is* in the Academy, and the other to speculate about why Jung isn't in the Academy *more*.

The first institute is the C. G. Jung Institute in Küsnacht, Zürich. On their website in 2012, they described themselves as "founded in 1948 as an institute for training and researching analytical psychology and psychotherapy."[1] I want to challenge this statement; when Jung inaugurated the Institute, that was not his intention at all, or perhaps more accurately stated, it was not *all* of his intention. I believe this statement obfuscates his original mission, and a look back at the latter will afford us a clue regarding the marginalization of Jung in the Academy. I take as my primary text "An Address on the Occasion of the Founding of the C. G. Jung Institute, Zürich, 24 April 1948."[2]

But wait. Already here we encounter our first problem. Jung didn't inaugurate the C. G. Jung Institute that day. On April 24, 1948, Jung opened his address with these words: "It is a particular pleasure and satisfaction for me to have the privilege of speaking to you on this memorable day on the founding of an Institute for Complex Psychology."[3] According to Kirsch, this name was Jung's colleague Toni Wolff's preferred name for the Institute; she preferred the term *complex psychology* to describe Jung's psychology.[4] Jung did as well; Shamdasani stated that while Jung used *analytical psychology* in the beginning to designate his psychology, by the 1930s he renamed it *complex psychology*.[5] He references Woolf's distinction between the terms in a volume titled *The Cultural Signicance of Complex Psychology* which commemorated Jung's sixtieth birthday: analytical psychology "was appropriate when dealing with the practical methods of psychological analysis," whereas complex psychology was a broader term referring to general psychology including theoretical concerns.[6]

The word *komplex* in German shares similar multiple meanings with the word *complex* in English. We know Jung got his start with the word association experiments, which led him to the discovery of psychological complexes (*komplexes*). In the founding address of the Institute, he detailed how his theory of the complexes led to the discovery of psychological types, and that led to the theory of the unconscious, which then led to the discovery of the collective unconscious. Once that happened, Jung noted, "The scope of our researches was extended without limit."[7] So complex psychology literally started with the complexes, but *komplex* in German also shares another meaning in common with English's *complex*. In 1954, Jung wrote, "Complex psychology means the psychology of 'complexities' i.e., of complex psychical systems in contradistinction from relatively elementary factors."[8] In simpler terms, the psyche is complex, and complex psychology takes that into account.

Finally, *complex* also refers to what arises when many different parts come together into an interconnected whole (as in the military industrial complex). Analytical psychology was one part of Jung's interest, but complex psychology contained innumerable other parts of interest to him. In the address, Jung suggested some of the concerns of complex psychology, which include folklore, mythology, physics, spirituality, religion, biographical studies, parapsychology, literature, symbolism, history, family and relationship dynamics, cultural studies, and the humanities. These concerns are academic and theoretical and not merely professional and practical, but Jung's followers, in what Shamdasani calls "a startling disregard" for Jung and complex psychology, held to the name *analytical psychology* and focused the Institute on training professional analysts and psychotherapists.[9] We have for all intents and purposes lost the term *complex psychology* and its multidisciplinary connection to the wider academic world, though, of course, many Jungian analysts are still making those connections through their research and writing. According to Shamdasani, "The history of Jungian psychology has in part consisted in a radical and unacknowledged diminution of Jung's goal" and "obscures the question of what exactly Jung set out to achieve."[10]

Now let's jump forward a few decades to another institute.

In the late 1970s/early 1980s in Santa Barbara, California, Dr. Stephen Aizenstat and a small group of committed individuals founded Pacifica Graduate Institute (initially named the Human Relations Institute) and offered a master's degree in Counseling Psychology with an emphasis in Depth Psychology. According to Pacifica's website, soon thereafter a doctoral degree in Clinical Psychology was added, again, with an emphasis in Depth Psychology.[11] Both degree programs were professional programs leading to licensure that prepared students to practice depth psychology as counselors and therapists inside the clinical encounter and the therapeutic container. Both degree programs heavily emphasized not only depth psychology but mythology and the humanities; both had a wildly innovative and creative curriculum which was not afraid to emphasize the word *soul*. Indeed, the motto of the school, *animae mundi colendae gratia* (for the sake of tending the soul in and of the world) was heavily influenced by Hillman's idea that soul is not just in us but in the world, that the world has a soul of which we are all a part.[12]

By the beginning of the 1990s, Pacifica was well enough established to seek accreditation, and it encountered an academic mythological beast—WASC, the Western Association of Schools and Colleges. Accreditation agencies are creatures that don't like the taste of wildly innovative and creative curriculum; they like their programs bland, uniform, and recognizable—comfort food, to stretch the analogy. In order to win WASC's approval, much of the *depth* got dropped out of the curriculum, and courses in mythology and the humanities were necessarily, albeit reluctantly deemphasized. Of course, accreditation was important, because it allowed Pacifica to grant financial aid, significantly opening doors for a broader class of students to enter, but some of the faculty felt the loss of the soul of the school in this more narrow focus on professional accreditation. The mission seemed now to be "for the sake of tending the soul of the patient or client" at the loss of the wider world the Institute had initially sought to tend and attend. So, some of these faculty members gathered together in the mid-1990s to dream forward a new degree: one that would be accredited, yes, but one that was not a professional degree and would not lead to licensure, and thus would have more freedom to return to the more radical embodiment of the mission. That degree was in Depth Psychology, and now, sixteen years later, there are four separate specializations in depth psychology. The specialization Susan and I chair is in Jungian and Archetypal Studies.

When my colleagues and I designed the program and the curriculum, we very intentionally set out to create a place which would fulfill Jung's original intention fifty years earlier with the Institute for Complex Psychology. I often liken us to a *think tank* for extending without limit the best theories and practices from Jungian, post-Jungian, imaginal, and archetypal psychology into the wider world. In our specialization, we take seriously Hillman's belief that soul is not just within us but also in the world, and together we create a beloved community of what I call *cultural therapists*, dedicating ourselves to tending that part of the world's soul which calls to each of us.[13]

Samuels once stated, "If depth psychology wants to treat the world, then it had better do so as part of a multidisciplinary project."[14] This was Jung's intention with complex psychology—to create such a multidisciplinary project. At Pacifica in the Jungian and Archetypal Studies program, our students and faculty are doing just that. Our students are attorneys, health care workers, executives, engineers, educators, environmentalists, journalists, ministers, scientists, novelists, and yes, sometimes therapists. They come to us with degrees in business, history, media and communication studies, literature, medicine, ethnic studies, social work, art history, and yes, sometimes psychology. Many find their way to us in midlife just as Jung would have predicted, facing a crisis of meaning and seeking to live a more authentic life, but some come to us in the first third or the last third of their lives as well. Some come knowing what they want to do with the degree, but most come in answer to an intuitive vocational call, a teleological urge from the unconscious—they know they must be here though they don't yet know why. Everyone who comes seeks an education for individuation, rather than an education for information. Everyone who comes takes part in individuating the field of depth psychology by making more connections between it and the wider world. And yes, some become teachers and take Jung into the Academy, introducing a new generation of students to his work and its ongoing relevancy and reach.

I see us all as bridge builders, taking our own disciplines and connecting them to Jungian psychology's theories and practices, enacting complex psychology. We are dipping our collective toes into every disciplinary pool; we are in our own small way fulfilling Jung's original 1948 visionary call for extending the scope of our research without limit. We are a rare breed; you can count on one hand the number of academic institutions with such an offering.

To be clear, I am not asserting that there would be handfuls of academic institutions with such degree programs if it weren't for the revisioning of the Institute for Complex Psychology by Jung's followers, but to be honest, I am curious, and I obviously lean toward some culpability. Nor am I devaluing the importance of training institutes for analysts and psychotherapists, but I do agree with Shamdasani that a rather radical diminution of Jung's vision occurred post-1948, and I wonder how much we can connect that diminution with the marginalization of Jung in the Academy today. To my questions about how the past has influenced the present, I add my curiosity and wonder about how the present may influence the future and how programs like the one at Pacifica may send forth a new generation of scholars who will bring Jungian ideas into the Academy and beyond.

Research-led Teaching and Teaching-led Research by Susan Rowland

My part of this joint paper by two faculty of Pacifica Graduate Institute offers a case study of research-led teaching and teaching-led research. For the M.A./Ph.D. in *Depth Psychology in Jungian/Archetypal Studies,* one course I teach is called "Imaginal Ways of Knowing: Active Imagination, *The Red Book* and Psychic Creativity." In the course of teaching my research on Jung's *Red Book* and active imagination, I found myself structuring new research on the relationship of a Jungian idea, *active imagination,* to a conceptual development from another academic discipline to psychology.

I discovered both a historical parallel and an epistemological connection between Jungian active imagination and what is now known in literary studies as *close reading*. The link is a potentially exciting one for it substantiates the dual heritage of literary and psychological theory in Romantic philosophy, and before that in Renaissance alchemy and magic.[15] Let us begin with three quotes from Jung:

> Active imagination ... means that the images have a life of their own and that the symbolic events develop according to their own logic—that is, of course, if your conscious reason does not interfere.[16]

> A dream is too slender a hint to be understood until it is enriched by the stuff of association and analogy and thus amplified to the point of intelligibility.[17]

> No, it is not art! On the contrary, it is nature.[18]

Of course, Jung does not present active imagination as a theory of reading, but as a way of encouraging the spontaneous growth of images from the unconscious and of using them as a mode of healing. When a patient is depressed or overwhelmed by feeling of dread, he or she is prompted to allow the sheer power trapped in the unconscious to produce an image, or to meditate upon a potent dream symbol. By relaxing conscious control, the overwhelming Other will develop the images of its own accord. Either with the analyst or alone, patients can then work on finding a rapprochement with this *active*, previously alien, part of themselves. Ultimately, the *active* in active imagination encompasses ego as well as the unconscious. In this sense active imagination is a way of improving and enhancing individuation, that healing development of an ever deeper connection between ego and unconscious archetypal energies.

But active imagination, as the term denotes, means that the images have a life of their own and that the symbolic events develop according to their own logic—that is, of course, if your conscious reason does not interfere.[19]

In teaching my course on active imagination, I realized how difficult it was for the students to relax ego control sufficiently to allow the images to develop lives of their own. We had lively debates and exchanges upon the actual definition of Jung's active imagination and whether the psyche could or even should be starkly divided into ego versus image as Other. At one point my contribution to the online class was as follows:

Active imagination is to try to cultivate an ego where the Other is not separate from our sense of ourselves as rational beings. When we dream we are doing involuntary active imagination. What Jung proposed was letting a dream happen when we are still awake. Let something, some image *be powerful and do what it wants, not what you, the person you know as you, wants.*

A breakthrough came when I realized why active imagination was not so alien to my own scholarly practice: it was because the process deeply resembled the way I had been taught to read as a student of literature.

Literary studies is a discipline suggestively born at the same time as depth psychology in the late-nineteenth century. While the psychologies of Freud and Jung insisted upon the reality of the unconscious as their basic ontology, literary studies or *English* in the US and UK, had to find a way of making knowledge from studying literary texts. So *close reading* was developed as a way of generating meaning from just the words of literature themselves; it forbade delving into the author's life or intentions or considering the historical context of the work.

Close reading is a *perverse*, counter-intuitive practice for the modern person. It involves focusing on words, phrases, and their sounds and shapes on the page to invoke their almost infinite possibilities to spark interpretations. Put another way, close reading means allowing the words on the page to come alive and be the directors of the reader's attention. For close reading, everyone's interpretation of a particular text will be different. In this sense close reading as a technique resembles Jung's active imagination and amplification together. Close reading gives the words of literature an originating ontology; their subsequent liveliness and energy points to links and analogies just as amplification allows the first image to speak to other images.

Of course, when discussing this striking similarity with my students I also have to distinguish for them the disciplinary differences. For active imagination, the psyche is real; for close reading, the images in the form of words are real, and the role of the psyche in their creativity is severely downplayed by the literary theory that developed close reading, New Criticism.

Struck by the historical coincidence of literary studies and depth psychology, my suspicions were further intrigued by discovering that the eruption of both ways of working with images was very closely aligned in time. Close reading arguably begins with a book called *Practical Criticism* in 1929 and Jung begins to develop active imagination in "The Transcendent Function" in 1916.[20,21] With further research I began to see an uncanny relationship between these two approaches to the image in an equal and opposite *repression.*

The originators of close reading were emphatic about excluding psychology from literary criticism despite their heritage in Romanticism that insisted upon the supreme significance of the imagination as a creative force in nature and human nature. For the new critics, close reading was an art generated by the literature itself. By contrast, Jung refused, famously in the quote above from *Memories, Dreams, Reflections,* to countenance art as an authentic participant in active imagination. For him, active imagination was *nature*, meaning psychic nature alone.

Through teaching this course to Jungian doctoral students on active imagination, I decided to propose that we allow the two disciplines to learn from each other. Close reading can admit the creative psyche; active imagination can be embraced as an alchemical art of nature. Indeed, my teaching-inspired research into the history of active imagination and close reading has discovered their entwined heritage in hermeneutics, Romantic philosophy, alchemy, and, ultimately, magic—for we are dealing with creativity in the enlarged sense of creation. Magic is, in this sense, an art of (psychic) nature in learning to work with images, figures, gods, or, in Jungian terms, archetypes, with an existence beyond the personal.

Thus, active imagination becomes an *art to be learned and practiced* in the service of Soul as connected to Cosmos. Because both are skills practiced until they become arts, close reading and active imagination, now indistinguishable from each other, are activities of what the Renaissance called the intellect—not the ego, but ego-united-with-soul by training and practice in imaginative creativity. To be precise, close reading and active imagination are magic because the division between ego and unconscious has been eroded through the art. Practicing this magic remakes who we are as children of a creative earth.

NOTES

1. *C. G. Jung Institute*. Accessed Aug. 22, 2012, at http://www.junginstitut.ch/main/Show$Id=1101.html. The description has since been changed.

2. C. G. Jung, "An Address on the Occasion of the Founding of the C. G. Jung Institute, Zürich, 24 April 1948" (1948), in *The Collected Works of C. G. Jung*, vol. 18, ed. and trans. Gerhard Adler and R. F. C. Hull (Princeton, NJ: Princeton University Press, 1977).

3. Jung, CW 18, § 1129.

4. Thomas B. Kirsch, *The Jungians: A Comparative and Historical Perspective* (New York: Routledge, 2001), p. 17.

5. Sonu Shamdasani, *Jung and the Making of a Modern Psychology: The Dream of a Science* (New York: Cambridge University Press, 2003), p. 13.

6. *Ibid.*, p. 14.
7. Jung, CW 18, § 1131.
8. Shamdasani, *Jung and the Making*, p. 14.
9. *Ibid.*
10. *Ibid.*, pp. 13, 15.
11. Pacifica Graduate Institute, "Pacifica: The Origins and the First 38 Years." Accessed Oct. 14, 2014, at http://www.pacifica.edu/about-pacifica/history-of-pacifica.
12. *Ibid.*, "James Hillman." Accessed Aug. 22, 2012, at http://www.pacifica.edu/James-Hillman-tribute.aspx. This web address is no longer available.
13. James Hillman & Michael Ventura, *We've Had a Hundred Years of Psychotherapy—and the World's Getting Worse* (New York: HarperOne, 1993).
14. Andrew Samuels, *The Political Psyche* (London: Routledge, 1993), p. 30.
15. Duncan Wu, *A Companion to Romanticism* (Oxford and New York: Wiley-Blackwell, 1999), pp. 35–47; See also Joe Cambray's chapter in this book.
16. Joan Chodorow, ed., *Jung on Active Imagination* (Princeton, NJ: Princeton University Press, 1997), p. 145.
17. C. G. Jung, "Religious Ideas in Alchemy: An Historical Survey of Alchemical Ideas" (1944), in *The Collected Works of C. G. Jung*, vol. 12, ed. and trans. Gerhard Adler and R. F. C. Hull (Princeton, NJ: Princeton University Press, 1968), § 403.
18. C. G. Jung, *Memories, Dreams, Reflections*, ed. Aniela Jaffe (London: Fontana Paperbacks, 1989), p. 210.
19. Chodorow, *Jung on Active Imagination*, p. 145.
20. I. A. Richards, *Practical Criticism: A Study of Literary Judgement* (New York: Mariner Books, 1929/1956).
21. C. G. Jung, "The Transcendent Function" (1916), in *The Collected Works of C. G. Jung*, vol. 8, ed. and trans. Gerhard Adler and R. F. C. Hull (Princeton, NJ: Princeton University Press, 1968).

Chapter Nine

Jung and Laboratory Ethnographies
Lab as Locus of Transformative Research

Farzad Mahootian and Tara-Marie Linné

Introduction

Toward the end of his life, Jung's strongest concern was the collective shadow and the unintegrated nature of the Western psyche.[1] While still a medical student in his early twenties, he had penetrating insight into the destructive potential of an unbalanced psyche driving the ever-accelerating advance of science and technology.[2] In his Zofingia lectures, Jung quotes Immanuel Kant to make this strong point about ethics and science:

> Morality is paramount ... the reason and purpose of all our speculation and inquiries. ... God and the other world are the sole goal of all our philosophical investigations, and if the concepts of God and the other world had nothing to do with morality they would be worthless.[3]

Commenting on this passage, Marie-Louise von Franz notes that,

> After a polemical attack on materialism in general, Jung continues, asserting that we should start a 'revolution' on the part of our leading minds 'by *forcing* morality on science and its exponents. ... In institutions which offer training in

physiology, the moral judgment of students is deliberately impaired by their involvement in disgraceful, barbarous experiments, by a cruel torture of animals which is a mockery of all human decency.'[4]

Little psychological progress has been made regarding this issue after two world wars and Jung's apocalyptic pronouncements in his last years. The undeveloped sense of self-consciousness and moral consciousness characteristic of science is exemplified in the unrealistic image promulgated by positivism. The twentieth-century founders of positivism believed in science as an objective and apolitical antidote to Nazi Germany's extreme abuse of humanity and science during WWII. The ideal of a value-free science, free of cultural and social bias, seemed perfectly rational to them as it does to contemporary philosophy of science. The psychological and epistemological naïvete of this position was explicitly apparent to Jung in his early understanding of the dyadic structure of psychotherapy, a point to which we return in later sections. Quantum theoretic understandings of physical experiments demonstrated the epistemological shortcoming of positivist ideals of objectivity. During the 1920s two theoretical physicists, Werner Heisenberg and Niels Bohr, formulated a new mode of understanding science. Its impact on positivist philosophy of science was not widely acknowledged until the 1950s, from within mainstream Anglo-American philosophy of science and from outside the tradition, and especially during the 1960s by N. R. Hanson, T. S. Kuhn, and others.

Since the 1970s, governments of industrialized nations have taken steps to monitor the societal and ethical impacts of science and technology. Scholarship in fields collectively known as Science and Technology Studies (STS) have begun to develop more concrete, complex, and humanly plausible images of science, warts and all. By the end of the century, government programs were established with the aim of making science and technology more socially conscious.[5] Movements addressing the shadow side of science appeared in news media as efforts to reform the peer-review process, controversies over treatment efficacy in medicine, and ethical concerns about certain polarizing areas of research (e.g., genetically modified organisms, stem cell research, human enhancement, the safety of nanotechnological products, etc.). These movements have brought needed attention to such concerns. What is often lacking is a sophisticated understanding of basic psychological process, which Jung ingeniously defined in terms of integration, projection, transference, archetype, shadow, and the collective unconscious.

We focus on a specific subset of STS known as *laboratory engagement studies* (LES) whose explicit purpose is to stimulate and/or amplify the reflexive awareness of scientists in order to heighten their awareness of the broader societal impacts of their research and to inculcate the notion of *responsible innovation*. LES is a response to the lack of significant integration between physical and social sciences. In the late 1990s, the National Science Foundation (a federal funding source for basic and applied research in the USA) reshaped its requests for proposals and award criteria in order to address this lack of awareness and integration. Programs like the ongoing National Nanotechnology Initiative were funded at a substantial level in order to advance nanotechnology research and development, foster interdisciplinary partnerships, and bridge the gap between science and society. Several LES projects have been carried out over the last decade. They vary in duration, from as much as twelve weeks to several years. In this paper we will focus on a case study from Erik Fisher's "Socio-Technical Integration Research" project (STIR), which embedded ten social scientists for a period of about twelve weeks, in over twenty international research laboratories, in order to observe and interact with physical scientists. STIR is based on Fisher's pilot study of decision-making at the lab bench level in a nanotechnology lab for a period of nearly two years.[6]

With few recent exceptions, LES generally lack psychological sophistication.[7] We propose that the relationship between embedded social and physical scientists bears significant similarities to key structural and dynamical features of psychotherapy. Furthermore, we contend that psychological analysis of such encounters can deliver significant insights and that a Jungian diagnosis of science is particularly relevant to improving the efficacy and utility of LES.

On the centenary of Jung's 1912 Fordham lectures, we trace Jung's development of key tenets of analytical psychology to explore the potential impact of his approach to LES. We contend that the perspective and methodology of analytical psychology, with respect to inter- and intra-psychic processes, amplify responsible scientific and technological innovation and is relevant to improving the design of LES.

Origins of Laboratory Ethnography and Engagement Studies

LES methodology is designed to counterbalance the unconscious side of science by increasing self-reflexive awareness and social consciousness within science research projects. This experimental design has emerged out of fundamental insights culled from ethnography studies of research labs first carried out in the late 1970s by Latour and Woolgar, whose idea was to enter the lab in the semi-fictional mode of the so-called *ignorant observer*.[8] By bracketing their previous understandings of science, they hoped to attain some level of objectivity. Since that time, science studies has developed beyond hands-off observation modalities of traditional anthropology to *embedding* social scientists and humanists in research laboratories. Furthermore, contemporary studies allow and plan for the possibility of embedded social scientists to morph from the role of observer to that of contributing participant. Interactions between the embedded social scientist and the physical scientist begin to take place across their respective disciplines inside of what Peter Galison has called *trading zones*.[9] A variety of relational forms may occur in this zone ranging from exploitation to collaboration; at their best, collaborators develop a language that enables them to work together without full-scale adoption of the jargon of one or the other discipline. The process generally moves from trust-building to the development of *interactive expertise*; eventually a pidgin or creole emerges between physical and social scientists that enables the observer to become some kind of co-contributor.[10]

When such engagements are successful, a transformation of both parties occurs in which each experiences one's own activities, assumptions, and achievements from the alien perspective of the other. Beyond interdisciplinarity, this is a type of introspection that one rarely finds in ordinary professional circumstances. The result is a new and deeper internal understanding of research and its societal impact. The effects of LES have been largely positive in that they: 1) enable scientists to reflect on alternative perspectives within the research project in real time (e.g., concerning research protocols, strategies, etc.) and 2) stimulate and amplify scientists' reflections on the impact of their research on their immediate community and society at large. In the language of STS, these embedded social scientists and humanists engage in *midstream modulation*, a dialogical process wherein they inquire, reflect, and give feedback to the physical science researcher about their implicit and explicit activities and decisions.[11,12]

The STIR protocol's midstream modulation of research projects is comprised of three stages. These are defined briefly in the *Encyclopedia of Nanoscience and Society*:

> *de facto* modulation, the 'normal' shaping of research projects by a variety of cognitive, social, and material factors; *reflexive* modulation, in which researchers become aware of the role played by these factors, including their own position within larger interacting systems; and '*goal-directed*' [or '*deliberative*'] modulation, by which researchers deliberatively alter their decisions in light of clearly defined societal goals, concerns, or values.[13]

Mahootian's systems-based re-description of LES highlights some features of the interaction that are common to psychotherapy.[14] In the LES process, interactions between social scientists and physical scientists undergo occasional shifts of intensity and duration; at some point during the course of the study, the physical scientists spend more of their time engaging questions raised by the social scientist. It is clear that the *dyadic* relationship facilitates the progress of reflective introspection. To what extent LES systems dynamics bear resemblance to the processes of imagination and transference/counter-transference is an intriguing question.

Of importance here is the concept of *entrainment* wherein the activities of one member of the dyad sync up with those of the other—in the context of LES, the social scientist is often entrained by the physical scientist as part of the initial phase of gaining interactional expertise and building trust. The LES case study in a later section of this chapter captures some of the details of this process. The process of entrainment in the systems-based re-description of LES closely resembles Allan Schore's identification of elements within the relationship between infants and their primary caretakers.[15] Furthermore, Joe Cambray's understanding of the way that psychotherapy is facilitated by *resonance* and *mirroring* in the analytical field between patient and analyst is similar to LES dynamics.[16] While the context of therapy is different than that of LES, the dynamics that occur within the dyad are similar.

Jung's Theory of the Psyche: The Fordham Lectures

In "The Theory of Psychoanalysis," his 1912 series of nine lectures delivered at Fordham University 100 years ago, Carl G. Jung outlines the basic tenets of the nascent field of psychoanalysis.[17] He used this occasion to modestly challenge the shortcomings of the ideology with respect to his clinical experience. The lectures critique Freud's premise that sexuality is the basis of all unconscious thought and neuroses. The primacy of sexual trauma and the psychological mechanism of repression emerged through studies of hysteria. Jung describes the historical development of the theory of neurosis, originally stated as the *shock* or *trauma theory*, which later evolved to incorporate real and then imagined trauma through infantile fantasies.[18] Jung reflects on the influence of innate predisposition (i.e., an insufficient affective development or readiness to process the trauma) versus influence from the environment.[19,20] Of particular interest to Jung was the child's interaction with the parent complex, the internal images which form a person's early fantasy system, and eventually lead to the attitude that is projected onto the therapist in the transference.[21,22] Jung presents the view that trauma, real or imagined, is repressed and remains as a persistent unconscious constellation in the predisposed individual until activated by a conflict-laden pathogenic moment.

Signs of the impending schism between Jung and Freud emerge from Jung's critique of what he referred to as the *transgressions* of Freudian psychology, specifically, Freud's premise that sexuality is at the basis of all unconscious processes.[23] Jung did not believe in a purely sexual basis for the "preliminary phenomena of early infancy." In schizophrenic patients he observed the tendency to withdraw "object interest in general" rather than to withdraw their erotic interests only.[24,25] Jung re-envisions an *energetic* conception of psychic life in proposing a dynamic unity of primitive power that contains a genetic component and is indefinite as to content rather than comprised solely of psychosexual libido as Freud claimed.[26]

In essence, Jung conveys the importance of internally constructed fantasies emerging from interpersonal relationships or from withdrawal of libido (as in schizophrenia) while relinquishing the search for an etiology of pathology to be found in a single external event of the past. Jung's objection to Freud's term *polymorphous perverse* relates to his recognition of psychological phenomena beyond pathological processes that occur in the developmental spectrum of all individuals.[27] Sonu Shamdasani notes in his introduction to the 2012 edition of the Fordham lectures that Jung's initial title was "Mental Mechanisms in Health and Disease."[28]

This is the soil from which sprung Jung's longitudinal perspective on the psyche for his groundbreaking work, *Wandlungen und Symbole der Libido (Psychology of the Unconscious)*, revised in 1952 as *Symbols of Transformation* (CW 5). Published in German in 1912 and referred to in his Fordham lectures, this work was essentially the investigation of what Jung perceived as an individual (schizophrenic) fantasy system.[29,30] We can trace Jung's interest going from the psychological impact of real-life experiences (e.g., sexual trauma) to internal fantasies of infants and schizophrenics. He recognized that persistent unconscious psychological constellations (energetic complexes acquired through life experience or inheritance) exist in the psyches of all individuals, including scientists.

Jung's "Theory of Psychoanalysis" lays the foundation for his ideological emancipation from Freudian psychoanalysis, whereas *Wandlungen* elaborates upon the transitional development of Jung's larger paradigm and wider stratum of the psyche through extensive symbolic parallels and an archetypal context.[31] Expanding the parameters of the unconscious to include collective contents far beyond Freud's personal unconscious, Jung opened the door to multilevel consideration of influences that extend across time and space.[32] This allows us to see cross-cultural, shared collective experiences, which in turn serves to deepen our sense of connection to a larger humanity, a perspective that continues to bear considerable significance in our age of globalization and interest in responsible innovation.[33]

Between these two works, we witness the transformation of Jung's ideas beyond neuroses to the envisagement of psychic processes, ranging from psychopathology to psychological integration, and applicable across all cultures and historical periods.[34] In his Fordham lectures, Jung downplays the differences between his ideology and Freud's, but, through his authorship of *Wandlungen*, we ascertain that he was well aware that his view of the unconscious differed considerably from Freud's. *Wandlungen* intensified Jung's interest in exploring the archaic myth that was ordering his own life, eventually leading to his own self-analysis and the development of analytical psychology throughout his life.[35]

Jung refined his belief in a developmental journey evolving toward *wholeness*.[36,37] This *process of individuation* requires integrating the complementary complexes that characterize analytical psychology.[38] Jung claimed that particular processes (e.g., psychotherapy) are conducive to effect a change and expansion of consciousness. He assigned a similar role to dream interpretation, his technique of active imagination, and the use of artistic expression to help elaborate the ongoing dialogue that exists between the unconscious and conscious aspects of the human psyche.[39]

Analytical psychology embraces the interaction of the individual psyche within the world and restores the non-rational component of the psyche within the evolution of human consciousness. Jung states, "History teaches us over and over again that, contrary to rational expectation, irrational factors play the largest, indeed the decisive, role in all processes of psychic transformation."[40] Jung rescued the unconscious from debased connotations of Freud's id, and provided a compensatory function for one-sided leanings of Western culture.

Perhaps Jung's strongest contribution was his recognition of the primacy of the unconscious and its chronological priority in the development of the psyche. Jung states, "our conscious scientific mind started in the matrix of the unconscious mind," whereas "[Freud] derives the unconscious from the conscious."[41,42] Another significant contribution is his cartography of the psyche and discovery of complementary opposites whose dynamic interactions produce emergent phenomena towards integration. Jung found the polarities of nature in the structure and dynamics of the psyche and charted a course for our developmental strivings toward optimum human growth. Jung developed his theory that energetic constellations, acquired through life experience or by phylogenetic dispositions, dwell within the recesses of the human psyche, that complexes hold primacy in shaping perception and action, and that communication between the conscious and unconscious leads to extensive personality integration via imagery and symbolism.[43]

Science, Complementarity, and Transference

Jung often stated that modern science is unconscious of itself, of its sources and impacts. *Technoscience*, the merger of modern science and technology, is emblematic of Western culture. Jung's diagnosis of the psychological imbalance of Western culture can be applied to technoscience in the hope that change to the *process* of science-making can improve its course. Though the production of scientific knowledge is a collective enterprise, actions at the scale of the individual continue to shape key aspects of the outcome. LES focuses its efforts at this level of individual decision. Jung did not strive to be a social leader, but rather focused his attention on the transformation of the individual, envisioning a process of individuation to reconcile even the opposites of the individual and the collective.[44] By choosing LES as the focus of our critique of science we too focus on the individual. The role of complementarity in the epistemology of science frames the optimal dyadic relationship for transformation.

In Niels Bohr's understanding of complementarity within the context of quantum physics, observations gathered by one experimental set up (e.g., to measure dynamics data) exclude the very possibility of collecting other complementary observations (that measure kinematical data). There is an *unavoidable coupling*, as Bohr puts it, between measuring device and observable object.

> This very problem has indeed been brought to the foreground in an unexpected way by the discovery of the universal quantum

of action which expresses a feature of wholeness in atomic processes that prevents the distinction between observation of phenomena and independent behavior of the objects.[45]

The wholeness of atomic processes results from every observation of atomic processes where "any definable subdivision requires a change of the experimental arrangement giving rise to new individual effects."[46] Bohr states unequivocally that both in physics and beyond, the circumstances of observation *constitute* that which is observed: "*complementarity* simply characterizes the answers we can receive by such an inquiry, whenever the *interaction* between the measuring instruments and the objects form an inseparable part of the phenomena."[47]

Thus complementarity is relevant whenever a method of observation is constitutive of that which it measures, e.g., whenever the method of observation and the observed object exist on the same scale of space, time, and/or energy, the interaction between them *constitutes both*. Bohr said that complementarity between physical factors exemplifies "logical relations which, in different contexts are met with in wider fields."[48] Such relations are relevant beyond physics and are embodied in other fields of practice, such as anthropology in general, and LES in specific. This is also the case in psychotherapy, wherein patient and therapist exist on the same scale and take on the role of observer and observed in turn, both intra-psychically and interpersonally.

We contend that complementarity is a *meta*-scientific concept that defines an *interpretive framework* for experimental findings and theories. Complementary relations embodied in LES are refined by the application of depth psychology to broaden the interpretive framework of this situation. Bohr's concept of complementarity informs us that any individual's perspective, including the scientist's, is one mode of looking at a larger reality best grasped through several mediated viewpoints. We will review a case demonstrating that, in the research laboratory, embedding a humanist (or social scientist) can stimulate reflexivity and thus alter the perspective of researchers during research.

Given Jung's insistence that the "analysis of the analyst" is essential to the process of analysis itself, Jungian insights can optimize such ethnographic interventions.[49] He recognized that "in any effective psychological treatment the doctor is bound to influence the patient;

but this influence can only take place if the patient has a reciprocal influence on the doctor. You can exert no influence if you are not susceptible to influence."[50]

This is consistent with Bohr's idea of complementarity, that any objective and complete account of quantum phenomenon *must* include a description of the instrument and the theoretical framework employed to observe it. In quantum physics, the experimental setting for observing certain features of an atomic system excludes the possibility of observing others. Any complete account of quantum systems must *necessarily* include an account of the methods of observations and interpretation that were employed. The situation in psychotherapy is analogous but much more complex.

In "The Psychology of the Transference," Jung introduces a diagram (Figure 1) with the following statement: "The pattern of relationship is simple enough, but, when it comes to detailed description in any given case, it is difficult to make out from what angle the relationship is being described and what aspect we are describing."[51] Whether the context is quantum physics or the human psyche, one must attempt to account for the target *and* the vantage. These accounts are *complementary*, as a description of the target phenomenon is *incomplete* without an account of the vantage from which that description originates. This is simpler in physics than in psychotherapy because of the greater degree of manipulation and control in the case of instrumentation.

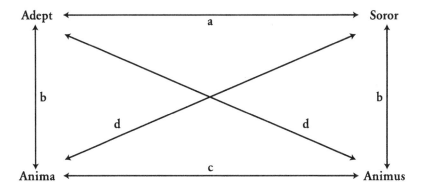

Figure 1. Jung's diagram of transference phenomena. (from "The Psychology of the Transference," CW 16, p. 221)

Jung's scheme identifies the composition of the individual human psyche in the context of its *interactions*.[52] Freud and Jung identified the psyche's primary division between the conscious and unconscious. Jung further claimed the primacy of the unconscious and the personal imperative—for the patient *and especially for the analyst*—to integrate the conscious and unconscious psyche for mental health. In their compensatory relationship, changes in one effect changes in the other. Jung's methodology of dyadic interpersonal process allows for the expansion of consciousness through interactions, and, by self-reflexively accounting for such interactions, the eventual integration (recognition and reclaiming) of unconscious material.

Figure 2 shows Jacoby's modification of Jung's transference diagram to address the space of psychotherapy, specifically, the analyst-patient field. By extracting the diagram from Jung's alchemical context, Jacoby made the web of relations applicable to the therapeutic context. A key difference with Jung's view is implicit in the change of terms from Adept and Soror to the *egos* of Patient and Analyst. While the upper and lower halves of both diagrams correspond to the conscious and unconscious psyche, Jacoby restricts conscious therapeutic interactions to *ego*-consciousness. Perhaps for the sake of diagrammatic simplicity *ego* is meant to stand in for other aspects of consciousness.

Jacoby illustrates the relation *e* in the diagram by commenting on a patient's dream: "The astonishing fact is the extent to which her

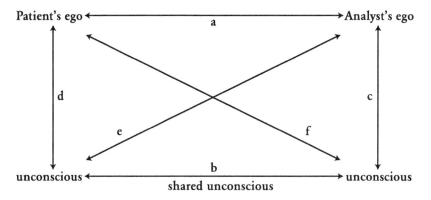

Figure 2. Jacoby's analyst-patient field. [Adapted from Jacoby's *The Analytic Encounter* (1984)]

unconscious grasped my own wavelength in dimensions which were far away from her consciousness."⁵³ The dream was *constellated* by the analytic encounter. Jacoby cites Jung's description of relation *b*: "The patient, by bringing an activated unconscious content to bear upon the doctor, constellates the corresponding unconscious material in him ... [Therefore] contents are often activated in the doctor which might normally remain latent."⁵⁴

Cambray refers to Jacoby's diagram in his discussion of the synchronistic dimension of empathy in the analytic field.⁵⁵ He articulates the mutual influence of the dyad through *resonance* via empathy and synchronicity which function as emergent channels of the field. Cambray's use of complex adaptive systems to explain synchronicity is congruent with the systems-based description of interactions between social and physical scientists in LES. We have couched these interactions in systems dynamics language, using the term *entrainment*—a specific case of resonance. In Cambray's conception of dyadic resonance within transference, we see a rich potential for psychological exploration in the science laboratory.

Key Features of Analytic Psychology Applicable to LES

1. Archetypal symbolism in the framework of analytical psychology

Jung remarked, "we have plunged down a cataract of progress which sweeps us on into the future with ever wilder violence the farther it takes us from our roots ... not to speak of the terrible perils to which the most brilliant discoveries of science expose us."⁵⁶ In archetypal symbolism, the undeveloped self-consciousness of science lies in the interaction between *Logos* and *Eros*, the dualities intrinsic to LES. *Logos*, traditionally symbolizing aggression and the masculine principle, is associated with the mind and word which penetrates, discriminates, and divides; *Eros*, symbolizing the feminine, is associated with the body, receptivity, containment, love, emotions and relationship. Von Franz wrote,

> We might say that Jung was not only a 'leader of minds,' because he showed that individuation is not possible without the differentiation of Eros. Perhaps Jung will be remembered as a knight who restored to the community the feminine principle of Love, or Eros.⁵⁷

Elsewhere she remarked, "The masculine drive toward activity and Faustian aggressiveness—caught in the maternal womb of the mandala—can only there be transformed into a new creative form in which the destructive initiative of our existence can be integrated."[58]

2. Typologies

Jung's explanation of psychological dualities led him to propose a framework of personality characteristics that are predominant in everyone to varying degrees (see Figure 3). In *Psychological Types,* he further describes how these characteristics are expressed through the two psychological attitudes of introversion and extroversion.[59] Subsequent researchers have expanded on these findings to construct corresponding assessment tools (e.g., the *Myers-Briggs Type Indicator,* MBTI) that are now used in diverse fields.[60,61] The four sets of combinations, which describe the ways in which we relate to the world, are the following: Extrovert/Introvert—where one focuses attention and derives energy from others or from within oneself; Sensing/Intuition—the type of information attended to most often, i.e., facts or impressions; Thinking/Feeling—how judgments and decisions are made, from a cognitive or feeling dimension; Judging/Perceiving (a category not developed by Jung but added by subsequent researchers)—how you prefer your lifestyle and outer world to be structured, i.e., whether you prefer to utilize the judging functions (Thinking/Feeling) more than the perceptual functions (Sensing/Intuition), or vice versa. American culture tends to overvalue Extroversion, Sensing, Thinking, and Judging. The combinations of four letters which correspond to sixteen different personality types are indicative of one's strengths and challenges, e.g., ESTJ, INFP, etc.[62] Unique interactions emerge between letter combinations within and between people, an understanding of which would be conducive to working with the dyadic configurations that emerge between scientists in LES.

Von Franz describes the four functions as providing a basic orientation for ego consciousness.[63] Everyone cultivates and differentiates one orientation more than the others and relies on it for adaptation. A second or third function may also be developed, but the fourth (opposite of the main function) remains largely unconscious

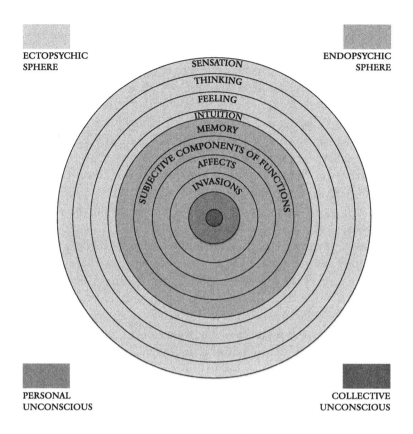

Figure 3. Jung's Concentric Diagram of the Psyche. [Adapted from Jung's Tavistock Lectures (1968)]

whereby Jung designated it the *inferior* function. This is germane to LES and our discussion regarding the undeveloped inferior function or shadow side of science. Development of the *thinking* function at the expense of the other three functions would have a negative impact on the development of the latter and diminish the sense of morality and humanity. Elsewhere, we have discussed in greater detail the interactions among the four functions in the context of the special role of intuition in Jung's psychology and Alfred North Whitehead's philosophy.[64] A contemporary of Jung, Whitehead developed a conceptual and cultural critique that addressed specific imbalances in the historical development of Western science.[65]

3. The Ego Complex and the Personal and Collective Unconscious

According to Jung's diagram of the psyche (Figure 3), the types reside within the ecto-psychic sphere of egoic consciousness, existing in dynamic interaction with one another and in the exchange between the person's inner and outer worlds.[66] Several arenas (e.g., memory, body awareness, emotions, etc.) comprise the endo-psychic sphere, the egoic dimension that manifests itself in will-power (perhaps also a complex within consciousness). The relevance of Jung's diagram for LES is its delineation of the complexities that each participant brings to the dyadic process. LES are likely to err in assuming that participants are self-aware and that the totality of their mental activity is conscious.

The unconscious aspect of the human side of science, and of LES researchers, is germane. Depth psychology postulates that the innermost level of the psyche of each LES participant is unknown, even to the participant. It is the goal of the psychotherapeutic process to unearth these subliminal elements that exhibit a strong influence on a patient's consciousness and life. The reality of the unconscious can be understood through the conscious or liminal lens of both therapist and patient. The presence of the dyadic Other affords space and a container for catching the unconscious projected, split off elements that can then be revealed, as in a mirror, and reclaimed.

Theoretically, the ego of the LES scientist, and of a patient, creates a protective barrier around unconscious material to ward off anxiety and the unpleasant thoughts and emotions internally triggered when suppressed material intrudes on consciousness. The defense mechanisms of denial, repression, rationalization, projection, etc., suppress material unacceptable to the ego. These psychological mechanisms have been studied extensively by the neo-Freudian school. Like Jung, contemporary relational theorists propose that dynamics such as splitting and projection are more primitive and fundamental, initially emerging during infantile stages of development to define the Self in relation to others.

4. Projection

Projection is a psychological mechanism employed by the ego to transfer subjective material outwards. A primary impetus for this phenomena is an activated unconscious emotion. For Jung, transference and counter-transference are specific forms of projection.⁶⁷ Projection and transference happen unconsciously and involuntarily.

As LES consist of intimate dyadic arrangements, we surmise that dynamics occurring within the ecto- and endo-psychic sphere, and the realms of the personal and collective unconscious, will be projected among various partners onto their scientific work to varying degrees. As Jung posits, transference is

> a phenomenon that can take place quite apart from any treatment, and is moreover a very frequent natural occurrence. Indeed, in any human relationship that is at all intimate, certain transference phenomena will almost always operate as helpful or disturbing factors.⁶⁸

He also states, "[transference] is a perfectly physical phenomena that can happen [to the therapist] just as it can happen to the teacher, the clergyman, the general practitioner, and last but not least—the husband."⁶⁹

Review of a Laboratory Case Study

Social scientist, S, was embedded in a fertility lab for a period of twelve weeks as a STIR researcher.⁷⁰ There was an initial period of adjustment as in every case of embedding, to a greater or lesser degree. For S, it included observing the written and unwritten routines and practices of the lab; for the lab, it involved adjusting to the presence of an outsider and responding to questions framed by a non-specialist.

By all accounts, S's presence in the lab and her agenda to establish the STIR program of observations and interactions constituted an inevitable disruption of routines. At the most basic level this disruption is due to the fact that once S entered the lab she was consuming both the time and space of lab team members. The efficacy of the systems approach is grounded in the inevitability of spatiotemporal location, an awareness that is further amplified by the disruption that accompanies even the mildest of interactions—dealing with this inevitability is a fact of life in any anthropological field study.

Once the initial phase was stabilized (the regular schedule of ongoing laboratory presence and periodic interactions around the STIR decision protocol established), S, in accordance with the STIR engagement study design, noted, and shared her observations of *de facto* modulation with the lab personnel.[71] Soon thereafter, as has been the case with other STIR studies, S was invited to do lab work alongside the researchers she was there to study. Speaking metaphorically on the basis of the systems approach, this is an instance of entrainment of the social scientists by the physical scientist; S was initiated into the routine of lab life as a *genetics laboratory researcher* and was literally trained in lab techniques (e.g., sample prep, etc.). Her spatiotemporal signature matched those of the researcher training her. The *outsider* had taken on some of the language and skills of the insiders she came to observe and engage; in the process she gained a deeper level of trust with one collaborator. Together, they probed some nascent and unresolved ethical reflections about the ongoing practice of extraction and use of blood samples from lab workers. S's role in mediating the laboratory researcher's reflections eventually resulted in the explicit codification of such practices in their lab. S's acquisition of interactional and contributory expertise enabled her to gain the trust of her collaborators and to continue to address insider concerns articulately. S was now entrained with respect to the language and activities of the lab. This laid the groundwork to entrain her collaborators by facilitating their acquisition of interactional expertise sufficient to reflect upon the societal impacts of their own laboratory practices. The facilitation of this kind of temporary reversal of roles is precisely the transformation that was conceived in the STIR pilot study.

Under the influence of S's questions and interactions, laboratory objects and practices became labile and responsive to re-description, even to the point of the social scientist and lab researcher adopting each other's terms and concepts. The enhanced responsiveness, afforded by a temporary loosening of professional self-other identity, supported further episodes of reflexive modulation for both S and the genetics lab researchers. S's STIR study eventually resulted in her entrainment of the lab manager in basic ethnography and "STS 101." The lab manager was not only sensitized to the social context of his laboratory with gained awareness of the ways in which the lab could be perceived *from the outside*, he also became actively involved in shaping those same perceptions. This re-description of his role resulted in observable changes in behavior, e.g., co-authoring a paper about the lab with S. This also led to the lab's launching of a patient outreach newsletter.

The Transformative Process

The US National Science Foundation (NSF) uses the term *transformative research*, in a way that is related to, but distinct from, Jung's use of the concept of transformation (discussed below). Our own use of the term in the chapter subtitle intends both literal and figurative senses simultaneously. Before proceeding to examine Jung's approach, we include the NSF's definition for reference:

> Transformative research involves ideas, discoveries, or tools that radically change our understanding of an important existing scientific or engineering concept or educational practice or leads to the creation of a new paradigm or field of science, engineering, or education. Such research challenges current understanding or provides pathways to new frontiers.[72]

1. The Transformative Process in Analytical Psychotherapy

Depth psychotherapies use various techniques to bring unconscious contents into consciousness for the sake of personal transformation. The hallmark of Jung's approach was his use of word association, dream analysis, active imagination, and artistic materials. Each method is effective in eliciting images from the unconscious. Also noteworthy is analytical psychology's overarching perspective on dualities: a cultivation of the dialectical play of opposites with the ultimate goal of their integration within consciousness. Broadly speaking, this suggests that 1) both therapist and patient endeavor to engage equally with unconscious and conscious features of the patient's material; 2) the phenomenon of healing and transformation comes through a *transcendent function* (or inner guidance) that emerges out of the interaction of conscious and unconscious material; and 3) the movement, mixing, and interaction of contents is counterbalanced with a patient, caring, embracing ambiance (like the alchemical *vas*) which allows the patient to sustain the tension (arising from a seeming conflict of opposites) long enough until a new narrative is born. Jung emphasizes that psychotherapy involves not merely the intellect but also "confirmation [of the issues] by the heart and the actual release of suppressed emotion."[73] Engaging the emotions provides further orientation for the patient.

2. The Transformative Process in LES

Transformation occurs in LES in a way that is similar, yet markedly different from a depth psychotherapeutic process. For the sake of comparison, we would divide the total LES experience into the following four consecutive stages: 1) introduction of participants and the LES project during which ideological and relational bonds are formed, *releasing* and exchanging scientific information; 2) building interactional expertise, trust, and a common language to enhance communication and understanding across disciplinary fields; 3) engagement in reflexive discourse, including social impact; and 4) transformation, the emergence of new ideas and insights between the physical and social scientist that could potentially lead to changes in the participants and the science research design.

Egoic defense mechanisms such as projection would likely occur in the earliest stages while anxiety is high due to the novelty of the situation. Transference and counter-transference phenomena would likely emerge in the second phase as LES relationships deepen and conscious and unconscious fantasy formations become more entwined over longer periods of time. Attachment issues would appear in more intimate contexts.

The crux of the transformative process in LES lies in the engagement and interactional dialogue that transpires between the physical and social scientists through the latter's application of the interaction protocol. Exploring moral issues within the intersubjective space helps to provide alternative perspectives within a relational sphere potentially resulting in greater objectivity and internalization.

The methodology provides opportunity for sustained reflection and, although structured, invites open discourse. Circumambulating participants' responses around the theme of social responsibility allows for the emergence of critical and creative thinking. Structurally, the interactional format embodies the dialogic encounter that Jung felt was significant to the process of gaining insight. The depth of dyadic engagement in LES likely stimulates the participant's imaginative capacities in a preliminary fashion, somewhat similar to a Jungian analyst's aim of intentionally and skillfully activating imagination through analytic dialogue.

The social scientist may also serve a psychological function of personifying the physical scientist's ethical self. This enables the latter's inner dialogue, analogous to Jung's use of active imagination. Alternatively, we might consider the presence of the social scientist as an adjunct to the physical scientist's *observing* ego, analogous to a psychotherapist's relationship to a patient. Incorporation of societal concerns beyond the self is reflected in the most advanced levels of human development proposed by psychological theorists such as Jung, Piaget, and Kohlberg. As such, LES have the potential to promote the intrapsychic development of participants, as well as helping to integrate scientific methodology with concerns of societal welfare.[74,75]

The one-on-one encounter of the LES design is highly relational, as is the topic of social impact. Infant research and developmental theory has emphasized the optimal effect of positive human contact. The relational effect promotes consideration of one's impact on others, not from a detached *objective* view, but rather from a humanistic one in recognizing and experiencing the relational connection between all things, scientific and nonscientific.

Comparison of LES and Therapy

Table 1 presents a summary of general similarities and differences, recognizing that there are many more than the ones addressed here. The features listed in the left column were selected as primary categories that best reflect standard practice for both disciplines. The individual entries that appear under the column headings of Depth Psychotherapy and LES are general descriptions—there are many variations even within the standard practice of each discipline. The components listed here comprise the backdrop of our discussion.

In previous sections we noted general similarities with respect to the complementarity of factors inherent within LES, psychotherapy, and quantum physics. The wholeness of quantum phenomena and the arbitrary location of the line between instrument and object suggest the following parallels: 1) In physics, the line moves by virtue of

Table 1. Comparisons between LES and Psychotherapy

Feature	Depth Psychotherapy	Lab Engagement Study
Training	Therapists undergo professional training process	Post-docs and graduate students adapt in real-time or undergo brief training
Implementation	Therapists study and apply psychological theory	LES apply interview protocols
Context	Therapists encounter a broad variety of cases	LES encounter a broad variety of research topics, but limited to laboratory settings
Primary focus	Patient	Physical Scientist
Methods	"Left brain" and "right brain" techniques (dialogue, debate, analysis, art, active imagination, etc.)	"Left brain" (dialogue, debate, analysis, problem-solving, rational synthesis, etc.)
Goal	Intentionally working with the unconscious; expansion of consciousness; integration	Expanding consciousness and integration with social and ethical standards
Approach	Exploratory, confrontational, revelatory, and educative	Educative, supportive, and enhancing
Meaningful Narrative	Tailored to the individual patient	Articulate social, political, ethical context of science
Boundary conditions	Consistent meeting time, place; therapist skill set, patient's personality structure, symptomology	Varies by project goals, methods; personality of researchers—principal investigator, humanist, physical scientist
Contextual Systems	Influence of social service agencies, healthcare insurance programs; other third party sources	Influence of research policies, social and political values, science agency research priorities

variations in the structure and function of the measuring device and the design of the experiment. Different arrangements of instruments and experimental settings may give rise to complementary objective states, thus making corresponding properties and measurements of the object accessible; 2) In successful psychoanalysis, working with the unconscious, the transference, and other projective phenomena, the therapist and patient gain access to different, complementary, and sometimes mutually exclusive psychological complexes; and 3) In successful LES, collaborators begin mirroring each other to the extent that they adopt each other's concepts and practices in a temporary reversal of roles. This mirroring is an occasion for the physical scientist to think through the categories of the social scientist and consider questions that are normally excluded from conscious consideration, i.e., unasked questions of which the scientist is professionally (if not personally) unconscious.

Despite a sophisticated methodological design that includes a relational element, LES investigators do not seem to account for the full effect of their interactions in the lab. Phenomena in the realm of feeling, sense, and intuition are not sufficiently attended to despite the fact that significant relational exchanges occur at these levels. LES realize the influence of the presence of a social scientist at the concrete level of laboratory participation and verbal exchange, but they do not recognize the co-constitution of psychological reality and meaning, the matrix out of which the ideas of the physical scientist are born. This demonstrates a failure to recognize Bohr's idea that, in the act of observation, instrument and object are coupled and form an integral whole; at that moment, instrument and object are co-constituting. In both physical and psychological contexts, the mutual exclusion of certain types of observations precludes the possibility of seeing the entire, whole matrix at once. Both sciences require the integration of multiple perspectives that are irreducible, yet collectively form a whole.

Intersubjective processes are intrinsic to both psychoanalysis and LES. Analytical psychology offers an encompassing perspective that explicates relational complexities not formally discussed by LES. From its inception, psychoanalysis has articulated a keen awareness of the web of intersubjective relations that occur during therapy sessions. Freud and Jung developed the concepts of *transference* and *counter-transference* because they grasped the necessity of accounting for such dynamics. Jung recognized the important interplay of intra- and inter-psychic processes in the co-construction of meaning. In its short history, psychoanalytic theory has experienced a paradigm shift from a focus on intra-psychic conditions to refocusing on inter-psychic ones, from psychodynamics to object relations. The developmental psycho-neurobiological model currently emerging from empirical findings in neuroscience, infant research, and attachment theory holds that the brain is dynamically formed through relationship.[76]

We began this chapter by remarking that STS has developed a more concrete, complex, and humanly plausible picture of science, moving well beyond former positivist ideals of it. Incorporating an enlarged perspective on intrapersonal and intersubjective processes via the framework of analytical psychology, would enrich STS by rendering the LES approach more complex and comprehensive. Analytical psychology offers LES an alternative contextual analysis of its current methodological design. Furthermore, it suggests alternative theoretical grounds upon which more exploration and experimentation could be conducted. Ideally, all LES scientists would engage in fostering their own process of individuation within the context of scientific research. The paradigm example of this is Nobel laureate physicist Wolfgang Pauli, who underwent analysis with Marie-Louise von Franz and Jung's assistant, Erna Rosenbaum, and maintained lifelong correspondence with Jung. The development of Pauli's scientific thought went hand in hand with his psychological development.

Conclusion

Jung was one of the strongest leaders of the twentieth century movement to reconceptualize science. It is surprising that over one hundred years later his footsteps are still fresh. In broadening the parameters of the unconscious, Jung made depth psychology relevant to the world beyond the consultation room. An interdisciplinary thinker, he challenged the compartmentalization of knowledge as indicated by his deep collaborations with eminent sinologist R. Wilhelm and physicist W. Pauli with whom he developed the familiar yet difficult concept of synchronicity. In his foreword to the Fordham lectures, Jung dismisses the idea that he is introducing a "split in the psychoanalytic movement," since "schisms only occur in matters of faith." Psychoanalysis, on the other hand is concerned with knowledge in the manner best captured by William James, whom Jung cites favorably on the point that theories are "*instruments, not answers to enigmas, in which we can rest. We don't lie back upon them, we move forward, and, on occasion, make nature over by their aid.*"[77] Despite Jung's tremendous effort at moving knowledge forward by expanding our collective consciousness in dynamic accord with our collective unconscious, science has not been especially receptive to his radical ideas.

In the Fordham lectures, we witness Jung's lengthy response to criticisms surrounding psychoanalytic theory in 1912. Despite its many strengths, depth psychology continues to be questioned by the prevailing rationalism of mainstream science and to struggle for recognition within academic circles. Conceptual bias continues to cycle through political, social, and economic realms leading to scarce funding for psychological research and minimal insurance coverage for mental health care.

On a positive note, attitudes toward Jungian concepts may indeed be shifting as our culture begins to catch up with a man ahead of his time. The *Psychiatric Annals* devoted its December 2011 issue to measuring occasions of coincidence, signaling a willingness by mainstream medical psychiatry to take Jung seriously.[78] Measuring synchronicity may be an important step, but other psychological dimensions such as the imaginative, poetic, intuitive, aesthetic, and visionary may not be as amenable to scientific investigation. Furthermore, as Otto Kernberg notes, "the subtlety, complexity, and richness of the psychoanalytic process cannot be captured in the necessarily restricted quality of particular research projects."[79] In fact, Jung conducted experimental studies, but the depths of his psyche were best revealed through his own self-study.[80] Irwin Hoffman believes that the *privileged status* of doing systematic empirical research rather than in-depth case-studies is "unwarranted epistemologically and is potentially damaging both to the development of our understanding of the analytical process itself and to the quality of our clinical work."[81] Hoffman redefines knowledge in psychoanalysis, in terms of a *nonobjectivist hermeneutic* paradigm, noting that "the individual case study is especially suited for the advancement of 'knowledge'—that is, the progressive enrichment of sensibility—in our field."[82]

Whether conducting an individual case study or systematic empirical research of larger scale, the question for depth psychology remains—how do we get conscious and unconscious phenomena to emerge cooperatively within the context of qualitative or quantitative empirical research? The challenge is alive today as it was in Jung's time. Jung and Bohr taught us that, whether in physics or psychology, the mind is the ultimate tool with which we make *distinctions*—a point we should carefully consider in shifting the position of key distinctions as we merge disparate disciplines and approaches. As humanistic and scientific studies continue to cross-fertilize and grow together, we will inevitably erase some established lines, shift others, and draw new ones where none were previously suspected.

A review of psychoanalytic literature identifies three trends in the discussion of the place of empirical research. Michael Rustin has noted "the need for empirical research into the outcomes of treatments, for integration with other scientific disciplines concerned with the mind, and for the codification and unification of psychoanalytical theories."[83] Collaboration between analytical psychology and the field of science and technology studies has the potential to develop what Rustin calls "a more active relationship to academic methods of inquiry." Collaborative design and implementation of laboratory ethnographies of this type may potentially enhance research that is transformative of science at the frontiers of discovery and self-discovery. Analytical psychology has the potential to strengthen the capacity for reflexive understanding within cutting edge research by catalyzing deep self-understanding as the necessary psychological pre-requisite for responsible innovation. Reciprocally, analytical psychology stands much to gain by demonstrating, in this manner, the value of the dyadic methodological approach in empirical science. As the capstone of the psychoanalytic tradition for over one hundred years, the clinical method is naturally positioned to wed the physical and social sciences, or as Jung might have said, to perform the *magnum opus* of transforming both.

NOTES

1. C. G. Jung, "The Psychology of Jung: Passions of the Soul," *Mind and Matter*, vol. 3, IKON Television (Princeton, NJ: Films for the Humanities and Sciences, c1992, c1991), VHS.

2. Marie-Louise von Franz, "C. G. Jung's Rehabilitation of the Feeling Function in Our Civilization," *Jung Journal: Culture & Psyche* 2 (2, 2008): 9–20.

3. *Ibid.*, p. 9.

4. *Ibid.*

5. See, e.g., Erik Fisher, "Lessons Learned from the Ethical, Legal and Social Implications Program (ELSI): Planning Societal Implications Research for the National Nanotechnology Program," *Technology in Society* 27 (3, 2005): 321–328; and *National Nanotechnology Initiative Strategic Plan 2011*, objective 4.3.2.

6. Erik Fisher, "Ethnographic Invention: Probing the Capacity of Laboratory Decisions," *NanoEthics* 1 (2, 2007): 155–165.

7. Lisa M. Osbeck, Nancy J. Nersessian, Kareen R. Malone, and Wendy C. Newstetter, *Science as Psychology: Sense-Making and Identity in Science Practice* (New York: Cambridge University Press, 2011).

8. Bruno Latour and Steve Woolgar, *Laboratory Life: The Construction of Scientific Facts* (Princeton, NJ: Princeton University Press, 1979).

9. Peter Galison, *Image & Logic: A Material Culture of Microphysics* (Chicago, IL: University of Chicago Press, 1997).

10. Michael E. Gorman, ed., *Trading Zones and Interactional Expertise: Creating New Kinds of Collaboration* (Boston, MA: MIT Press, 2010).

11. Erik Fisher, Roop L. Mahajan, and Carl Mitcham, "Midstream Modulation of Technology: Governance from Within," *Bulletin of Science, Technology & Society* 26 (6, 2006): 485–496.

12. See the work of Bruno Latour, Peter Galison, Harry M. Collins, Karin Knorr-Cetina, Nancy J. Nersessian, Michael Gorman, Eric Fisher, and Katie Shilton.

13. Daan Schuurbiers, "Midstream Modulation," in *Encyclopedia of Nanoscience and Society*, ed. David H. Guston (Thousand Oaks, CA: SAGE Publications, Inc., 2010), pp. 426–427.

14. Farzad Mahootian, "Lab as Dynamic System: Refining Midstream Modulation," *NanoEthics* (forthcoming, 2015).

15. Allan N. Schore, "Effects of a Secure Attachment Relationship on Right Brain Development, Affect Regulation, and Infant Mental Health," *Infant Mental Health Journal* 22 (1–2, 2001): 7–66.

16. Joseph Cambray, *Synchronicity: Nature and Psyche in an Interconnected Universe* (College Station, TX: Texas A&M University Press, 2009), p. 82.

17. C. G. Jung, *Jung contra Freud: The 1912 New York Lectures on the Theory of Psychoanalysis* (Princeton, NJ: Princeton University Press, 1915/2012).

18. *Ibid.,* p. 8–9.
19. *Ibid.,* p. 14.
20. *Ibid.,* p. 48.
21. *Ibid.,* p. 52.
22. *Ibid.,* p. 108.
23. *Ibid.,* p. 37.
24. *Ibid.,* p. 22–25.
25. *Ibid.,* p. 38.
26. *Ibid.,* p. 36–37.
27. *Ibid.,* p. 46.
28. *Ibid.,* p. vii.
29. *Ibid.,* p. 129.

30. C. G. Jung, *Symbols of Transformation: An Analysis of the Prelude to a Case of Schizophrenia*, vol. 5, *The Collected Works of C. G. Jung*, ed. and trans. Gerhard Adler and R. F. C. Hull (Princeton, NJ: Princeton University Press, 1912/1956), p. xxx.

31. *Ibid.,* p. xxv.

32. C. G. Jung, *Memories, Dreams, Reflections* (New York: Random House, 1961), p. 401. Jung incorporates Freud's unconscious realm as the *personal unconscious* in his own model.

33. *Ibid.* Jung's unconscious includes "unconscious qualities that are not individually acquired, but are inherited, e.g., instincts as impulses to carry out actions from necessity, without conscious motivation … [and also the] archetypes … the instincts and archetypes together form the 'collective unconscious.'"

34. Jung, CW 5, p. xxix.

35. *Ibid.*, pp. xxiv–xxv.

36. C. G. Jung, *The Structure and Dynamics of the Psyche*, vol. 8, *The Collected Works of C. G. Jung*, ed. and trans. Gerhard Adler and R. F. C. Hull (Princeton, NJ: Princeton University Press, 1960), § 557.

37. C. G. Jung, *The Practice of Psychotherapy: Essays on the Psychology of the Transference and other Subjects*, CW 16, § 219.

38. M. L. von Franz, "The Process of Individuation," in C. G. Jung, ed., *Man and His Symbols* (London: Aldus Books Ltd., 1964), p. 158–229.

39. Jung, *Memories, Dreams, Reflections,* p. 161.

40. Jung, CW 5, p. xxvii.

41. C. G. Jung, *Analytical Psychology: Its Theory and Practice* (New York: Random House, 1968), p. 43.

42. *Ibid.*, p. 8.

43. Jung, CW 8, § 99–101.

44. M. L. von Franz, "C. G. Jung's Rehabilitation," p. 18.

45. Niels Bohr, *Atomic Physics and Human Knowledge* (New York: John Wiley & Sons, Inc., 1958), p. 99.

46. *Ibid.*

47. Niels Bohr, "Quantum Physics and Philosophy—Causality and Complementarity," in *ESSAYS 1958–1962 on Atomic Physics and Human Knowledge* (Bungay, Suffolk: Richard Clay & Co., 1963), p. 4.

48. *Ibid.*, p. 7.

49. Jung, CW 16, § 165.

50. *Ibid.*, § 163.

51. *Ibid.*, § 422.

52. Mario Jacoby, *The Analytic Encounter: Transference and Human Relationship* (Toronto: Inner City Books, 1984), p. 25.

53. *Ibid.*, p. 34.

54. *Ibid.*, p. 42.

55. Cambray, *Synchronicity*, p. 82.

56. Jung, *Memories, Dreams, Reflections,* p. 236.

57. M. L. von Franz, "C. G. Jung's Rehabilitation," p. 18.

58. Marie-Louise von Franz, *C. G. Jung: His Myth In Our Time* (New York: Little, Brown & Co., 1975), p. 147.

59. C. G. Jung, *Psychological Types,* CW 6.

60. For a standard MBTI reference, see Naomi Quenk, *Essentials of Myers-Briggs Type Indicator Assessment* (New York: John Wiley and Sons, 2000).

61. Douglass J. Wilde presents an empirically-based critique of the original MBTI categories in *Jung's Personality Theory Quantified* (New York: Springer, 2011).

62. John Beebe proposes a contemporary extension of typologies in a developmental context in "Understanding Consciousness Through the Theory of Psychological Types," in Joe Cambray & L. Carter, eds., *Contemporary Perspectives in Jungian Analysis* (New York: Brunner-Routledge, 2004).

63. M. L. von Franz, *C. G. Jung: His Myth*, p. 47.

64. Farzad Mahootian and Tara-Marie Linné, "Jung and Whitehead: An Interplay of Psychological and Philosophical Perspectives on Rationality and Intuition," in Lisa M. Osbeck and Barbara S. Held, eds., *Rational Intuition: Philosophical Roots, Scientific Investigations* (New York: Cambridge University Press, 2014).

65. Alfred North Whitehead, *Science and the Modern World* (New York: Cambridge University Press, 2011).

66. C. G. Jung, *Analytical Psychology*, p. 49.

67. *Ibid.*, p. 153.

68. *Ibid.*, p. 171 (footnote 14).

69. *Ibid.*, p. 172 (footnote 16).

70. Embedded social scientist Shannon Conley (S) recounted her experience as a STIR investigator in, "Engagement Agents in the Making: On the Front Lines of Socio-Technical Integration," *Science and Engineering Ethics* 17, (4, 2011): 715–721.

71. See note 13, above.

72. US National Science Foundation, "Definition of Transformative Research." Accessed on Dec. 13, 2013, at http://www.nsf.gov/about/transformative_research/definition.jsp.

73. Jung, CW 16, § 134.

74. Claire Allphin discusses theories of moral development and the ethical attitude within the analytic process in "An Ethical Attitude in the Analytic Relationship," *Journal of Analytical Psychology* 50 (2005): 451–468.

75. Luigi Zoja discusses the new ethical frontier within depth psychology in *Ethics and Analysis: Philosophical Perspectives and Their Application in Therapy* (College Station, TX: Texas A&M University Press, 2007).

76. Allan N. Schore, *Affect Dysregulation and Disorders of the Self (Norton Series on Interpersonal Neurobiology)*, vol. 1 (New York: W. W. Norton & Co., 2003).

77. Jung, *Jung contra Freud*, p. 4.

78. *Psychiatric Annals* 41 (12, 2011).

79. Otto F. Kernberg, "The Pressing Need to Increase Research in and on Psychoanalysis," *International Journal of Psycho-Analysis* 87 (2006): 924.

80. C. G. Jung, *The Red Book: Liber Novus*, ed. Sonu Shamdasani (New York: W. W. Norton & Co., 2009).

81. Irwin Z. Hoffman, "Doublethinking Our Way to 'Scientific' Legitimacy: The Desiccation of Human Experience," *Journal of the American Psychoanalytic Association* 57 (5, 2009): 1043–1069.

82. *Ibid.*, p. 1043.

83. Michael J. Rustin, "Varieties of Psychoanalytic Research," *Psychoanalytic Psychotherapy* 24 (2010): 380–397.

Part III
Jung: The Humanities and Beyond

Chapter Ten

Jung, Psychic Reality, and God

Ann Belford Ulanov

Jung and the Academy

We celebrate at this great Fordham University its invitation a hundred years ago to C. G. Jung to deliver nine lectures and daily seminars on his emerging insights into the depths of human psyche. Jung's work aimed to contribute to healing psychic suffering and to bring psychic reality into the domains of knowledge to which our pattern-making and symbol-forming psyches contribute resulting in an organizing force of knowledge. Running through Jung's entire corpus is his concern with matters religious, amounting to more than 6000 references to God.[1] Indeed, he found after emerging from his own descent to deepest psyche, now available to us in *The Red Book*, that his path to pursue what he found through his own experience was to comparatively study religions, myths, and alchemies of many cultures in order to discern the link between the psyche's transformation of the individual toward unity and the world made visible as an interconnected whole. Central to this comparative study is Jung's "question of the relationship of the symbolism of the unconscious to Christianity as well as to other religions"; "not only do I leave the door open for the Christian message, but I consider it of central importance for Western man."[2]

To take on Jung's work (and the Academy) brings before us both trouble and rich potential. Because of Jung's inclusion of religious instinct as native to psyche, he is placed in religion departments, not psychology, implying, along with Freud's objections to Jung, his is not a real psychology. The Academy and psychoanalytical training institutes feel nervous about Jung because he sees God as central to our psyche. In religious academies, such as seminaries, for example my own and those where graduates of the Psychiatry and Religion Program at Union hold faculty positions, an equal nervousness abounds because of Jung's insistence that any experience of God is through the psyche; that is, psychic reality must be factored into any exploration of religion. So trouble looms from both sides of what turns out to be a fence, or a transitus space, or a gap—however we want to describe it—where Jung brings together psychic reality and God's reality, seeing both as valid and interconnected. The nervousness results in banishment of Jung's work from psychology departments despite his description of analytical psychology as natural science and his groundbreaking discoveries, such as the Word Association Test, a true psychological research tool to track complexes in personality and in culture. In religious institutions nervousness results in ignoring the relevance of psychic reality in interpretation of sacred texts, theological doctrines, discernment of ethical principles, and performance of worship.

Nonetheless, rich potential exists in universities and seminaries as this conference illustrates. Our conference evokes the true space of such learned places, described by Cardinal Newman's "Idea of a University,"

> where a multitude ... keen, open-hearted, sympathetic, observant ... come together and ... learn from one another ... and they gain for themselves new ideas and views, fresh matters of thought, and distinct principles for judging and acting day by day.[3]

Paul Tillich ends his tenure at Harvard with words of gratitude for the wonder of a university:

> The greatest thing ... [is] the opportunity ... to carry through the experiment to which my whole life was dedicated, the reunion of what eternally belongs together but what has been separated in history ... we call it the religious and secular.

> The religious question is the question of meaning of human existence and existence generally. ... What am I, for what do I live? ... Is being a whole big accident, or has it an ultimate inner aim? ... The question arises in every section of man's cognitive approach to reality.[4]

Jung is trouble to both psychology and religion and gets into trouble because he had to bring them together for all kinds of personal reasons: his gripping childhood dreams and fantasies that posed questions to him and of which he said, "I knew I had to find the answer out of my deepest self, that I was alone before God, and God alone had asked me these terrible things"; his discovery out of such aloneness that "The Divine Presence is more than anything else. ... This is the only thing that really matters. ... I wanted proof of a living Spirit and I got it"; his *beatific vision* about which he would not speak and with it a God who sometimes "kicks us, as with Jacob, and you punch back"; and his losing his soul and embarking on the journey in *The Red Book, Liber Novus* to find it.[5,6,7]

Jung finds the psyche to be a medium through which God speaks to us, hence the psyche is not where the buck stops but is another means to that ultimate authority. "It is only through the psyche that we can establish that God acts upon us but we are unable to distinguish whether these actions emanate from God or the unconscious."[8] Jung stands for God and for psyche, as well as their relationship, their interconnectedness: "the main interest of my work [is] ... with the approach to the numinous ... [that] is the real therapy and inasmuch as you attain to the numinous experiences you are released from the curse of pathology." And even more amazing, as he reflected to Victor White in 1945, "My personal view ... is that man's vital energy or libido is the divine pneuma ... and it was this conviction which it was my secret purpose to bring into the vicinity of my colleagues' understanding."[9] That was Jung's personal mission.

Personal Equation

I want to recognize three aspects of Jung's purpose that directly affect our religious lives, by which I mean our relation to the god around which we revolve even if we say there is no god. The first, which he called the *personal equation*, figures into intractable splittings in adamantly held positions that oppose each other (which Jung wrote about in *Psychological Types*, his first published book after his *Red Book* experiences).[10] The personal equation means we are unconsciously identified with our point of view; we see the mote in our neighbor's eye and miss our own beam. We cannot attain objectivity. Jung writes, "The effect of the personal equation begins already in the act of observation. *One sees what one can best see oneself.*"[11] Jung describes here what quantum theory in science came also to assert—that the observer is part of what is observed; the means to study phenomena objectively inevitably includes the subjective element of the viewpoint of the observer that affects what is observed.

Personal equation is a problem if we do not know it is an inevitable factor in our observation and search for so-called objective truth; "The essential thing is to differentiate oneself from these unconscious contents ... and at the same time to bring them into relationship with consciousness."[12] Objectivity is permeated with subjectivity. What we take, for example, as revered religious tradition, is created out of subjectivities of a former era. This personal equation applies to all obstinate oppositions between us, e.g., divisiveness of race, creed, neighbors arguing over placement of a fence, couples caught in venomous divorce, combatting theorists of psyche, businessmen seeking to defeat instead of collaborate, and, as Newman says, in "fresh matters of thought."[13]

The Red Book ends with Jung saying he can go no further; he must deal with the barbarian in himself and for that he must go back to the Middle Ages. Such a return must be made when faced with an obstacle we cannot get past. We return to a prior position, collectively as well as personally, to see the roots of the present impasse.[14] The libido (and remember, for Jung, libido is also the divine pneuma, the divine spirit) has split into two halves, and we cannot see the merit of the other's viewpoint. "Barbarism consists in one-sidedness, lack of moderation"; "the inability to be anything but one-sided is a sign of barbarism."[15]

From this we can see what Tillich means when he says he seeks the reunion of what eternally belongs together but has been separated in history. Jung is trying to discern causes of the split between Freud and Adler, and between Freud and himself. Behind this lurks the cause of all splits; here, the background of the split between the ideal of reason and progress was blasted by the bloodbath of trench warfare of World War I and repeated in a second World War and many *smaller* wars throughout the twentieth century including the one we called the Cold War. Our hopes when the Berlin Wall came down that this would end such lethal divisions were smashed by a new kind of enemy that marks the twenty-first century—one of infiltration rather than the clear lines of iron curtains, of us and them, but more like an immune disorder that infects the whole system. We call it terrorism. We suffer its force when we do not know if the guy next to us in the plane is going to start lighting his shoes to blow up the aircraft, if the man now using the bathroom we had just used is trying to detonate the bomb fuse in his underwear, or if the station wagon parked too long in Times Square will explode to kill hundreds.

On the positive side, recognizing our personal equation changes our expectation of attaining an objective psychology (or any branch of knowledge). We must include our subjective lens of our observation and that introduces a gap between what we see and what is there. On the negative side, when we do not recognize our personal equation, we split away from others' views, dismiss them, even kill them, for not accepting what we assert as the truth, due to our unconscious identification with our view and identification of our view with truth. To see our personal equation is no *academic* issue unrelated to life with colleagues in our department or our psychoanalytical association, nor to the *barbarians* in ourselves. (Can we even say the *terrorists* in ourselves?)

Jung must return, and with him all of us, to the Middle Ages because the medieval man had a root to the solution to the problem of Jung's *barbarian*—the one lurking under his identification with his own personal equation, which for Jung is with his thinking. The medieval man recognizes "the idea of the imperishable value of the human soul" and that means in Jung's barbarian too. If each individual soul is of lasting value, then every person is, and all their parts are too. They must be recognized and included, not left undeveloped in the unconscious ready to attack like barbarians at the gate opposite the superior, developed parts of us. Furthermore, the superior parts usually affect just such an identification with the collective values dominant in one's culture that may further civilization but at the expense of our individuality that lies in our inferior, undeveloped functions. We may believe we are civilized and not see the barbarous state of our actual individuality.[16] It does not help society nor ourselves simply to let loose these undeveloped sides of ourselves; they must be claimed and developed, not inflicted on our neighbor.[17] Jung sees his *I* as an unbearable barbarian he must live with "until you are capable of making it bearable."[18]

Further still, when Jung takes up medieval theology in *Psychological Types*, he traces a long pattern of theological controversy about personal equations, psychological attitudes, and functions, that is, subjective elements related to the quest for what is real. Does our personal equation, when we are conscious of it, contribute to seeing the real or occlude our perceptions? This question lurks behind many controversies, such as in the arguments about the humanity/divinity of Christ, nominalism/realism, and same or merely like substance in transubstantiation.[19] In my view, Jung is also trying to resolve relation of his God-images, confronted in *The Red Book,* to God. He knows the psyche is real. He knows his experience of God is real, because of its *unshakeableness*.[20] How do they go together, or not? Jung also knows he can get no further with the stubborn complexes that bedevil him and influence his personal equation. Two stand out in *The Red Book*, one to do with feeling, the other to do with soul, Self, and God.

Jung said his superior developed capacity was thinking and identifying with its virtues, but it left his feeling at the mercy of decay; and therein lies, for him, and for each of us in our own neglected capacity, the barbarian.[21] Jung's neglected feeling confronted him in *The Red Book* in the personification, indeed in the personage, of Salome.[22] Jung shudders, recoils from her as insane, the bloodthirsty murderer of the Holy One (John the Baptist). She develops into a wise, loving woman wanting to give herself to Jung, who gasps and refuses, exclaiming she would stifle his freedom.[23] Go, live your life, he says; I cannot carry it—thus revealing where his feeling complex is stuck. He cannot reconcile his freedom with loving intimacy with another. He does resolve this impasse to some degree, saying finally he will serve love, but not on the lived level of life with another.[24] In *Memories, Dreams, Reflections* he expresses sorrow for hurting others, leaving them abruptly when they no longer serve his need, but he was pressed by the inner *daimon* and he knows that at its core "life is 'steel on stone.'"[25]

Jung's other major complex strikes a similar theme to do with his freedom, now in relation to soul, to Self, and to God. Near the end of *The Red Book*, Jung argues hotly that the soul must not steal off with a precious human treasure. The soul prevaricates, resists, and finally comes clean that she has stolen the warm, red-blooded love of humans, of Jung here, to take to the heavens, to God. Jung says NO! That is mine, and belongs to me, to give or withhold; give it back! And furthermore, soul, you must serve humanity, not the heavens or God; we are not going to labor here for you there. Give your energy "for the earthly fortune of humankind!" The soul consents.[26] This means all the energy, the libido (remember, it is divine pneuma), does not go off into the soul's salvation but pours back into the human heart for humans together in this life.

Jung also fights with the Self and with God to get his own self in order to have his self. This is the first mention of his pivotal idea of Self, I believe, where he distinguishes Self from his *I*-ness and Self from God: "the self is not God, although we must wrestle with God for the self. Since God is an unfathomable, powerful movement that sweeps away the self into the boundless, into dissolution ... we must strive to free the self from God, so that we can live."[27,28] Then, once he owns his own self, he can choose to give it to God. But if his self stays with God from the beginning, in psychological terms, he is flooded by the unconscious and in its grip; he does not have this energy, this libido, this divine pneuma for himself and his development. His *I*-ness disappears. We must fight God for the Self, then we can give ourselves to God, or not.[29]

Related to this is our creating of God out of ourselves, which is a highest act of love and of our developed self, what Jung calls an act of the Above. But he is commanded to sacrifice those images of God to which, over his own protest, he finally submits.[30] This is an act of the Below and means that those God-images, all that libido, again the divine pneuma, flows back into the Self and stirs up God from Below, the *Deus Absconditus*. (This wrestling the Self for the self is, again, the first instance of Jung noting the Self as different from *I*-ness, from ego, functioning as a centering force in the whole psyche, conscious and unconscious.) Once free of the Self and therefore able to sense this Self bigger than the ego and not under ego control is one means through which that which transcends the ego makes itself felt, so to speak.

Hence, Jung will say the images we find and create for God and those of this Self are practically indistinguishable, although he also says, "The psychic nature of all experience does not mean that the transcendent realities are also psychic" and "the self never at any time takes the place of God though it may perhaps be a vessel for divine grace."[31,32] I understand Jung to be saying we must carry our Self and through it God reaches us.[33]

The Bridge

The second item of importance is what Jung found to bridge our inner warring opposites. Creative fantasy constructs a bridge between intransigent positions and our symbol-making capacity that is the pull of *life itself*.[34] When a symbol appears that makes the "bridge going across," rigid oppositions, warring personal equations between people and nations and between conscious and unconscious parts of ourselves, get lifted into a new level; the problem in its old form of either/or is superseded by a new symbol that lifts the conflict into a both-and form providing for the libido to flow again into living.[35,36]

The clinical significance for the patient of this idea is of incalculable value, and for the analyst too, as the coming about of this new *third* is not the result of technique or clever interpretation. The analyst contributes knowledge of its possibility, readiness, and alertness to the coming of the new that always surprises. This is the *third* thing, a term only recently taken up in contemporary analytical schools, indicating a new representation missing from old opposing factions that now re-visions in a new image, attitude, possibility of behavior, and renewed life as mysterious as it is effective.[37] Jung even calls God in the *Liber Novus* "sheer effectiveness."[38] The patient's old conflict, for example, to drink again or get sober, to try to forgive only to want to wreak vengeance, to connect the disparate elements in an elusive business formula only to have them scatter, to find a space of warm meeting with an estranged partner only to fall back into isolated distance from each other—all these human problems—yield their fixed static positions. The new thing that appears spontaneously goes beyond and supplants the opposition of this side versus that side with the new.[39] We do not invent it but receive it with amazement.

I have written elsewhere of many examples of this happening.[40] The idiosyncratic details of each person's experience is of great significance, for there we find both the demons we confront, namely our complexes that grip and compel us and by which we are *torn asunder* in *agonizing disunion*, indeed our madness, and also there we find our particular creativity that hides in the complex and appears in the symbol that heals it.[41,42] For example, Jung could not give himself to Salome nor receive her love, but he submits himself in devotion to love itself by the end of the book and recognizes in his autobiography its final sovereignty.[43,44] So caught and frightened of losing his freedom, of being bound by "an iron ring," Jung nonetheless finds his fear transformed into willing service, another devotion, now not to love but to the reality of psyche and its mediating function of what is beyond psyche: "I dedicated myself to the service of the psyche, I put my trust in the thing I felt to be ... *sub specie aeternitatis* ... for the sake of that goal I was ready to take any kind of risk."[45]

When that *third* thing appears, an experience of our psyche and of beyond psyche conjoin. Libido that has stalemated in the opposition of two personal equations confronting each other, or two sides of conscious and unconscious in our complex, dams up this energy. When the resolving new symbolic form appears, the demon of the complex is superseded by a new symbol that in effect dissolves the old opposition and presents us with a new task. A new path summons our energy; the damned-up libido flows into this new direction. We feel release from madness, and further, the barbarian gains energy to develop.[46] The social significance of this new path is incalculable, for just to release on others the barbaric, undeveloped parts of us and of our group results in unimaginable horrors—from massacre of citizens in a movie premiere, to camps of enslaved citizens tortured and killed, to bombings of civilian neighborhoods. To find paths for energy of outlier parts now devoted to a shared goal, combining different points of view steadies and renews our communal existence. We feel this steadiness in ourselves too, for the opposition we played out with our neighbor now lands squarely in ourselves, our own experience of the *yea* and *nay* of life.[47] We accept different points of view in ourselves as our task to resolve, hence developing all the psychological functions in our personality.

To develop only one function and identify with it as superior promotes civilization but oppresses the other functions which we also need in order to live a life of

> intensity and beauty. ... His individuality is wholly on the level of his inferior, undeveloped functions, and he is simply a barbarian. ... The differentiated function procures ... the possibility of a collective existence, but not the satisfaction and *joie de vivre* which the development of individual values alone can give.[48,49]

Still further, we feel granted new life in relation to purpose that is ours particularly and benefits others around us. We feel life-giving energy in us, flowing toward, indeed, serving what matters, what is meaningful, our very own devotion to God or to whatever we revolve around as if it is a god. It is as if we move from a black and white world into Technicolor. We find our very own relation to the wholeness of the whole, and live, in the words of poet Wallace Stevens, "This self, not that gold self aloft."[50]

One other note of great importance, in which I cannot go into detail here, I will just toss out for mulling: the relation of this creative fantasy, this pull of life, to Jung's later formulation of synchronicity as a culmination of decades of thought.[51] The impasse of complexes cannot be solved by consciousness because we are caught in one side of the conflict and then the other; we cannot consciously produce by will, the energy, the divine pneuma of libido, to lift a symbolic content into awareness that "alone can produce an irrational solution of a logical antithesis."[52] Nor can we, via our unconscious, produce a solution to the complex because in our unconscious all contents and psychic functions are "indistinguishably merged in the original and fundamental activity of the psyche."[53] When an unconscious content receives a value, and hence, enough energy to cross the threshold of consciousness, a breakthrough from conflict results. It appears as a lucky idea, or hunch, chance, scrap, indeed what the revolutionary wordsmith James Joyce calls *accident*.[54] Jung too says "we blunder into the work of redemption unintentionally."[55] An odd idea or intuition or emotional resonance or body hint that we stumble upon arrests us; we follow it like a dog beckoning us in a dream, its dot of light alerts, casting a little beam toward the *middle way*.[56] These sparks are "worthless in so far as nothing clearly distinguishable can be perceived from their configuration ... but valuable in so far as it is just this undifferentiated state that gives them that symbolic character which is essential to the content of the mediating will."[57] The nonrational coincidence of causally unrelated contents that affects us with great emotion in this creative fantasy presages the theory of synchronicity.[58] We experience personally within our own psyche a transcendence of conflict that brings us experience of a transcendence without, in life itself, as if the ordinary workaday world is pierced by another reality that convicts us of our connection to it and its connection to us. Jung's description, "the redeeming symbol is a highway, a way upon which life can move forward without torment and compulsion," calls to mind Paul Klee's paintings "Highway and Byways" and "Glimpse of the Land of Plenty," both of 1929.[59]

Jung's God-Images in *The Red Book*

But of which god is Jung speaking? We come to my last item of Jung's purpose, to put before us God and God-images and their relationship. Jung reached the conviction that God is a "psychic fact of immediate experience. ... God has general validity inasmuch as almost everyone knows approximately what is meant by the term 'experience of God,'" and again as a psychic fact that "I observe but I do not invent."[60,61] God as the "highest value operative in the human soul" is differently located in different people and cultures, spanning the arc from those who reject any idea of God at all to those whose god is instituted by the religious tradition to which they belong. But, psychologically speaking, in our personality we revolve around something as if it is the god, the center of our attention: "There are men [sic] whose God is in the belly ... and others for whom God is money, science, power, sex" whatever situates the highest good.[62]

What was it for Jung? Following his soul, he experienced psychic reality as utterly different from conceptions of psyche then dominant in psychology or in Freud's views. So he resigned his university position and his position in the psychoanalytic group and descended into the depths, indeed fell into them. There, his soul confronts him with images for God different from credited conventions in religion. From these engagements Jung sees the difference between our images for God and God. Our God-images exist as real, actual images that perform the creative mediating function of symbol linking us to real, unfathomable God, incomprehensible to our comprehending capacities. An inevitable gap exists between God and our God-images while they remain vital for psychological functioning in people and for society.

A second conviction grips Jung: the God of "the spirit of the depths" differs from the God of "the spirit of the times." This *Deus Absconditus*, the hidden God, lives outside our conceptions of God, outside even our traditional images of God.[63] This raises for all of us what images of God hold us and what hidden ones find us.[64] Any effective priest knows church sermons and rituals must make space for people's personal God-images if the scriptural images are to connect and bring life to the parishioner.

This undiscovered deity, the left-out one, brings all that is excluded by dominance of our accepted God, and whose arrival always summons our response and proves unforgettable even if we do not understand it. God-images appearing in the psyche bring us closer into the mysteries of the wholeness of the whole in relation to God revealed in religion over the ages. The devil is linked to the *Deus Absconditus* as "our other standpoint" that brings what we left out, for Jung, a joyous figure of redness who dances in contrast to Jung's leaden-footed seriousness. Jung responds that "joy is … the greening of life."[65] But the hidden god also brings experience of evil as the devil, who lacks any positive force, is just a shadow parasite who would steal the gold of the gods and make nothing where something is. Indeed, hell is described as utterly impersonal where nothing happens, nothing personal occurs, but just a surging back and forth and nothing comes of it.[66] Thus, for Jung, the terrible fact of evil is brought into the precincts of God.

Jung's whole direction in *The Red Book* is downward to the Below— "the God climbs down to mortality," and Jung's soul tells him to "climb down into your depths, sink!" and he sees that "he who goes into himself climbs down," and Philemon, who emerges as a figure of holiness and speaks for the larger self and for God, says "to enter even deeper into the God."[67] Here are the God-images that encounter Jung in *The Red Book*; he experiences them as other than himself and also as aspects within himself—the renewing child, the mythopoetic Izdubar, the sheer force of Abraxas and of the body Hap, and the loving and suffering Christ.

The child is that part of us and of life itself that is of "inexhaustible freshness and adherence" to which we can have recourse at any time. It is free from preconceptions and presuppositions, "undisturbed by conscious assumptions" and evoking in us "divine astonishment ... to behold its wonders."[68] Jung speaks of himself as a child, even as the servant of a child God. He finds this humiliating yet "from his hand everything unexpected came to me, everything living." Jung says for developed persons this may always be the case, whereas for undeveloped persons the God-image may be more exalted.[69] More astounding still is the implied fact, which becomes explicit, that where there is a child there is a mother. The mother is the creative fantasy capacity of the human psyche leading into life, thus placing psychic reality at the heart of religious experience. This does not mean a reduction of religious experience to psyche but a discovery of the valuable mediating function of psyche; it is another channel through which God reaches us. To critics who attack Jung as replacing God with psyche, he exclaims, "I can't even replace a lost button with my imagination but have to buy a new real one!"[70]

The psyche with its imaginative, metaphor-making, and image-receiving nature, its "maternal womb of creative fantasy," fashions symbols for God to represent a content that at bottom is "incomprehensible."[71] Being dispossessed of the God of "the spirit of the times," Jung becomes empty, a beggar, to discover that "he who climbs down into his darkness reaches the staircase of the working light."[72] In this sense, then, Jung feels the maternal womb function in himself, giving birth to the child God, thus retrieving for him not just evil in the precincts of God, but also the feminine: "I am a mother to the God." "He was born as a child from my own human soul. I had conceived him with resistance like a virgin."[73] This does not deify the human nor the psyche for

> when God enters my life, I return to my poverty, for the sake of the God ... to bear all my ugliness and ridiculousness, and also everything reprehensible in me. I thus relieve the God of all the confusion and absurdity that would befall him if I did not accept it.[74]

Thus Jung's experience of God inaugurates his devotion in service to God. He will honor God by carrying his own conflicts as his to suffer and solve and not load them onto Christ to do it for him. Jung also sees the child as a god outside himself and draws upon the Orphic figure Phanes, painting him in picture 107 and citing wonderful descriptions of him, such as "the immortal present ... the gushing streams ... promise and fulfillment."[75]

Christ comes up at the beginning of *The Red Book*, though Jung does not encounter him in person until the end of the volume. Jung sees right away he must enter into the mysteries of Christ and not leave them projected outside himself onto Christ doing all the work of suffering and redemption: "the depths will force you into the mysteries of Christ. We are not redeemed through the hero, but becoming a Christ." He says,

> at one time I believed I was a Christian, but I had never been a Christ. ... To be Christ oneself is the true following of Christ. ... God becomes human. He becomes apparent in you and through you, as a child. ... You can't learn it through the description, it can only become in you.[76]

A third God-image confronting Jung is called Izdubar, a giant, mighty bull-man with a double axe from the east seeking to reach the sun in the western land and become immortal, thus associating Izdubar with solar myths and a mythopoetic religious consciousness.[77] Jung tells him of science in the west—that the earth is round, that there is space unending around it, that we can measure the sun's distance from the earth, that there are flying machines and ships, that the sun rises and sets, and no, we are not immortal. Izdubar sobs and throws away his axe as no good against the *unreplenishable* empty space and because he can never reach the sun and immortality. Jung's science, he wails, has poisoned him; "Logos has paralyzed him." His mythopoetic consciousness is felled by secular science. Jung feels great love for Izdubar and does not want to abandon him, but take him west to find medicine to heal him. But the giant is too big for Jung to carry. Then Jung hits upon this insight: Izdubar is a fantasy, real as an image. In fantasy, he can squeeze the giant into the size of an egg and then carry him toward healing. Jung mourns Izdubar, loves him, and sings incantations to him. He says if we leave the god outside us, his weight is too heavy; if we take the god inside, we take him with us.[78] Later Jung opens the egg and Izdubar, renewed, is transformed and becomes the sun. The mythic consciousness and the religious sense of a god thus relocates from *outside* reality to *inside* reality, a psychic imagining where we sense our part in a dying and rising god-image.

Jung wants to rise with the sun but knows we humans are but *hollow forms* and so negates this god who rises up, and Jung descends into empty depths. There, he writes, "you will succeed in dissolving the formation in you ... [and] thus regain your freedom."[79] I understand Jung to say when he creates a God-image his force goes into it and it can live as a God outside him but he feels thereby emptied of his force. To see this God-image as a real psychic image withdraws its force back into Jung's self and restores his freedom. He no longer pours all his force into a God-image of God he forms as if outside himself, but takes all that energy back into himself free to have a Self and choose to offer it to God. On the one hand, no God-image "stands firm," but, on the other hand, he has his Self and the choice to offer it in devotion, so the issue of God inside or outside does not remain the issue. But Jung's experience asks what may our God-images be? Has all our strength poured into those images as if God exists only outside us, leaving us weak and empty? If we accept our images of God as real psychic images within us, what function do they play?

The fourth God-image in *The Red Book* comes in two parts. Jung hears Philemon's sermons to the dead who come back because they failed to live their animal part even though they were believing Christians. They rejected the God of love and the order of community and unity and killed one another, and they did as they pleased to the earth, greedy for "its shiney ore," fatal to "the ox with the velvet eye."[80] So Philemon teaches them the God who dissolves unity, is chaos without measure and blasts humanity. This image is named Abraxas who is the

> radiant source of vital force ... the sun and ... the eternally sucking forge of emptiness ... producing truth and lying, good and evil, light and darkness in the same word and act; Abraxas is terrible, lord of toad and frogs ... the manifest opposition of creation to the Pleroma and its nothingness. ... Abraxas is creative

> drive, form and formation ... the creative and the created ... blind creative libido ... that gets transformed in man through individuation like a pregnancy.[81]

A lesser part of Abraxas is Hap, the son of frogs, who joins the Christian God and Satan:

> He is the flesh spirit, the blood spirit ... the extract of all bodily juices, the spirit of the sperm and the entrails, of the genitals, of the head ... the feet ... the joints ... the bones ... the spirit of the sputum and entrails, excretions.[82]

Christ appears as a shade in the garden and Philemon speaks with deep gratitude and honor to Christ who has done all he can for humanity. With anger, he says men have not learned and still cry out for help, for Christ to do redemption for them; they "make demands on you and forever remind you your work is incomplete." Christ lived his own life, but men fail to do so. Christ's work "will be completed when men manage to live their own life without imitation."[83] This hearkens back to Jung's first intimation that imitating Christ is not sufficient; we must be Christ, that is, enter into our own work of redemption, to serve God beyond our God-images, by doing the work in our own psyches, dealing with the Abraxas' sheer force of blind libido by differentiating it into our own lives and together in society. The human becomes a site of transformation that means wrestling with and finding our paths of service to the whole. Jung exclaims, "I accepted all the joy and every torment of my nature and remained true to my love, to suffer what comes to everyone in their own way."[84] We too must discover our own ways of acceptance and devotion.

Philemon, the Self figure, lives in his garden that turns out to be Christ's garden, implying the centering Self in human psyche aligns with and shows in images indistinguishable from images of God. Christ says in his garden, "I bring you the beauty of suffering. That is what is needed by whoever hosts the worm."[85] I understand this to mean our suffering partakes of Christ's which helps us in facing the worm of corruption.[86]

The result, as far as it goes, for remember Jung breaks off writing *The Red Book* mid-sentence, saying he must live with his barbarian "until you are capable of making living with you bearable," is discovering that as we become differentiated from blind libido and individuate its force in our particular lives, we engage intimate relation of God-image with God beyond our images.[87] At great distance in the zenith stands a star; "this is the one God of this one man, this is his world ... his divinity ... the God and goal of man. ... To this one God man shall pray ... prayer throws a bridge across death."[88] This God we do not create, but serve.

Conclusion

To sum up, we, in our psyches, become the vessels in which transformation occurs.[89] It occurs, and we are not this mystery, but we are in the midst of it and required to participate and respond to it for transformation to occur (for ourselves, and through us for our world). So, we must reckon with what Jung discovers and ask how transformative work of redemption applies to us, for Jung sees us as the gateway of the procession of gods. He means, I believe, our god-creating capacity and the multiplicity of gods in human history. Each of us finds her or his or their god, which, like our lone star, burns more brightly as we live in relation to this god. God beyond our God-images rests also in our psyche but connects to something far outside our psyche. Jung writes, "you are the suffering heart of your God, love him, live from him," so God is not reduced to a psychic function in Jung's experience but recognized as alive, a force, what matters most. God is not dead, nor reduced to human soul; the emphasis falls on our relation to God in our daily living—"All your love and worship due him."[90] Our response is to live our lives to the fullest, "all we could think and could be, we should think and be. For who should live your life if not you?"[91]

Jung began finding his soul in 1913. He later said, in 1945, it was his secret intent to put before his colleagues that our human libido is the divine pneuma. Thus, Jung brings together psychological and religious questions, for, finally, Jung sees his journey as not madness but discovery of patterns of human psyche that belong to all of us, with which we each must reckon.

Twentieth-century images structured the whole of reality in terms of height and depth, what Jung called the Above and the Below. He climbed down to "the spirit of the depths." From there Jung brought us to see in religion and psychology the addition of not-knowing to systems of knowledge, of paradoxical to intellectual intelligence, of what he will call synchronicity to causality, of flesh and blood to spirit, of chaos to order, and of our work of transformation in relation to God's. Jung's discoveries ask, what are your, mine, our experiences of the depths now, in our time?

Jung uncovers his own complexes of feeling and freedom that enforce his personal equation. The implied question addresses us: what are our complexes with which we fall into identification, thus forging our personal equation? Can we get aware of it? How do we digest that our so-called objectivity always includes our subjectivity? Can we accept that our faith in God also shows the hidden God who must be included? Can we see our theory of psyche includes our personal equation? Can we accept that our neighbor has the same process with God-images and with psyche and believes in something different as the god, different as the psyche? Can we unite in our differences instead of killing each other?

Jung encounters hidden God-images, the absconding god who runs off with our certainties. Can we bear a similar experience and enlarge our God-images and reckon with including what we left out and what is left out in our official doctrines? In discovering his God-images, Jung finds each one brings its pairing with its effects on his psyche. His God-image of the child affects a freshness in him, even a rebirth, and that acquaints him with the feminine nature of the womb of his own psyche's creative fantasy in which is born the new releasing symbol. The child image brings freshness; the mother image brings experience of the psyche's power of creative symbol-making. Izdubar, a God-image of mythopoetic religious consciousness, meets secular science and affects a realization of our pictures of God as images, not God, images that we love and mourn their passing, not to kill but to relocate as our pictures of the unpictureable. Abraxas and Hap bring into consciousness sheer force and chaos, bundles of opposites, and body fluids and guts, to which our own individuation is our response. Our work is to differentiate and pursue our own symbols and religious symbols that bridge those opposites and release the divine pneuma of libido into human living. Christ who lives his life to the fullest enters our living and suffering as we enter into his life.[92] We become "vessels of creation in which the opposites reconcile" offering our efforts at transformation to his redemptive grace.[93]

The implied question put to us is, what are our God-images? Jung's data says we all have God-images even if we reject the notion of God. Our God-images relate to, connect with, and are defeated by God beyond our God-images. Our God-images are not the same as Jung's; they express our own personal creating from our particular lives and cultures and religious traditions. We need to know these and feel their effects upon us. In a sense, we thus construct our ladder to God, which, like Jacob's, breaks off before the unfathomable God. The questions ask: What are these pictures? What are our ladders? What are our experiences of the God in and beyond all our pictures?

These God-images live and act in us, whether we know them or not. Jung's journey says get conscious of them; enter into the mystery of your own life through which God gets born into our shared lives with each other. Through each of us the blind creative libido, the divine pneuma, the spirit of God, may transform the Below and the Above through our living our lives. As Jung says, "you find the beginning of individuation, out of which the divine child arises … actually born in many individuals … a spirit in many people, yet one and the same everywhere." From such shared context, we in the Academy have a chance to keep united the range of knowledge with what ultimately concerns us from the heart.

NOTES

1. D. R. Dyer, *Jung's Thoughts on God, Religious Depths of the Psyche* (York Beach, ME: Nicolas-Hays, 2000), p. xii; and see pp. 91–96.

2. C. G. Jung, *Memories, Dreams, Reflections* (New York: Pantheon, 1963), p. 210.

3. Cited in M. P. Hederman, *The Haunted Inkwell, Art and Our Future* (Dublin: Columba Press, 2001), p. 71.

4. P. Tillich, "Farewell Address," The Busch-Reisinger Museum, May 24, 1962; and "Addressing Harvard's Board of Overseers," Nov. 24, 1958; both on the program of "The Paul Tillich Lectures," Memorial Church, Harvard University, Cambridge, MA, May 1, 2012.

5. Jung, *Memories, Dreams, Reflections*, p. 47.

6. C. G. Jung, *Letters*, vol. 1, eds. Gerhard Adler and Aniela Jaffe (Princeton, NJ: Princeton University Press, 1973), Jan. 30, 1948, p. 492.

7. C. G. Jung, *Letters,* vol. 2, eds. Gerhard Adler and Aniela Jaffe (Princeton, NJ: Princeton University Press, 1973), Feb. 17, 1954, p. 156.

8. C. G. Jung, "Answer to Job," in *Psychology and Religion: West and East, The Collected Works of C. G. Jung,* vol. 11, ed. and trans. Gerhard Adler and R. F. C. Hull (New York: Pantheon, 1958), § 757.

9. Jung, *Letters*, vol. 1, Oct. 15, 1945, p. 384.

10. C. G. Jung, "Psychological Types," CW 6, § 9.

11. *Ibid.*

12. Jung, *Memories, Dreams, Reflections*, p. 187.

13. Hederman, *The Haunted Inkwell*, p. 71.

14. C. G. Jung, *The Red Book, Liber Novus,* ed. and trans. Sonu Shamdasani, Mark Kyburz, and John Peck (New York: W. W. Norton & Co., 2009), pp. 330, 354.

15. Jung, CW 6, §§ 118, 346; and see also §§ 123, 124, 150, 172, 178, 314.

16. *Ibid.*, § 161.

17. *Ibid.*, §§ 111, 113.

18. Jung, *The Red Book*, p. 330.

19. Jung, CW 6, chap. 1.

20. Jung, *The Red Book*, p. 338.

21. *Ibid.*, p. 366.

22. *Ibid.*, p. 246.

23. *Ibid.*, pp. 245–246, 324–325.

24. *Ibid.*

25. Jung, *Memories, Dreams, Reflections*, p. 357; and Jung, *Letters*, vol. 2, May 29, 1953, p. 119.

26. Jung, *The Red Book*, p. 344.

27. Jung, CW 6, § 183, note 37.

28. Jung, *The Red Book,* pp. 338–339.

29. *Ibid.*

30. *Ibid.*, p. 291.

31. C. G. Jung, *Visions*, vol. 2, ed. Claire Douglas (Princeton, NJ: Princeton University Press, 1997), p. 1538.

32. C. G. Jung, "Good and Evil in Analytical Psychology" (1959CW 10, § 874.

33. Jung, *The Red Book,* p. 337, note 24; and p. 339, note 37.

34. Jung, CW 6, §§ 84, 174, 182, 185, 187.

35. Jung, *The Red Book*, p. 239.

36. Jung, CW 6, §§ 174, 182, 185, 187.

37. *Ibid.,* §§ 136, 171.
38. Jung, *The Red Book,* p. 340.
39. Jung, CW 6, §§ 171, 184.
40. A. B. Ulanov, *The Functioning Transcendent* (Wilmette, IL: Chiron, 1996).
41. Jung, CW 6, § 175.
42. A. B. Ulanov, *Madness and Creativity: Meditations on Clinical Work in Relation to Themes in Jung's The Red Book* (College Station, TX: Texas A&M Press, 2012).
43. Jung, *The Red Book,* p. 356.
44. Jung, *Memories, Dreams, Reflections,* p. 353.
45. *Ibid.,* pp. 192, 194; and see also Jung, *The Red Book,* p. 324.
46. Jung, CW 6, §§ 172, 178.
47. *Ibid.,* §§ 95, 137.
48. *Ibid.,* § 111.
49. *Ibid.,* § 113.
50. Holly Stevens Knopf, ed., *Letters of Wallace James Stevens* (New York: Knopf, 1966), p. 176 as cited by D. LaGuardia, *Advance on Chaos: The Sanctifying Imagination of Wallace Stevens* (Hanover and London: University Press of New England, 1983), p. 69.
51. Jung, "Answer to Job," CW 11.
52. Jung, CW 6, § 180.
53. *Ibid.*
54. See Hederman, *The Haunted Inkwell,* pp. 148–149.
55. Jung, *The Red Book,* p. 338.
56. Jung, CW 6, § 443.
57. *Ibid.,* § 181.
58. J. Cambray, *Synchronicity: Nature & Psyche in an Interconnected Universe* (College Station, TX: Texas A&M University Press, 2009).
59. Jung, CW 6, § 146; and W. Haftmann, *The Mind and Work of Paul Klee* (London: Faber and Faber, 1954).
60. C. G. Jung, "Spirit and Life", CW 8, § 625.
61. C. G. Jung, *Dream Analysis,* ed. W. McGuire (Princeton, NJ: Princeton University Press, 1984), p. 511.
62. Jung, CW 6, § 67.
63. *Ibid.,* §§ 150, 427; see also A. B. Ulanov, *The Unshuttered Heart: Opening to Aliveness/Deadness in the Self* (Nashville, TN: Abingdon, 2007), p. 228f.

64. See A. Ulanov and B. Ulanov, *The Healing Imagination: The Meeting of Psyche and Soul* (Einsiedeln: Daimon, 1991/1999), chap. 4; A. B. Ulanov, *Finding Space: Winnicott, God, and Psychic Reality* (Louisville, KY: Westminster John Knox Press, 2001), chap. 1; and Ulanov, *The Unshuttered Heart*, chap. 8.

65. Jung, *The Red Book*, p. 261.
66. *Ibid.*, pp. 229, 230, 320, 322.
67. *Ibid.*, pp. 239–240, 280, 310, 339.
68. *Ibid.*, p. 234, note 58; and pp. 238, 365, 368.
69. *Ibid.*, pp. 234, 327.
70. Jung, *Letters*, vol. 1, Jan. 13, 1948, p. 487.
71. Jung, CW 6, §§ 171, 182, 185.
72. Jung, *The Red Book*, p. 272.
73. *Ibid.*, pp. 244, 249–250; see also p. 246, note 162; and p. 299, note 201.
74. *Ibid.*, p. 303.
75. *Ibid.*, p. 301, note 211.
76. *Ibid.*, p. 253, note 228; p. 254, notes 233, 238; and pp. 255, 283.
77. *Ibid.*, pp. 278–288.
78. *Ibid.*, p. 283.
79. *Ibid.*, p. 287.
80. *Ibid.*, p. 352.
81. *Ibid.*, pp. 350–351, 370; p. 354, note 123.
82. *Ibid.*, p. 339.
83. *Ibid.*, p. 356.
84. *Ibid.*, p. 356.
85. *Ibid.*
86. *Ibid.*, p. 359; Jung takes up this theme in CW 11, §§ 414–421, 447–448.
87. Jung, *The Red Book*, p. 330, note 354.
88. *Ibid.*, p. 354.
89. *Ibid.*, p. 252, note 211.
90. *Ibid.*, p. 371.
91. *Ibid.*, pp. 233, 249; see also p. 246, note 163; p. 247, note 164; and p. 254, note 138.
92. *Ibid.*, p. 253, note 228.
93. *Ibid.*, p. 252, note 211.

Chapter Eleven

Discussion of Dr. Ulanov's Chapter

William J. Sneck, S.J.

It is a great privilege and honor for me to share the podium with Professor Ann Ulanov. I well remember her coming to Loyola University in Maryland to receive from our Pastoral Counseling Department one of her many honorary doctorates.. She graciously spent the day with our Pastoral Counseling students and faculty, made a presentation, and interacted with those present.

As a priest, enthusiastic about C. G. Jung, I'd heard a critique from co-religionists that Jung seems to identify the *Self* with God, and I'd asked Prof. Ulanov to comment. She remarked that, from her reading of Jung, she concluded that *Self* and God are not identical, but it is through the *Self* that God and we interact, come into contact, and have relationship. Her paper presented here reminds me of that exchange from years ago, because her reflections sound to me like an extended meditation on her insight, then, for example, "Jung finds the psyche as a medium through which God speaks to us, hence the psyche is not where the buck stops, but is another means to that ultimate authority." Quoting Jung, Ulanov states,

> 'the self never at any time takes the place of God though it may perhaps be a vessel of diving grace.' I understand Jung to be saying we must carry our self and through it God reaches us.

> Placing psychic reality at the heart of religious experience ... does not mean a reduction of religious experience to psyche but a discovery of the valuable mediating function of psyche; it is another channel through which God reaches us. To critics who attack Jung as replacing God with psyche, he exclaims, 'I can't even replace a lost button with my imagination but have to buy a new real one!'

I find Prof. Ulanov's humble style very winning as she often modestly interjects: "From my reading of Jung, I conclude"; "I understand Jung to mean"; "I understand Jung to be saying"; etc.

Next, her summary of the complicated collection of five God-images in *The Red Book* is most helpfully clarifying. She outlines Jung's thoughts on "the renewing Child, the mythopoetic Izdubar, the sheer force of Abraxas, the body, Hap, and the loving and suffering Christ."

Dr. Ulanov offers more than a *merely academic* paper, however, and challenges us, her listeners, to question ourselves with such queries as the following:

> What are *our* (italics mine) complexes, with which we fall into identification thus forging our personal equation? Can we get aware of it? ... How do we digest that our so-called objectivity always includes our subjectivity? ... Can we accept that our faith in God also shows the hidden God who must be included? ... Can we see our theory of psyche includes our personal equation? ... Can we accept that our neighbor has the same process with God-images and with psyche and believes something different as the god, different as the psyche? Can we unite in our differences instead of killing each other?

While all these wonders are very helpful for our personal prayer and reflection, the last one is most relevant for our current worldwide geopolitical situation. Thus, in the spirit of Jung himself, Prof. Ulanov extends her own pondering beyond the therapeutic setting to the whole planet.

Let me close with a few brief comments on the title of our conference and this book, *Jung in the Academy and Beyond*. I discern among us a spirit of discouragement that Jung isn't seriously accepted by the Academy. This term seems to mean psychology departments in many U.S. schools, the American Psychological Association, and insurance companies—the latter, part of *the Beyond*. One example is in Frances M. Parks' chapter, "The Fading of C. G. Jung in the Academy," where she noted that among seventy-seven "evidence-based practices" listed by the APA Presidential Task Force, only two from many psychotherapeutic techniques seem acceptable. I want to suggest that this is much too narrow a definition of the Academy.

Here are four more hopeful signs: Jennifer Selig and Susan Rowland inspired and encouraged me with their chapter, "Putting the 'Academy' in 'Jung': Research-led Teaching and Teaching-led Research in a Jungian/Archetypal Studies Doctoral Program." Their exciting program at Pacifica Graduate Institute in Santa Barbara, CA, offers M.S. and Ph.D. programs in Depth Psychology with four subspecialties.

Secondly, in my own University, Loyola of Maryland, our Pastoral Counseling Department, approved by the American Counseling Association (ACA), requires doctoral students to take two of five theory courses: Freudian, Adlerian, Cognitive-Behavioral, Humanistic-Existential, and *Jungian,* of which I teach the latter two.

Next, I have a colleague who regularly gets reimbursed by insurance companies when she submits as her theoretical approach and practice, "Cognitive-Therapy-Based Jungian Psychotherapy!"

Finally, we cannot forget the great impact of Jung in the arts, especially cinema, and the wide usage of Jung's Personality Theory, as popularized by the Myers-Briggs Type Indicator (MBTI), in business and the churches.

Even if Jung isn't *accepted* by the above, narrowly-defined Academy, he *is* alive and well in other branches of academe and *Beyond.*

CHAPTER TWELVE

UNBARRING SHEOL
UNCONSCIOUS ILLUMINATIONS ON THE HISTORY, FORM, AND RECEPTION OF THE HEBREW BIBLE

Tiffany Houck-Loomis

A small minority of biblical scholars have had the courage to take up Jung as a conversation partner as a way to engage the use of narrative, symbolism, and imagery within the Bible through a method articulated most clearly by scholar Wayne Rollins as a *Jungian psycho-hermeneutical* approach to the Bible.[1] The two Jungian methodological techniques that tend to be employed by this minority are that of amplification and active imagination. Rollins goes further to suggest Jung offers eight different challenges to biblical hermeneutics ranging from how the field understands the Bible itself to how the scholar understands herself in relation to this text, and then proposes techniques one may add to one's method of scholarship increasing depth and a new way of reading. This work, alongside a small handful of others' including Schuyler Brown, David Halperin, Andrew Kille, and Walter Wink's, has attempted to forge new ground amidst the dominant domain of historical criticism within the field.[2] What I wish to add to this previous conversation and the current conversation regarding Jung in the Academy is not only how we might employ Jung in our methods of scholarship or glean bits of his theory to enliven our current modes of engagement, but discuss Jung's contribution to naming that which has been left out, and thus, what carries enormous and potentially explosive possibilities in the future of scholarship, particularly within the field of biblical scholarship. In being able to name what has been left out, in a phrase *unbarring Sheol*, Jung's method can offer a modality of wholeness and healing to this particular field.

Biblical Scholarship and the Threat of the Unconscious

There lives an enormous fear of the unconscious, even the potential of the unconscious, within the field of biblical scholarship. The fear manifests in the rubric by which biblical scholars are measured. The scientific methods employed most rigorously, which seek to parse up the text into bits in hopes of discovering the ancient landscape out of which the texts of the Bible arose, give the scholarly world something tangible to hold onto. There is merit in this enterprise, and, at the very least, it is interesting to hypothesize about where certain texts may have originated, in what historical context, and from which theological or ideological perspective within a particular community or conflation of several ancient communities. This is only one kind of investigation, however, leading to one kind of knowing. Jung argues that there is another kind of knowing that, when disallowed, cut off, or silenced, has the potential of infecting the entire system. This infection can lead to potentially explosive consequences. As Jung says, "we are constantly living on the edge of a volcano, and there is, so far as we know, no way of protecting ourselves from a possible outburst that will destroy everybody within reach."[3]

The intellectual pursuits in the biblical field disguise the potential for, or inevitability of, an outburst by overvaluing conscious pursuits and disallowing room for the unconscious to inform, transform, and reform our methods and research. The dominant current within biblical scholarship has been influenced by a kind of mass-minded thinking. When treading into new territory or giving credence to another voice, the voice that comes from somewhere deep within yet simultaneously comes from without and is not in service to the dominant culture, this new territory or other voice is met with suspicion at best. At worst, this new perspective is met with disregard, even contempt, and is thus, silenced.

As an objective reality, the psyche is experienced symbolically, presenting itself in dreams, images, and within the field of transference and counter-transference, between two individuals mediating to our consciousness that which cannot be directly or tangibly experienced.[4] Symbols are not coerced; they come to us, they have us rather than us having them, and, in this way, the symbol is not ours, but rather is something objectively Other that we can enter into relationship with *as if* it were "issued from an intelligent, purposive, and as it were, personal source."[5] In this way, Jung understands the unconscious *as if* it were an autonomous being with its own set of experiences and a particular view to ponder. The symbolic image then, according to Ann Ulanov, "makes a bridge from what is known to what is unknown."[6]

If we reject being in relationship with the unconscious or deny its existence entirely, we run the risk of becoming over-identified with our symbols or lacking symbols altogether, and thus risk being taken over by the unconscious all the more. As Jung says, "By understanding the unconscious we free ourselves from its domination."[7] Particularly for biblical scholars who are charged with or have chosen for their vocation the task of hypothesizing, working with, interpreting, and enabling others to play with sacred texts that are, for many, a living symbol, there seems to me an enormous responsibility to be aware of one's own psychic life. The purpose of this is not only pertinent for one's own scholarly work, but also for any understanding the scholar hopes to have of the ancient communities she reads about in the text and the stories they tell. Thus, acknowledging the unconscious and working to see the symbolic images it presents provides a bridge from what is known in the scholar to what is unknown in the scholar as well as to what is known and unknown within the sacred text itself.

One's unconscious is actively at work in any translation or interpretation posited whether acknowledged or not. If one is open to the unconscious, in relationship with it, and listening to the dream images, the symbols, and their affect, as if they have something valuable to show and teach, then she may be able to recognize when her interpretation is simply a working-through-of some past trauma or experience, enmeshed with the social and or cultural interpretation of a given text, or, when it wrestles with this interpretation, is in relationship with it, and yet allows space for something new to inform.

If we do not, as Ann Ulanov says, "pretend to a perfectly detached position from which we view events, past or present," then we allow for something other in our interpretations; there is more room made in our own scholarship and in our teaching.[8] The new serves as a bridge to something beyond, an experience that connects one to one's deeper self and to others and to something new within the living symbol of the text itself.

The Bible as Symbol

Taking the Bible as a living symbol, in the Jungian sense, which previous scholars who seek to use a Jungian hermeneutic have not gone so far as to do, one can approach the Bible similarly to the method by which Jung proposes one investigates the psyche. As Jung says,

> A symbol is an indefinite expression with many meanings, pointing to something not easily defined and therefore not fully known. ... The symbol therefore has a large number of analogous variants, and the more of these variants it has at its disposal, the more complete and clear-cut will be the image it projects of its object.[9]

Our purpose is now two-fold. Not only is there one's own psychic work with which to be in process, but also there is a new way proposed to engage the Bible. Rather than approaching the Bible to find out what it is, I, as a scholar, seek to know and argue, thrusting my own unconscious contents upon it; I now approach the Bible to see what it seeks to show about itself. In doing my own psychic work, I no longer need the Bible or my mere conscious translation and interpretations to hold certain parts of myself that I cannot hold; nor do I need it, or them, to perform a regressed or inferior function in my own life. Rather, I can open myself up to something new that can come from the symbol itself offering new insights, new ways of understanding Self and Other, and now, something can come up between myself as the scholar and the text as a symbol. As Ann Ulanov says, "the purpose of Jung's investigation is to grasp what the psyche says and shows about itself, its structure, and its dynamics, not to find out what he as the experimenter wants to know."[10] In this method a space is now created or opened up—a space that is disallowed if I become enmeshed with the ego, trapped in consciousness alone. Within the space created, I can be in relationship with the symbol rather than consuming it or being consumed by it. Rather than placing demands on the text about what I, the scholar, want to know, in relationship with my own history, culture, and the collective (and the affect generated upon my psyche by and through each of these), I am now able to be in a different kind of relationship with the symbol and allow more space to explore Self and Other.

The symbol cannot be made-to-order, and it does not require intellectual knowledge. Rather, if the symbol is real, it will evoke a spontaneous and affective experience.[11] If one cannot understand the symbol, or, if belief in the symbol begins to fade, then one must resort to conscious or intellectual understanding of the symbol.[12] Perhaps one reason why consciousness pursuits are privileged is due to a lost experience of whatever it is the Bible, as a symbol, is pointing toward. From this lack of understanding or experience, perhaps belief in the symbol has begun to fade and what is resorted to is intellectual knowledge from the ego complex rather than from the totality of the Self. How, then, does one restore the loss or the break? Can the symbol be revived for the scholarly world?

This question brings me to what Ulanov, expounding on Jung, explains as the *third*, or the transcendent, coming in through the shadow of the *fourth*, or the muck and mire of one's psychic life. Jung's theory of the *third* was articulated in his article on the transcendent function wherein he describes the compensatory nature of the unconscious on the side of consciousness and consciousness on the side of the unconscious. Through Jung's synthetic-constructive method which treats the objective reality of the unconscious or the objects coming from the unconscious, though symbolic in form, as informing one of the subjective potential, or subjective tendencies, one can transition from a one-sided stuck place to a place of union and, therefore, movement.[13] This theory provides a method for the reader to relate the text to his or her experience but also as a way of opening other possible interpretations of the text when one is involved in the work of historical and structural analysis. Jung urges us to rid the separation between conscious and unconscious for it is in their union and their conversation between one another that wholeness, unity, and genuine community are enabled.[14]

If, however, the scholar knows nothing of the potential for transcendence, of transitioning from one attitude to another, of making space for being in relationship with both conscious and unconscious contents and with others amidst the differences, or of experiencing other possibilities for what the symbol might be communicating, the scholar lacks the ability to help others develop in this way. This has ramifications for scholarship and for education. If the scholarly world overvalues consciousness, as I believe it does, Jung's challenge would then be for compensation. The compensatory function in this case would come from the side of the unconscious.

The unconscious compensates whether we are aware of it or not. When there is no awareness or acknowledgement of such compensation one can become arrested in a complex. Biblical scholarship is in the grip of an ego-complex; we have fallen into partial if not whole identity with consciousness believing we can have some mastery over the texts, or that all there is to know about the texts comes from our rational, scientific methods and that these methods will lead to some truth or awareness that will be universally held.[15] Belief in one's singularly intellectual tools without regard for one's psychic tools, regardless of how honed one's intellectual tools may be, has the potential of cutting one off from deeper communication internally and externally. As Rollins says, "It is important when approaching Scripture to have as clear a read as possible on "who this is who reads," for the protection of others for the protection of Scripture and for one's own protection."[16]

Unbarring Sheol: Implications for Historical-Critical Findings

Jung says the ego is merely a subject of one's consciousness, whereas the Self is the subject of one's totality, including all that resides in the unconscious.[17] The questions for biblical scholarship are the following: What are we neglecting, ignoring, repressing, or projecting when we place value only on ego knowledge, on the side of consciousness at the expense of the whole self? What does Jung offer biblical scholarship in terms of healing, making space, and reawakening the symbol? How do we unbar Sheol?

In light of Ulanov's work adding to Jung's notion of the feminine, I would argue that the way for transcendence, the *third*, for conjunction of the opposites in the biblical world is, as they say, through the *fourth*.

Ulanov describes the *fourth* as the undifferentiated matrix of all that we have split off from consciousness. We find in it the *bad*, what we consider evil, whatever works to dismantle or destroy our ideas of the *good*.[18] She goes further to point out that we also find the missing feminine in the *fourth* (matter, earthiness, material), and argues that the "feminine still stands too much in the shadows despite all the advances made through feminism."[19] This helps to explain why methods such as Feminist/Womanist criticism, reader-response, and sociological and ideological criticisms have arisen within biblical scholarship yet remain on the fringes, the periphery, and are not yet integrated within the dominant field. The *fourth*, that which remains in the unconscious, as Jung says is the

> fly in the ointment, the skeleton in the cupboard of perfection, the painful lie given to all idealistic pronouncements, the earthiness that clings to our human nature and sadly clouds the crystal clarity we long for ... but at the same time it is ... the basis for the preparation of the philosophical gold.[20]

Biblical scholarship is uncomfortable with methods that honor subjectivity because they are messy, too open-ended, and lack clarity.

As I was working on this chapter and mulling over what I believe Jung has to offer the Academy, particularly in the field of biblical scholarship in light of his concepts of the transcendent function, the objectivity of the psyche, and its symbols of the unconscious, it became apparent to me that what I was writing about in terms of a method of scholarship parallels is what I see within the Hebrew Scriptures themselves. Throughout the Pentateuch and the historical books of Joshua, Judges, Samuel, and Kings, we find a very particular, rigid, and determined set of instructions the Hebrew community is to live by if they are to receive the benefits of the Covenant, land, progeny, safety, and power. What is also read in these books is a fairly clear explanation for why the Israelites ended up in exile. The exile is justified by explaining the Covenant and Israel's actions against Covenant loyalty. The explanation justifies the Assyrian and Babylonian invasion and eventual decimation of the Israelite community as a consequence of Covenantal disobedience.

One can map out through the historical books and some of the prophets how the Covenant becomes more rigid and exclusive through exile and post exile.[21] This one dominant voice in the Hebrew Bible seems to name the *bad* and then dramatically cut it off—first, beginning with how the Northern Kingdom is portrayed as "doing evil in the eyes of the Lord," and then later mandating the exclusion of any foreign women or any foreign presence within the community as a way to keep the *bad* out. Thus, the Northern Kingdom becomes the villain; the foreigner is thrown out, often by being dragged by their hair; perfect obedience to the Covenant is mandated; and centralized worship is instituted. This seems to me strikingly parallel to one's psychic process when one has lost the ability to connect with one's symbols. When one is trapped merely within conscious understanding because there is no space created for union with what is beyond or with the other parts of one's self, rigidity ensues. Survival, be it psychical or physical, is felt to depend on ridding oneself or community of the *bad* as well as a rigid obedience to the socially-constructed *good*.

The Hebrew Bible contains more than this one voice, however. Another voice speaks up and challenges the rigidity of the Covenant, not because of its rigidity, but because there was a break, a loss, and the characters in these stories engage this loss—the loss Israel experienced in the exile. Rather than shoring up strict ideologies, finding a way to blame the *bad* within, and mandating an extermination of the *bad* without in order to make sense of the devastation of the exile, this counter-voice sits with the disappointment, the loss, the emptiness, the Other. The voice of Job and the message of the book of Jonah in the Hebrew canon reflect the counter-position or the *shadow*. In Job, we read of a man who diligently obeyed the Covenant on behalf of himself and his children and still suffered enormous loss, loss of progeny and essentially loss of land (his cattle, houses, and crops). Yet he refuses to be held responsible for disobedience. He holds the counter-voice, or in Jungian terms he holds the *shadow*, in his refusal to take responsibility or to be condemned by the *bad*. The story this book tells essentially dismantles the *good* previously upheld within the Hebrew canon.

In Jonah the prophet character is sent on a mission to rescue that which has been named *evil* within the Hebrew canon, namely, Israel's oppressor Assyria. The message in these books speaks of a God beyond the Covenant, beyond right-doing, beyond obedience. These stories, containing a God beyond human control, enable a new kind of knowing and being in relationship with this wholly other divine. These stories include the *fourth*, the dirt and grime, the dark, the *bad*, and the destructive functions of the *shadow*.[22] In Job's refusal to take the blame for the devastating losses he incurred and in Jonah's inability to escape the call to rescue the *evil* Israel tried to protect itself against, these stories hold the other side of what Israel held to be the *good*.

As Ulanov suggests, however, there is also the constructive side of the *shadow* which protects and allows for slow growth. In the story of Job we have an example of a seed being germinated in the *shadow*, the counter-position to the community who upheld the split. The story of Job speaks of a refusal to be cut off or silenced. Throughout the story, Job's silence at times infuriates his friends. His refusal to take the blame causes them to cast more blame. Job holds onto something of his own, his body and his experience, and in doing so a new perspective slowly grows. At the denouement, Job hears from God, not what one might expect, but something new. This God that speaks is not the God of the Covenant, at least not how the Covenant portrays God. This God is wholly Other, mysterious and unknown, the *Deus Absconditus*. In Job's own willingness to carry the *shadow*, the exported *bad* of the community, and remain protected by the *shadow*, allowing something new to grow, the *third* is experienced, communication with the Transcendent through Job's conscious/unconscious communication and union. What this adds to the Hebrew canon is parallel to the portrayal of Job's experience. The message of Job contains the left out, regressed, inferior, what is perceived as bad, the grit, earthiness, and the feminine of Covenant Theology. Job's willingness to confront the *shadow* of the collective or the group through his own *shadow* allowed him to intercede on behalf of himself and the group.[23]

As Ulanov says, "our perceptions of the fourth, however shadowy, makes possible our living in the third."[24] As can be read within the Hebrew Scriptures themselves, inclusion of the *fourth* allows for living in the *third*, a more opened, expansive space that allows for difference and a new kind of consciousness. This too is the challenge to biblical scholarship coming from the very texts we study. In loosening the grip ego consciousness has had over us, practiced through directed thinking, one is enabled more space to hear from the other parts heard and experienced in the second kind of thinking, or in Jungian terms, non-directed thinking. As Ulanov says,

> A third kind of thinking lies between the one and the two as a union of nondirected and directed thinking. ... Drawing on both conscious intent and unconscious expressiveness, this sort of thinking is a process, to-ing and fro-ing from center to circumference of the issue or image at hand, building up a content.[25]

This is the challenge of Jung for biblical scholarship. To open into this third kind of thinking means to unbar Sheol, all that has been left out and repressed, the stuff of matter, earth, and the feminine, to allow the unconscious into our method and thus a new kind of knowing. It means sitting in the unknown, or the empty space, the gap where intelligence leaps to fill, out of its fear of not knowing, what may come into this space. This way is not comfortable, yet this is the way of the living symbol itself. The symbol guides us, shows us how to contain the *good* and the *bad* which shifts our orientation to both. To open up to this third kind of knowing we as scholars must open ourselves to and live in and through the *fourth*. The work of the biblical scholar is to engage this living symbol from the perspective of the Self rather than from the ego perspective. In this way the symbol remains open and alive and transformative for both the scholarly world and those we hope to teach. As Jung says,

> Consciousness behaves like some one who hears a suspicious noise in the attic and thereupon dashes down into the cellar, in order to assure himself that no burglar has broken in and that the noise was mere imagination. In reality he has simply not dared to go up in the attic.[26]

What would the future of biblical scholarship look like should it dare go up into the attic?

NOTES

1. Wayne Rollins, *Jung and the Interpretation of the Bible,* ed. David L. Miller (New York: Continuum, 1995).

2. Schuyler Brown, *Text & Psyche: Experiencing Scripture Today* (New York: Continuum, 1998); David Halperin, *Seeking Ezekiel: Text and Psychology* (University Park, PA: Pennsylvania State University Press, 1993); Andrew Kille, *Psychological Biblical Criticism* (Minneapolis, MN: Fortress Press, 2001); and Walter Wink, *Transforming Bible Study* (Nashville, TN: Abingdon Press, 1989).

3. C. G. Jung, "Psychology and Religion" (1937), in *The Collected Works of C. G. Jung,* vol. 11, ed. and Gerhard Adler and trans. R. F. C. Hull (Princeton, NJ: Princeton University Press, 1958/1969), § 25.

4. C. G. Jung, "Symbols of Transformation: Part Two," CW 5, § 180.

5. Jung, CW 11, § 36.

6. Ann Belford Ulanov, *The Feminine in Jungian Psychology and Christian Theology* (Evanston, IL: Northwestern University Press, 1971), p. 21.

7. Jung, "Commentary on 'The Secret of the Golden Flower'" (1957 CW 13, § 64.

8. Ann and Barry Ulanov, *Religion and the Unconscious* (Philadelphia, PA: The Westminster Press, 1975), p. 127.

9. Jung, 1911–12/1952, in CW 5, §180.

10. Ulanov, *Feminine in Jungian Psychology,* p. 20.

11. Jung, "A Psychological Approach to the Trinity" (1948), in CW 11, § 280.

12. *Ibid.,* § 280–281.

13. Jung, CW 6, § 708; CW 8, §§ 131–193.

14. Jung, CW 8, §§ 131–193.

15. Jung, CW 6, §§ 738, 742.

16. Wayne Rollins, *Jung and the Bible* (Atlanta, GA: John Knox Press, 1983), p. 99.

17. Jung, CW 6, § 183.

18. Ulanov, *Unshuttered Heart: Opening to Aliveness/Deadness in the Self* (Nashville, TN: Abingdon Press, 2007), p. 170; Jung, CW 12, §§ 31, 137.

19. Ulanov, *Unshuttered Heart,* p. 170.

20. Jung, "The Symbolism of the Mandala" (1944), CW 12, § 207.

21. See Martin Noth, *Überlieferungsgeschichtliche Studien* (Halle: M. Niemeyer, 1943); Rainer Albertz, *Israel in Exile: The History and Literature of the Sixth Century B.C.E.*, trans. David Green (Leiden, Boston: Brill, 2004); and Thomas Römer, *The So-Called Deuteronomistic History* (New York: T. & T. Clark, 2007).

22. Ulanov, *Unshuttered Heart*, p. 174.

23. Ann and Barry Ulanov, "Intercession," *Religion and the Unconscious*; Ann Ulanov, "Evil," *Unshuttered Heart*, pp. 141–146.

24. Ulanov, *Unshuttered Heart*, pp. 178–179.

25. *Ibid.*, p. 178.

26. Jung, CW 8, § 206.

Chapter Thirteen

The *Deus Absconditus* and the Post-Secular Quest

Amy Bentley Lamborn

Seekings and Soundings

In the mid-twentieth century, in the years following the Second World War, the Jewish philosopher Hannah Arendt described the modern world, plagued by doubt and deep uncertainty, as a spiritually secular world. Having fled twice from the Nazis and witnessed the horrors of the Second World War, Arendt was familiar with the doubt and uncertainty she described. Arendt rightly predicted that the problem of evil would become the most critical question of post-war Europe. And, like her fellow intellectuals who wrestled mightily with that critical question, she did so in the wake of God's death, that is, following the announcement of the death of God by Nietzsche, Marx, and Freud.[1]

By the *death of God*, Arendt understood that a certain kind of deity had died—specifically, the God of the theologians and philosophers, entangled in complex and abstract metaphysical systems. In *The Life of the Mind*, Arendt wrote,

> It may be wise to reflect upon what we really mean when we observe that theology, philosophy, and metaphysics have reached an end—certainly not that God has died, something we can know as little about as God's existence ... but that the way God

has been thought of for thousands of years is no longer convincing; if anything can be dead, it can only be the traditional thought of God.[2]

I begin with this extended reference to Arendt for two reasons. First, her words conjure up something of the spirit of the secularism which we must have in mind as we consider the meaning of the post-secular, a term that I will soon define more precisely. Second, Arendt's understanding of the death of God resembles Jung's explicitly psychological and symbolic interpretation of the phrase. In his 1937 essay "Psychology and Religion," Jung wrote, "(perhaps) we could say with Nietzsche that 'God is dead.' Yet it would be truer to say 'He has put off our image, and where shall we find him again?'"[3] Jung believed that God was still active as the *Deus Absconditus*, the hidden god, an unknown quality in the depths of psyche.[4]

Now, in this new millennium, the quest for the hidden God has become an urgent one among post-secular philosophers and theologians. While these thinkers have nuanced the term post-secularism in a variety of ways, there nonetheless remains a discernable definitional core. Post-secularism, in essence, attempts a double delimitation: of Enlightenment rationalism, including its preferential option for objectivity, on the one hand, and of Enlightenment secularism, including its suspicion of subjectivity and matters of faith or belief, on the other. Simply put, post-secularism seeks to combine a renewed interest in religious and spiritual matters with the practice of critical inquiry. So we are beginning to see fresh attempts to think of God other than the ways God has been traditionally thought, beyond the ways that, for many, no longer convince.[5]

This post-secularist sensibility is evident, for example, in philosopher of religion Richard Kearney's recent book, *Anatheism*.

> What comes after God? What follows in the wake of our letting go of God? What emerges out of that dark night of not-knowing, that moment of abandoning and abandonment? Especially for those who—after ridding themselves of 'God'—still seek God?[6]

Kearney advocates for a renewed quest for God *after* God—a quest that he describes as anatheistic:

Ana-theos, God after God. Ana-theism: another word for another way of seeking and sounding the things we consider sacred but can never fully fathom or prove. Another idiom for receiving back what we've given up as if we were encountering it for the first time.[7]

In this essay I explore three interrelated seekings and soundings that mark the post-secular quest: the Open, the Other, and the *Chora*. Each of these themes, I suggest, images a topos, or place, for the hidden God. Each evokes a potential phenomenological answer to the question of Jung's *where*: "(God) has put off our image, and where shall we find him again?"[8] My method, inspired by Jung, will be to stick as closely as possible to these images, insofar as I understand Jung's guidance and given the constraints of time. My aim is to identify points of correspondence between these philosophical and theological images and images of depth psychological process and, thus, begin to discern their symbolic potential.

The Open

Philosopher Charles Bigger has noted that following the death of God, "'what matters most' ... or, for that matter, anything mattering is in question."[9] So while the poets of the early nineteenth century celebrated the presence and movement of the Sacred as something that mattered, later poets "hollowed out a place seemingly beyond being where the yearning for the dead God could be expressed." According to Bigger, this hollowing out process culminated in Rainer-Maria Rilke's idea of the Open in the Seventh and Eighth *Duino Elegies*.[10]

We glimpse the Open in these oft-quoted lines, taken from the beginning of the Eighth Elegy: "With all its eyes, the animal sees/the open. Only our eyes are/as if reversed and set as traps/encircling it, all around its open exit."[11] It is difficult to say exactly what Rilke means by the Open, arguably the central image of the entire poetic cycle. Interpreters of the Elegies generally agree that the Open is an affective and ultimately ineffable concept. As David Oswald writes in the introduction to his translation of the Elegies,

> What Rilke means by the open ... goes beyond words into non-interpreted experience, which can be approached through the images he uses. It is something that animals, lacking our kind of

consciousness, can see; it resembles being in love without needing one's lover. … It is a quality of consciousness that he is after, a quality of 'being here,' a state of relationship with this world, without being possessed by its performance.[12]

Bigger describes this quality of consciousness as one in which the distinction between subjective and objective is overcome and a space is cleared for our letting-be of things rather than our constant appropriation of them.[13] The Open thus images an encounter with things as they give themselves, without distortion. Using the terms of analytical psychology, we say that we glimpse this quality of consciousness, however ephemerally, whenever we withdraw our projections from the outer world and recognize them as part of our own inner experience. It is a process by which we build up a symbolic consciousness.

So what can be said about the God who lies hidden in the Open? What does the Open offer the post-secular imagination in its quest for the God *after* God? Theologian Joseph O'Leary suggests that the Open has set off a *deconstructive ferment* in theological thinking.[14] The God hidden in the Open is a God who dismantles and relativizes our overly fixed images of God. Such divine-deconstructive activity, as I see it, has a *telos*—a goal that can, itself, only be evoked by images. "If we empty out the inherited God languages of all delusory stabilities and identities," O'Leary writes, "then that to which we reach out in using the word 'God' becomes a space of potentiating withdrawal."[15] What is potentiated in this empty, hollowed out space? Nothing less, it seems, than our encounters with an Other that resides beyond our projections, an Other that transcends our categories of subjectivity and objectivity, an Other, that might escape our otherwise limiting gaze.

The Other

What do we see when we look upon the letting-be of things as they give themselves in the Open? Philosopher John Manoussakis claims that "we see the Other (or we become aware of ourselves as seen by the Other—for it is not so much that *we* see the Other; rather, it is the Other that shows itself through the World to *us*)."[16] I think that the decisive point here has to do with the relationship between the "big O" Other and the *world*.

In the post-secular imagination there has been a movement away from the notion of radical Otherness, as in Emmanuel Levinas—a movement away from the idea of an utterly remote and removed Other. The post-secular Other is making a return from beyond Being and Time, back down into the seemingly mundane world. For it is here, in the midst of everyday embodied life, where we meet with Otherness. According to Kearney, the Other appears to us through the accidental and anecdotal. And so he argues that we are bidden to "revisit the primordial sphere of the everyday sayings, expressions, presuppositions, beliefs, speech acts, convictions, faiths, and commitments", for it is in this realm of our "primary speech" that we encounter the Other, vis-à-vis, or face to face.[17] Whenever we see the extra-ordinary in the ordinary, transcendent and immanent (as categorical descriptors of Otherness) mix and mingle, re-arranging and re-positioning each other.

This idea of Otherness resonates with fundamental notions of Jungian psychology. Following Jung's translation of the alchemical imagination, we claim that spirit is in matter, so matter matters. The ego can only build up its connection to the self in the midst of the matters of everyday life. The archetypal (transcendent) layers of psyche can only be reached through the personal (immanent) layers of psyche— all the particulars of embodied life, including the influences of family and culture. As Jungian scholar Roger Brooke puts it, the transformative moments and movements of individuation appear to be "less the retreat of psychic life from one's engagements with the world than the deliteralizing of these relations into metaphoric structures."[18] The process of individuation, Brooke claims, "does not evaporate incarnate reality but situates imaginal life."[19]

What about the God who lies hidden in the Other? What might the Other of the post-secular imagination offer the quest for God *after* God? For most post-secular philosophers, the paradigmatic Other is God, a God "curled at the heart of quotidian existence."[20] Here God appears hidden in the face of the Other. And discerning the Other requires a symbolic, *as-if* consciousness. For the face of the Other both *is* and *is not* God. It is both the site of divine disclosure and, also, always a target for our projections.

A symbolic, metaphorical consciousness is critical for the post-secular quest for God *after* God. "Metaphor," Kearney observes, "involves a transportation (*metaphora*) between self and other. And as such the metaphorical *as* contains within itself a mixed copula of *is/is not*."[21] The metaphorical consciousness is a symbolic consciousness in which the fictive (*as if*) is sustained as the figural. And it is the figural that stands to save God from the literal, for in this place of paradoxical tension, faith leaps.[22]

The *Chora*

But what if the Other we encounter is *faceless*—more absent than present ... without form or name? *Chora* has appeared as a distinctly postmodern image of God—or another site for encountering this God, "in the far extremities of the *via negative*," or way of negation.[23] The God imaged in *Chora* is the God of the abyss, the God we might meet up with in the abyss, the *abyssal* God, the God of the depths.

Before considering several key postmodern musings on *Chora*, we must recall the contours of what is perhaps its most significant premodern context. As a philosophical concept, *Chora* first appeared in Plato's *Timaeus* dialogue. There, Plato posits the possibility that the eternal and unchanging Forms and their Copies could not, on their own, exhaust the inventory of this world. And so he asks one of the most fundamental and perennial of all questions: what is the primordial origin of all that exists, of all things that come to be? After struggling to identify the conditions for the possibility of being, and a world of being, Plato argued for a third type, a *triton genos*, a category distinct from both Forms and Copies. *Chora* was the name Plato gave this elusive *third thing*, a mysterious placeless space that contains all being and becoming.[24]

Plato used a variety of images to describe this elusive *Chora*, including mother, receptacle, nurse, space, a base material for the making of perfume, a country or region, and a winnowing sieve used in the bread-making process. Common to each of these associations is the idea of a vessel or matrix, that which contains the possibility of emergence and the actuality of becoming.[25]

But, despite his metaphorical generosity, Plato insisted that *Chora* remain an untranslatable concept—a mysterious and ineffable thing—thus challenging our usual categories of reason and sense. Plato in fact argued that *Chora* could only be properly apprehended through a dream-like state of consciousness, a kind of fantasy-thinking or reverie.

This elusiveness and womb-like emptiness of *Chora* has rendered it an appealing conceptual plaything for a host of contemporary thinkers, including philosophers, psychoanalysts, and theologians.

Jacques Derrida, for example, seized on the placeless spatiality of Plato's *Chora* and appropriated it as a kind of deconstructive next-of-kin for his notion of *différence*. *Chora*, according to Derrida, is the abyssal chasm, the formless matter of form, the wholly other that transcends all rational categories. It is a barren and naked place that gives nothing—a tropic of negation, a sort of black hole that even swallows up Being itself.[26]

John Caputo, a philosopher of religion influenced by Derrida, argues that *Chora* overturns and negates even the Platonic system in which it first unfolded and thus emphasizes the *no-thing-ness* of *Chora*. "*Khôra* is neither present nor absent, active nor passive, the Good nor evil, living nor nonliving," he writes. "Neither theomorphic nor anthropo-morphic—but rather atheological and nonhuman—*khôra* is not even a receptacle, which would also be something that is itself inscribed within it."[27]

Alongside these cosmological and a-theological readings of *Chora*, we can productively place Julia Kristeva's psychoanalytic reading. Kristeva offers a psycho-semiotic interpretation by which she takes *Chora* to represent the earliest stage of psychosexual development; a pre-verbal/pre-linguistic domain characterized by a chaotic mixture of feelings, needs, and perceptions. *Chora* stands for the pure physicality and materiality of existence where there is as yet no differentiation between infant and mother, Self and Other—just a chaotic mix of drives. Nothing is as yet signed or signified.[28]

Theologian Catherine Keller links *Chora* with the *tehom* of the opening verses of the Book of Genesis—that deep and watery chaos that, as the story has it, exists before the beginning of creation, right next to the *tohu vabohu*, the formless void. Through her creative exegesis of the biblical *tehom*, Keller also claims the ancient sense of *Chora* as a generative matrix—a space for emergence and becoming.[29]

This small sampling of *Choral* reveries suggests to me two projective clusters—one that borders on a kind of nihilistic negation (devoid of any divinity) and another that is centered on the possibility of generation, emergence, and becoming, a primordial matrix (over which the divine spirit creatively hovers). There is a tendency to privilege one of these categories of projection over the other. Each has numinous qualities. Each harbors a potentially numinous appeal. Indeed, John Manoussakis compellingly argues that "(the) common language within which both God and *khora* appear creates proximity that contaminates both"; "God looks like *khora* and *khora* like God."[30] So, in this milieu of postmodern conflation, some have suggested that a choice is required of us: God ... or *Chora*? The dark night of the soul ... or the barren desert—a no-place with no ladders on which we might climb up toward a utopian view (heavenly or otherwise)?[31]

Others have suggested a third way with this *third thing* named *Chora*—namely, that of sustaining a paradoxical attitude. And it is in this way of paradox, where the opposites are held together, that I see the *Chora* revealing its *topos*, a placeless space for the hidden God. Kearney offers two examples of this paradoxical third way with this *third thing*. In an essay entitled "God or Khora," Kearney lays out his basic claim that *Chora* "is neither identical with God nor incompatible with God but marks an open site where the divine may dwell and heal."[32] This quote hints at the interconnectedness of the Open, the Other, and *Chora*.

Elsewhere, Kearney suggests that *Chora* might well be reinterpreted as "the primordial matrix of the world which God needs to become flesh."[33] This proposed reinterpretation of *Chora* evokes Jung's notion that matter and the feminine are the Fourth in relation to the Christian Trinity. Kearney references murals that decorate the interior of the Chora Church near Istanbul, Turkey. These fourteenth-century Byzantine works depict Mary, Mother of God, as "Khora tou akoretou," the "Container of the Uncontainable." Others portray Christ as "*Khora* of all the Living."[34]

Kearney's interpretative strategy with the *Chora,* and his associations to the artful interior of the Chora Church, call to mind some additional bits of Jung's writing about the *Deus absconditus*. Jung saw Christ as "the typical dying and self-transforming God." And he understood this process of dying and transforming, which is not unique to the Christian myth, as a necessary process. "The death or loss must always repeat itself," Jung writes. "Christ always dies, and always he is reborn."[35] The regeneration of a god-image depends upon the symbolic death of the god-image. The process is necessary psychologically.

Containment: The Uncontainable and Livingness

The Open, the Other, and the *Chora*: a letting-be space; a space of *deconstructive ferment* and *potentiating withdrawal*; a space opening onto an encounter with the Other; the divine "curled at the heart of quotidian existence"; the Other hidden in the face of the other; a faceless Other who thwarts our attempts to make meaning and sense; a placeless space where there is both chaos and destruction, generation and ordering, *disiunctio* and *coniunctio*.

In the Visions seminars Jung writes,

> The Self as the Deus absconditus can undo its own symbolism for a certain purpose. When an individual has been swept away up into the world of symbolic mysteries, nothing comes of it, nothing can come of it, unless it has been associated with the earth, unless it has happened when that individual was in the body. ... The Self wants its own destruction as a symbolic reality.[36]

What I see Jung describing is a destructiveness that works to free up the reality beyond our images of God—a reality that, referencing Rilke, refuses to be caught in all the traps we set in circles around it, all around its open exit. Ann Ulanov has movingly described the purpose of this destructiveness—a destructiveness that characterizes each of our three post-secular themes. "This plowing up from the depths," she writes, "this destroying our God-images to free God is the work of the *Deus Absconditus*, the God of the Depths, from the dark, from the light so bright it blinds."[37] This plowing up—this hollowing out—is the hallmark of the post-secular quest, the search for God *after* God, the anatheistic way of seeking and sounding the things we deem sacred but cannot fathom or prove, of getting back what we have given up as if it were our first encounter with it.[38]

I think the symbolic potential of the Open, the Other, and *Chora* is exquisitely expressed in the murals of the Chora Church, the Container of the Uncontainable and the Container of all the Living. In them, *Chora* does its ancient and contemporary work, functioning as a third space—between the divine logos and human embodiment, between self and Other, between destruction and aliveness ... between hiding and being found.

NOTES

1. H. Arendt, "Religion and Politics," in J. Kohn, ed., *Essays in Understanding* (New York: Harcourt, 1994).

2. Hannah Arendt, *The Life of the Mind* (New York: Harcourt, 1978), p. 10.

3. C. G. Jung, "Psychology and Religion," in *The Collected Works of C. G. Jung*, vol. 11, ed. and trans. Gerhard Adler and R. F. C. Hull (Princeton, NJ: Princeton University Press, 1958), § 144.

4. *Ibid.*

5. Phillip Blonde, ed., *Post-Secular Philosophy: Between Philosophy and Theology* (New York: Routledge, 1998).

6. Richard Kearney, *Anatheism: Returning to God after God* (New York: Columbia University Press, 2011), p. 3.

7. *Ibid.*

8. Jung, CW 11, § 144.

9. Charles Bigger, *Between Chora and the Good: Metaphor's Metaphysical Neighborhood* (New York: Fordham University Press, 2005), p. 23.

10. *Ibid.*

11. Rainer-Maria Rilke, *Duino Elegies,* 3rd ed., trans. David Oswald (Einsiedeln: Daimon Verlag, 2012), p. 81.

12. David Oswald, trans., "Introduction," in Rilke, *Duino Elegies,* p. 15.

13. Bigger, *Between Chora and the Good*, p. 23.

14. J. O'Leary, "Questions," in J. Manoussakis, ed., *After God: Richard Kearney and the Religious Turn in Continental Philosophy* (New York: Fordham University Press, 2006), p. 199.

15. *Ibid.*

16. Manoussakis, *After God*, p. 28.

17. R. Kearney, "Epiphanies of the Everyday," in Mannoussakis, *After God*, p. 12.

18. Roger Brooke, *Jung and Phenomenology*, 2nd ed. (New York: Routledge, 2009), p. 35.

19. *Ibid.*

20. Kearney, "Epiphanies," p. 5.

21. Kearney, *Anatheism*, p. 15.

22. *Ibid.*, pp. 14–15.

23. John Manoussakis, "Khora: The Hermeneutics of Hyphenation," *Revista Portugeusa de Filosofia* 58 (2002): 93.

24. Plato, *Timaeus 52a–b*, trans. Donald Zeyl, *Complete Works*, ed. J. M. Cooper (Indianapolis, IN: Hackett, 1997), p. 1255.

25. *Ibid.*

26. Jacques Derrida, *Acts of Religion* (New York: Routledge, 2002).

27. John D. Caputo, *The Prayers and Tears of Jacques Derrida: Religion Without Religion* (Bloomington, IN: Indiana University Press, 2002), pp. 35–36.

28. Julia Kristeva, *The Kristeva Reader*, ed. Toril Moi (London: Blackwell, 1986), p. 93; and see also pp. 94–98, 108–109, 115–117.

29. Catherine Keller, *Face of the Deep: A Theology of Becoming* (New York: Routledge, 2003).

30. Manoussakis, "Khora," p. 97.

31. Richard Kearney, *Strangers, Gods, and Monsters* (New York: Routledge, 2003), p. 202.

32. *Ibid.*, p. 194.

33. *Ibid.*, p. 211.

34. For more information on the art and intellectual history of the Chora Church, see Paul A. Underwood, *The Kariye Djami*, 3 vols. (New York: Bollingen Foundation, 1966).

35. Jung, CW 11, § 129.

36. C. G. Jung, *The Visions Seminar*, vol. 2 (Princeton, NJ: Princeton University Press, 1997), pp. 1313–1314.

37. Ann Belford Ulanov, *The Unshuttered Heart: Opening to Aliveness/Deadness in the Self* (Nashville, TN: Abingdon Press, 2007), p. 228.

38. Kearney, *Anatheism*, p. 3.

CHAPTER FOURTEEN

REVISITING CARL JUNG'S *SEMINAR NOTES* ON THE IGNATIAN *EXERCISES*

Harry W. Fogarty

> In 1939 I gave a seminar on the *Spiritual Exercises* of Ignatius of Loyola. At the same time I was occupied on the studies for *Psychology and Alchemy*. One night I awoke and saw, bathed in bright light at the foot of my bed, the figure of Christ on the Cross. It was not quite life-size, but extremely distinct; and I saw that his body was made of greenish gold. ... I had been thinking a great deal about the Anima Christi, one of the meditations from the *Spiritual Exercises*.
> —C. G. Jung, *Memories, Dreams, Reflections*

Years ago Jung's words leapt off my copy of *Memories, Dreams, Reflections* as I was engaged in the quest for a Ph.D. dissertation topic. I was rather enthralled with Jung and his work, but as a loyal graduate of Loyola College, then the Jesuit College of Fordham University, I was also pre-committed to Ignatius. But where were these *Seminar Notes* to be found? Like so many Jungian texts at that time, they were (and remain) only available unofficially, and only a select few could access them.[1] Since that time, and especially since the time of Jung's *Seminar*, both Jungian reflection on the process of active imagination as methodologically central to all of Jung's work (and as exemplified in other traditions) *and* Jesuit reflections on Ignatius's *Spiritual Exercises* have expanded exponentially.

In numerous texts in the *Collected Works*, in the *Visions Seminars*, and in this *Seminar* itself, Jung comments on Ignatius's *Exercises*. Studies comparing Jung's lectures and other interpretations of the *Exercises* have been authored; especially, post-WWII and post-Vatican II, Jesuit sponsored studies in Ignatian Spirituality have blossomed, such as those by Harvey Egan and Jules Toner on the processes of discernment, along with others focused on aspects of spiritual direction.

In this essay, I intend to briefly summarize Jung's *Seminar* and the overall flow of the *Exercises* so that we too can shape the Jung-Ignatius exchange. Also, in honor of Jung's 1912 Fordham lectures on the Theory of Psychoanalysis and to provide a specific focus for our consideration, I want to lift up one comment from those lectures as its motif is central to both the Jungian and Ignatian endeavors.

> [It] all depends on the attitude the patient takes toward his fantasies. Hitherto the patient's fantasying was a completely passive and involuntary activity. He was lost in his dreams. Even so called "brooding" was nothing but an involuntary fantasy. ... What psychoanalysis asks of the patient is the exact opposite of what the patient has always done. He is like a man who has unintentionally fallen into the water and sunk, whereas psychoanalysis wants him to act like a diver. It was no mere chance which led him to fall in just at that spot. There lies the sunken treasure, but only a diver can bring it to the surface.[2]

Jung returns often to this image of the treasure beneath the sea. For instance in *Psychology and Alchemy,* in discussing one of Wolfgang Pauli's dreams, "In the sea there lies a treasure," he comments on the disciples on the road to Emmaus and the encounter between Moses and Khidr found in Sura 18 from the Qu'ran, identifying both as stereotypic of the process of active imagination that possibly leads one to finding the *treasure*.[3] Likewise, what the treasure evokes is central to Jung's investigations of processes typifying transformation, such as his essay "Concerning Rebirth," and is supremely and extraordinarily manifested in his *Liber Novus, The Red Book*.

Jung and Ignatius arrived at their core methods and beliefs from within the context of their own *crises*. What they found became a vital contribution both as an exemplar and as a method.

Jung came to understand that active imagination was *the* method for a transforming dialogue to occur between aspects of oneself. In his view, personally constellated complexes (splinter psyches) engaging/engaged by the arising archetypal Self, manifesting the objective psyche—that is, opposites, or oppositional forces, interacting—yield the transcendent function. In such a living synthesis nothing is lost; rather, the unexpected is gained, The Transcendent. For example, Jesus Christ is experienced as fully human and fully divine. Thus, active imagination could continuously fuel one's process of individuation, including creative embeddedness in collective life. For as Jung noted often, there is no individuation except within and for the collective.

Ignatius came to know that spiritual colloquies provided an immediate and personal access to God's presence and God's gracious invitations within one's life for the sake of one's fullest joy in existence; such living, in turn, was made manifest in the service of others. More particularly, these conversations between oneself and God were entered into with heightened attentiveness to one's experience of the movements of the spirits—helpful and seductive spirits, that is, experiences of consolation and desolation within the time of prayer.

Simply, Jung and Ignatius offer a shocking and life-giving possibility: one might directly and experientially know one's Self more fully in a way that heals and makes one whole. Further such experiences would manifest objectively, inviting possibilities for discovering as well as directly apprehending the *treasure* we all seek. At last, one might no longer be in the grip of inordinate passions, no longer inflatedly one-sided.

A few words about the Ignatius's *Exercises* and Jung's *Seminar* on them shall serve as a setting for thoughts about this quest for living treasure one hundred years later.

The *Exercises* are divided into weeks, offer a detailed map for entering into a prayerful experience of God, and include Ignatius's infamous "Rules for Thinking with the Church": "What seems to me white, I will believe black if the hierarchical Church so defines." What we may not know is that the *Exercises*, although filled with examples and texts, are, in the main, a description of a dynamic process and various ways to undertake it. The dynamism, more than the specific exercises, is the core. Four weeks of exercises, scripted in part to the mysteries of Christianity, was a model inherited from Cisneros (mysteries) and from Avicenna (weeks).

What was and remains novel about the *Exercises*?

One embraces an attitude of submission to God, akin to Jung's saying that the experience of the Self is a defeat for the ego and that the ego must submit to the objective nature of the manifestations of psyche.

One awakens to, deepens, and nourishes the experience of being saved and called to the service of others as best suited to one's individual state, as with Jung's understanding of individuation.

One meditates in the manner best suited to oneself—the direction for prayer is not imposed, is person specific, may utilize the exercises Ignatius offers, may proceed in another manner, may be prayer using images, and may be prayer that is like the Jesus Prayer, that is, prayer of the breath, as is similar to Jung's understanding of active imagination in which dialogical process, not contents or specific manifestations, is central.

One prays in a fully embodied way. The "Application of the Senses" makes it clear that prayer is to be radically grounded within one's fullest bodily self-sense, or interior experience; additionally, prayer extends into all aspects of one's life—what state one is called to, how to live in a transforming way even if one's circumstances cannot change, how one is to relate to food (awareness of human hungers, both one's own and those of others), almsgiving, scrupulosity (OCD), and how one is placed in the church (community). Similarly, Jung focuses on dynamic change that in today's vocabulary we would say, following the work of Allan Schore among others, reshapes the organic structures of our ways of thinking, perceiving, and acting. Jung also notes that becoming well is not the same thing as getting rid of an illness; rather, we grow out beyond our neurosis. This means that the outer structure might not change but our relationship with it shifts, as Jung suggests in *The Commentary on the Secret of the Golden Flower*. Finally, we cannot change except in, with, and for the collective.

One learns how to understand experiences of consolation and desolation, in particular "consolation without prior cause," an autonomously-arising consolation not due to one's efforts, like the transcendent function, *and* how to deepen such experiences that are affective and often visionary. Likewise, Jung discusses one's sense of an arising symbol as the outcome of active imagination.

In brief, the *Exercises* detail a method through which one might be guided by one's own encounter with God resulting in salvific, transformative, and empowering experiences and directing one toward others, a process largely marked by autonomous interior manifestations of grace.

Many guided meditations are offered. A few guiding principles are required: One is to embrace one's place in life as a creature, "The First Principle and Foundation." One is to ask actively for what is desired. One is to embrace and work with the graces one receives. One's process is personally specific. One comes to know oneself and becomes fulfilled through the model and actual service of others ("Take, Lord, and accept all my liberty, my memory, my understanding, and my entire will, all that I have and possess. ... Give me Thy love and Grace, for this is sufficient for me"). *And* one is to know all these realities affectively as typified in the prayer Jung refers to, the *Anima Christi*.[4]

Jung's *Seminar* (given nearly 400 years after the *Exercises* were formally formatted and the Jesuit Order founded) was a further effort on his part to detail archetypal patterns of transformation in psychic life. Since he delivered it as World War II was erupting, with the dead veterans of past wars rising to summon Europe to peace not war in Able Gance's film *J'Accuse*, we might be reminded of the dead returning from Jerusalem to question Jung in *Liber Novus*. Having studied various aspects of yoga and other *Eastern* approaches, Jung was returning to the *West*. He recollects various initiatory rites such as the Eleusinian mysteries, approaches to contemplation such as Philo, the traditions of the Devotii, the work of a Kempis (who also earlier was such an essential aspect of his own *Red Book)*, and Cisneros. Additionally, he reviewed techniques of focusing and drew upon his own prior writings on the process psychologically speaking of the Christian Mass. All of his reflections mirror the quest for a sense of the Salvator, or *stone*, as a perpetual presence. He brings to his work much of the best writing and interpretation of the *Exercises* available at that time, such as those by Pryzwara; we might also recall that Jung and Hugo Rahner knew and corresponded with each other. He studies specifically the *Anima Christi*, the "First Principle and Foundation," "Take, Lord, and Accept,"

The Two Standards, the structure of an exercise (preparations, petition, colloquy, and the application of the senses), and the central place of the director who, Jung observes, is to adapt to the specificity of the exercitant. In brief, he considers much of the *meat* of the *Exercises*; particularly, he focuses on the prayer of the *Anima Christi* and some of the other images in the *Exercises*. Predictably, he notes parallels with his other researches. He is especially interested in the similarity between colloquy and active imagination. One might say that Jung was further amplifying his effort to demonstrate archetypal patterns of transformation through his consideration of the *Exercises*.

What Jung does not explore are the rules for the discernment of spirits. And although he speaks of the centrality of the director's adaptiveness, he does not grasp how fully this releases the process into one quite similar to what he outlines in his *The Psychology of the Transference,* with its focus on what arises interactively, where, so to speak, the director is also an exercitant, both submitting to archetypal manifestations of the Self, or grace, or an arising symbol.

Jung's critique of the *Exercises* and of *scripted methods*, such as today's guided affective imagery techniques, rests on his sense that what needs our meeting as we experience an activated complex may well arise with images not synonymous with our familiar collective icons. Just such realities are those that are lacking attention from us and offer to us the seeds for beneficial shifts in our consciousness. To some degree he is quite accurate here; however, he understates both the flexibility of the *Exercises* as directed and his own latent pre-commitment to a pattern of change that draws upon Christian and Occult Christian traditions, such as alchemy—consider the main motifs of *Liber Novus,* replete with conversations with biblical characters and narrative, a Kempis, and their descendants. Further he plays down how one is to engage in the community aspect of transformation, a topic of much more attention post-WWII.

In his defense, what is central to contemporary utilizations of the *Exercises*, a focus on the Rules for the Discernment of Spirits was much less well-articulated in the literature Jung had available; and, as he noted, he never himself made the *Exercises*. These reflections on discernment and especially on consolation without prior cause would have pleased him as they are so similar to his method of active imagination in which one experiences both oneself and the Other as manifesting in autonomous feelings, images, and dreams, e.g., for Jung himself in *Liber Novus* when the dead returned full of questions for him. One was, for Jung, to submit to what was Other (objective), and then talk back with it and engage in a continuous and evolving process of dialogue.

Further in his defense, what a Jesuit now thinks of, in considering the image of Christ, has been liberated substantially from old missionizing tendencies in which the paradigm of Jesus Christ was seen as mirrored in all other cultures and traditions. Contemporary Jesuit spirituality is infused with an attitude of true dialogue with other traditions, pedagogies of liberating non-oppression, post-colonial thinking, and transformational gender thinking. These definitely were not mainstream seventy-five years ago. Although, equally, we would be hard-pressed to show these concerns as fully central for Jung; his efforts to consider amplifications and archetypal patterns, at least, were headed in the direction of non-imposition of psychological colonization.

Where does this exchange stand now?

In their methods of active imagination and colloquy and the specificity of those experiences on a personal basis, both Jung and Ignatius lift up the most central and most basic interior possibility of personal liberation and transformation. What may occur in a grace-filled colloquy is similar to what may occur in active imagination. Both Jung and Ignatius require that one's transformation be part and parcel of life in the community; Ignatius was much clearer about this than Jung, one might say to the latter's eventual regret after World War II.

Although Jung may have failed at being as open as his method suggests, his is an open method—no pre-assigned belief system, but rather discovering one's true interior living experience of the Self. Undeniably, even with all the aspects of liberation theology and spirituality, the *Exercises* are Christocentric, seeing oneself over against the experience of Christ, which indeed Jung referred to as an Archetype of the Self. Yet, herein lies an invitation to Jungians. Perhaps more central than what Jung left out in his *Seminar*, the rules on discernment, is the question those rules address. Namely, by what criterion does one evaluate the process of one's own transformation? While it remains truest to evaluate where one is in one's own individuation journey from within, the very nature of *from within* needs its opposite, *from without*, from the community in a manner that transcends the immediate community yet remains rooted in it. Just as Jung himself was vulnerable to self-serving interpretations, we too risk swimming unwittingly away from the treasure the dive offers.

Perhaps our dialogues will not reference Jesus as manifesting the transcendent, the transcendently arising symbol, for us. Still we must wrestle with just how our transcendent symbol functions efficaciously for us lest we end up with fool's gold rather than true treasure.

NOTES

1. C. G. Jung, "The Process of Individuation—Exercitia Spiritualia of St. Ignatius of Loyola" (notes on lectures given at Widgenossische Technische Hochschule, Zürich, 1939–1940), trans. Barbara Hannah (Zürich: Privately Circulated).

2. C. G. Jung, "The Theory of Psychoanalysis," in *The Collected Works of C. G. Jung*, vol. 4, ed. and trans. Gerhard Adler and R. F. C. Hull (Princeton, NJ: Princeton University Press, 1961), § 417.

3. C. G. Jung, "Individual Dream Symbolism in Relation to Alchemy," CW 12, §§ 155–157.

4. St. Ignatius of Loyola, *The Spiritual Exercises*, trans. Louis Puhl, S.J. (Westminster, MD: Newman Press, 1963), #234.

CHAPTER FIFTEEN

A Feeling of Kinship with All Things
Analytical Psychology, Deep Ecology, and Phenomenology

Teresa Arendell

> Trees cannot exist without animals, or animals without plants, and perhaps animals cannot be without man, or men without animals and plants and so on. And the whole thing being one tissue, it is no wonder that all its parts function together, just as the cells in our bodies function together because they are part of the same living continuum.
>
> —C. G. Jung, *The Visions Seminars*

Carl Jung argued, with strong conviction, that the profound challenges facing us in modern life are psychological and spiritual at their cores. We live in the midst of a relentless ecological crisis. At unprecedented rates the natural world is degraded. Climate change, global warming, deadly toxins, and explosive population growth have an impact on the entire globe. Yet, despite the findings of science, the environmental movement, and the coming together of the theories and practices of depth and eco-psychology, we persist in our assaults on Nature. We live in the tension of opposites: participating in life and destroying it. Most scientists, scholars, and policy-makers look to science and technology for solutions to our global crises in climate and environment, crises caused by scientific and technological advancements. But the crisis, as Jung insisted, is one of human consciousness.

More than sixty years ago Jung exclaimed that a new story is emerging.[1] The new myth, he declared, weaves together forgotten and rejected aspects of the old, the spirits of the ancestral lands and the primordial in our psyches that which Jung often metaphorically referred to as the two-million-year-old man.[2]

Jung was not alone in his quest to expand human consciousness and to bridge the modern split between Nature and Psyche. For example, also arguing for a new cosmology, one which would end our human estrangement from the universe, was priest, earth scholar, and professor Thomas Berry (formerly of Fordham University). Throughout his life, Berry sought to come to understand creation and our destruction of Nature. "It's all a question of story [he wrote]. We are in trouble just now because we do not have a good story. We are in between stories … [having] not [yet] learned the new story."[3] James Lovelock, originator of the Gaia Theory (an earlier version referred to as the Gaia Hypothesis), argued for a reformed science and worldview which recognizes that the Earth is an organic whole. As a self-regulating system, Gaia is made up of the totality and shared systemic evolution of organisms, surface rocks, the ocean, and the atmosphere. The goal of the system is "the regulation of surface conditions so as always to be as favorable for contemporary life as possible."[4] And the Norwegian philosopher Arne Naess formulated the initial principles of and coined the term *Deep Ecology*. He argued for a changed story, one which is "not a slight reform of our present society, but a substantial reorientation of our whole civilization."[5] Nature and Psyche come together in the new myth whether as posited by Jung, Berry, Lovelock, or Naess—a story which brings together elements from the deepest levels of the unconscious with the emergent consciousness—the *old-new way*.[6]

Carl Jung dedicated his life to the study and exploration of the wilderness within—the inner landscape—a metaphor he used repeatedly as he sought to understand the Psyche. Jung also felt deep concern about humankind's diminished connection with and loss of awe for Nature—the outer world.⁷ Through the modern scientific worldview, urbanization, and advanced industrial technologies, and through the concurrent loss of connection with Nature, the world became disenchanted. The value of the imaginal, and of heart and soul, was diminished, and relatedness and mystery abandoned. "We have stripped all things of their mystery and numinosity; nothing is holy any longer."⁸ We lost connection with our own powers of spiritual and psychological healing. Anything wild is to be managed or eradicated; we became creator, center, and destroyer. We began to approach the world, using Thomas Berry's words, as a collection of objects rather than a communion of subjects.

Jung became increasingly explicit about his own psychic relationship to the natural world in his later years. Near the end of his memoirs, he observed, "Nature, the psyche, and life appear to me like divinity unfolded—and what more could I wish for?" Concluding his reflections, Jung wrote, "This is old age, and a limitation. Yet there is so much that fills me: plants, animals, clouds, day and night, and the eternal in man. The more uncertain I have felt about myself, the more there has grown up in me a feeling of kinship with all things."⁹

Analytical Psychology and Deep Ecology

Among the various developments in analytical psychology in recent decades has been the move by some Jungian analysts and scholars to integrate into their work aspects of the relatively new field of Deep Ecology. This integration of principles of deep ecology expands classical Jungian work with respect to human relations with the natural, wild world. Jung's psychology, according to Native American Studies scholar and author Vine Deloria, "forms a perfect background and justification for expressing environmental concerns."¹⁰ Australian Jungian Studies scholar David Tacey, seeking expressly to develop an ecological elaboration of depth psychology, wrote the following: "Eco-psychology is, in my view, one of the most important disciplines of our time. It has emerged from the works of Jung and Hillman and has followed their passion for discovering psyche in the world, and not merely inside the human mind."¹¹

The field Deep Ecology was just developing when Jung died in the early 1960s. The new discipline formed in large part from out of contributions from analytical psychology. The early theorist of deep ecology, historian and author Theodore Roszak, asserted that Jung's idea of the collective unconscious is the single most important concept in the creation of an ecological psychology.[12] Using Jung's concept, Roszak developed the notion of an *ecological unconscious* to refer to the intersection of Earth, Gaia, and Psyche.[13]

The two perspectives—analytical psychology and deep ecology—increasingly enhance the other in dynamic and important ways. Analytical psychology takes us predominantly, but not solely, into the inner world of Psyche. Deep ecology, also referred to as ecopsychology or green psychology, attends primarily, but not exclusively, to the outer world of Psyche. Naess wrote, "the essence of deep ecology is to ask deeper questions. The adjective 'deep' stresses that we ask why, and how, where others do not." These questions move us to a stance of self-reflectiveness. The questions address not only the inner world of Psyche, however. Naess also extended the reach of deep ecology to the collective level and stated, "We ask which society, which education, which form of religion, is beneficial for all life on the planet as a whole, and we ask further what we need to do … to make the necessary changes."[14] Naess advocated "rich living, simple means."

Analytical psychology and deep ecology share a methodological approach in their respective quests to explore the relationship between humans and the natural world. That common approach is phenomenology. At the core of this methodology are the emphases on the human-lived experience and the search for meaning. Knowledge is the outcome of experience. Phenomenology aims at rich description and interpretation of symbolic experiences of both the inner and outer worlds in the light of intuition, perception, and self-reflection. Jung, who considered all phenomena to be potentially symbolic, drew on collective and personal histories, dreams and creative imaginings, cultural products, and the characteristics of the sociocultural contexts in which experiences occur.[15] To this phenomenological mix, deep ecology adds a rich analysis of the destructive effects of technological-industrial capitalism, the system which pervades modern Western society and through which Nature is commodified and exploited.

Meaning is created when the object, as it appears in our consciousness, mingles with the object in nature.[16] The natural world—Nature—is rich, complex, and diverse. Numerous layers make up what Edward Casey, the phenomenologist deeply influenced by analytical psychology (particularly archetypal), described as the "modes of hiddenness of nature." Casey wrote,

> What counts phenomenologically is that this body, my body or yours or that of the raccoon who visits my house at night or that of the tree that stands sentinel in my yard, apprehends what is happening to it within a coherent world. ... The experience of these inhabitants cannot be left out of account, for there are no such worlds without such experience.[17]

Contemplation of Nature opens our perception of the dynamic and evolving whole of life.

A phenomenological understanding is existential, embodied, situational, and nontheoretic. We move back and forth between the unique and that which is shared, the meaning which is particular and the transcendent.[18] Human consciousness, integral to the life-world, is experienced and explored from multiple angles. Analysis is reflexive, involving the dialectic between experience and awareness, between studying the parts and the whole. After 1932, Jung frequently referred to his approach as phenomenological.[19] In 1937 Jung wrote, "I am an empiricist and adhere as such to the phenomenological standpoint. ... I restrict myself to the observation of phenomena," and Jung insisted that his standpoint is "exclusively phenomenological, that is, it is concerned with occurrences, events, experiences."[20] While Jung's use of the label phenomenological was new, it was wholly consistent with his earlier use of both the constructive and comparative methods.[21]

Jung was highly critical of the model of natural science, which came to be known as positivism, for its limitations in studying human life and its causal and reductionist views. Even as early as 1912, in both the Fordham lectures and a published essay, "New Paths in Psychology," Jung critiqued Freud for his materialist perspective. He argued that Freud's position was that experience can be reduced to *nothing but*. Jung insisted on granting psychic facts—*psychic realities*—their own value, reducible to neither physiological nor physical mechanisms. Jung, as a psychological theorist and clinician, was ahead of his time when he argued that all observations and interpretations are *subjective*, involving the characteristics of the perceiver as well as of the perceived. Evidence from both personal experiences, including the years of his intense self-analysis which began shortly after he gave the Fordham lectures, and clinical observations led Jung to develop the concepts of analytical psychology.[22]

Deep ecology is also critical of the methods of the natural and conventional psychological sciences. And, as with Jungian thought and practice, deep ecology draws upon symbolic images. Naess, appropriating from Taoism, advocated such practices as "to listen with the third ear" and "to think like a mountain." Deep ecology, as defined by Naess, asserts "that belief in an objective comprehension of nature is belief in a flat world seen from above, without depth, and … is a primary cause of our destructive relation to the land."[23] Naess distinguished deep ecology from shallow ecology; the latter holds the view that the major ecological problems can be resolved through conventional scientific means and without a transformation of the political-economic system. Deep ecology, in contrast, requires a thorough and deep transformation of both individual human consciousness and social institutions.

Deep ecology emphasizes the value of Nature and interrelatedness of all phenomena. All life has intrinsic value; nature is elemental to creation, worthy of reverence and respect. Ecology should not be concerned with man's place in nature alone but with every part of nature on an equal basis.[24] Consistent with the phenomenological approach and overlapping with analytical psychology, deep ecology prioritizes relational experience. The anthropocentric worldview—which claims that humans are the ultimate center of creation—is challenged and refuted. As Australian environmentalist and advocate for the globe's rain forests, John Seed stated, "Deep ecology critiques the idea that we [humankind] are the crown of creation, the measure of all being."[25]

Deep ecology, like analytical psychology, attempts to promote greater awareness, that is, greater consciousness, of our role in the world of nature. Humankind has caused the Earth-threatening ecological crisis, and both perspectives seek to understand the forces that press humans to destroy Nature. Wrote eco-philosopher David Wood, "We are pissing in the reservoir and then wondering why the water tastes funny." Shared is the following question: What are our impacts, collective as well as individual, on the biosphere?[26]

In his later work Jung theorized about the experience of the unity and interrelatedness of all things. He drew upon the alchemical notion of *unus mundus* or One World, and declared, "In some way or other we are part of a single all-embracing psyche."[27] Archetypal psychologist and Jungian analyst James Hillman wrote, "The deepest self cannot be confined to 'in here' because we can't be sure it is not also or even entirely 'out there.'"[28] In this unity—the *unus mundus*—human life is utterly inseparable from Nature. Naess asserted, "We may be said to be in, out and for Nature from our very beginning."

We are pulled into the depths, beneath the surface of conscious experience, through our encounters with Nature. The natural, wild world offers experiences of the numinous; it is the place where the Self may be realized according to both analytical psychology and deep ecology. Contact with the wild "gives us the heart and soul we need to continue our quest for the meaning of our presence in the vast universe."[29] A shared psychic drama evolves between Nature and the human soul. Activated is the human imagination—that *creative fantasy* which, according to Jung, is too often lost in the modern psyche. Our conscious awareness is changed, the relationship between the inner and outer worlds altered.

I am confident that, were Jung alive, he would be raising alarm about the plight of the Earth and the major role modern humankind plays in the unfolding catastrophe. The old story in which humans assumed and asserted dominion over all of Nature cannot be sustained. We are called to participate in the emerging new story—one in which the modern split between Nature and Psyche is bridged, and in which the Self is understood to be not only *in here* but also *out there*. The collaborative threads between analytical psychology and deep ecology offer the framework for an emerging myth regarding the relations between humankind and Nature.

NOTES

1. C. G. Jung, *Memories, Dreams, Reflections* (New York: Vintage Books, 1963), p. 285; C. G. Jung, "The Fish in Alchemy," in *Aion: Researches into the Phenomenology of the Self*, vol. 9, *The Collected Works of C. G. Jung*, ed. and trans. Gerhard Adler and R. F. C. Hull (Princeton,

NJ: Princeton University Press, 1978); and C. G. Jung. "The State of Psychotherapy Today," in *Civilization in Transition*, CW 10, § 304.

2. See C. G. Jung, "Archaic Man," CW 10.

3. Thomas Berry, *The Dream of the Earth* (San Francisco, CA: Sierra Club Books, 1988), pp. 123–124.

4. James Lovelock, *The Vanishing Face of Gaia* (New York: Basic Books, 2009), p. 255.

5. Arne Naess, *Ecology, Community, and Lifestyle* (Cambridge: Cambridge University Press, 1989), p. 45.

6. Gary Snyder, *Turtle Island* (New York: New Directions, 1974).

7. Jung used *Nature* in multiple ways. Susan Rowland, "Nature Writing: Jung's Eco-Logic in the Conjunctio of Comedy and Tragedy," *Spring Journal* 75 (2006): 275–297; and see also Meredith Sabini, *The Earth Has a Soul: The Nature Writings of C. G. Jung* (Berkeley, CA: North Atlantic Books, 2005).

8. C. G. Jung, "Healing the Split," in *The Symbolic Life: Miscellaneous Writings*, CW 18, § 254.

9. Jung, *Memories, Dreams, Reflections*, p. 359.

10. Deloria, *C. G. Jung and the Sioux Traditions*, p. 102.

11. David Tacey, *Edge of the Sacred: Jung, Psyche, Earth* (Einsiedeln: Daimon, 2009), p. 18; and David Tacey, "Ecopsychology and the Sacred: The Psychological Basis of the Environmental Crisis," *Spring Journal* 83 (2010): 329–351.

12. Deep ecology scholars come from various disciplines, in addition to analytical psychology, e.g., theology, green psychology, ecophilosphy, ecofeminism, and eco-psychology.

13. Theodore Roszak, *The Voice of the Earth* (Grand Rapids, MI: Phanes Press, 2002), pp. 301–02.

14. Arne Naess, "The Shallow and the Deep, Long-Range Ecology Movement: A Summary," in *The Deep Ecology Movement: An Introductory Anthology*, ed. A. Drengson (Berkeley, CA: North Atlantic Books, 1995), p. 3.

15. See Andrew Samuels, *Jung and the Post-Jungians* (London and New York: Routledge & Kegan Paul, 1985), p. 5.

16. Clark Moustakas, *Phenomenological Research Methods* (Newbury Park, CA: Sage Publications, 1994), p. 27.

17. Edward S. Casey, "Phenomenon and Place: Toward a Renewed Ethics of the Environment," in *Spring Journal* 76 (2006): 185, 193.

18. Max van Manen, "From Meaning to Method" in *Qualitative Health Research* 7 (1997): 345; and see also Linda Finlay, *Phenomenology for Therapists: Researching the Lived World* (Hoboken, NJ: J. Wiley, 2011).

19. Regarding Pauli's assessment that Jung's work was phenomenological *and* scientific, see Suzanne Gieser, *The Innermost Kernel: Depth Psychology and Quantum Physics. Wolfgang Pauli's Dialogue with C. G. Jung* (Berlin, Heidelberg, New York: Springer, 2005).

20. C. G. Jung, "The Autonomy of the Unconscious," in *Psychology and Religion: West and East*, CW 11, §§ 5–6.

21. Gieser, *Innermost Kernel*, p. 160.

22. See Jung, *Memories, Dreams, Reflections*.

23. Walter Schwartz, Obituary of Arne Naess, *The Guardian*, Wednesday, Jan. 14, 2009 at *http://www.guardian.co.uk/environment/2009/jan/15/obituary-arne-naess*; and see also David Abram, "Deep Ecology," in *The Encyclopedia of Religion and Nature,* ed. Bron Raymond Taylor (New York: Continuum, 2005).

24. Arne Naess, *Ecology, Community and Lifestyle: Outline of an Ecosophy*, trans. David Rothenberg (Cambridge: Cambridge University Press, 1989).

25. John Seed, "The Ecological Self," *EarthLight Magazine* 14 (4 2005): 2.

26. David Wood, "What is Eco-Phenomenology?" in *Eco-phenomenology: Back to the Earth Itself*, eds. Charles S. Brown and Ted Toadvine (Albany, NY: State University of New York Press, 2003), p. 229.

27. C. G. Jung, "The Spiritual Problem of a Modern Man," in *Civilization in Transition*, CW 10, § 86; see also Erich Neumann on "Unitary Reality" in *Art and the Creative Unconscious: Four Essays* (Princeton, NJ: Princeton University Press, 1974), p. 131; and John Dourley, "Archetypal Hatred as Social Bond: Strategies for Its Dissolution," in *Terror, Violence and the Impulse to Destroy*, ed. J. Beebe (Einsiedeln: Daimon Verglag, 2003), p. 156.

28. James Hillman, "A Psyche the Size of the Earth: A Psychological Foreword," in *Ecopsychology: Restoring the Earth, Healing the Mind*, eds. T. Roszak, M. Gomes, and A. D. Kanner (San Francisco, CA: Sierra

Club Books, 1995), p. xix; Hillman continues, "If we listen to Roszak, and to Freud and Jung, the most profoundly collective and unconscious self is the natural material world. Since the cut between self and natural world is arbitrary, we can make it at the skin or we can take it as far out as you like—to the deep oceans and distant stars. But the cut is far less important than the recognition of uncertainty about making the cut at all." (p. xxi).

29. Jane H. Wheelwright and Lynda W. Schmidt, *The Long Shore: A Psychological Experience of the Wilderness* (San Francisco, CA: Sierra Club Books, 1991), p. 187.

CHAPTER SIXTEEN

A JUNGIAN PERSPECTIVE ON THE MOST IMPORTANT ISSUE OF OUR TIME—CLIMATE CHANGE

Dennis L. Merritt

As Bill Clinton might say, "It's the environment, stupid!" Our devotion to science, technology, and the capitalist system has culminated in a unique moment in the human-environment relationship. Our species is at, or near, the peak of a prosperity bubble that could burst in many different ways. We have exceeded the carrying capacity of the biosphere and we are still multiplying.[1] Overuse of antibiotics has created deadly bacteria becoming immune to everything we have.[2] Coral reefs are dying as oceans become warmer and more acidic—signs of the very beginnings of the negative consequences of climate change. It will include massive droughts and floods, freak storms, the spread of diseases, water wars, and the elimination of twenty to thirty-five percent of species in the next forty years.[3,4] Climate expert James Hansen believes there may already be enough CO_2 in the atmosphere to push us over the tipping point.[5] The apocalyptic situations we are inexorably moving towards are truly in the archetypal domain, requiring archetypal analysis and suggestions for dealing with it. Enter Jungian ecopsychology, a topic I have been writing on for the past sixteen years and am about to publish the fourth and final volume of *The Dairy Farmer's Guide to the Universe—Jung, Hermes, and Ecopsychology*.

I discovered Jung while working on my doctorate in entomology at Berkeley starting in 1967. My area was insect pathology, using insect pathogens instead of chemicals to manage insect pests; Rachel Carson's *Silent Spring* had made a deep impression on me. I realized the ecological and political dimensions of Jung's concepts and was able to bring my two backgrounds together within the developing field of ecopsychology.

Psychology has been painfully late in addressing environmental problems. Jungian analyst and archetypal psychologist James Hillman summed it up in the title of his book: *We've Had a Hundred Years of Psychotherapy—And the World's Getting Worse*.[6] He noted that the environment we have ignored and mistreated is making its importance known to us through its pathologies, much like human pathologies made the reality of the unconscious known to Freud.[7] The collective psyche of our species is deeply disturbed by our collapsing faith in science and the redeveloping human limitations in confronting nature, and it has been more a heroic confrontation than an enlightened relationship. The field of ecopsychology began to emerge in the 1990s. It examines how our attitudes, values, perceptions, and behaviors affect the environment. It calls for a reformulation of our political, cultural, economic, and educational systems to enable us to live sustainably. Like deep ecology, it maintains that we are capable of a far deeper connection with nature that will serve as a natural basis for protecting the environment. Jung, who died in 1961, recognized the magnitude of the change in consciousness necessary for these things to happen when he foresaw a paradigm shift coming in the West, what he called a *New Age* and the *Age of Aquarius*, a shift that will certainly and necessarily have an ecological base.[8]

There are two focal points from a Jungian ecological perspective for facing these issues. First is Jung's challenge to become more conscious, which for Jung meant to bring as much light as possible into the unconscious. It is clear this must now include greater consciousness of our niche in nature and greater awareness of environmental problems. This requires a knowledge of science as well as the archetypal dynamics of the apocalypse that will emerge ever more strongly, prompting more polarization in our society and a movement towards unreflective extreme religious positions.[9] The second Jungian ecopsychological focus is on the archetypal energies imaged by Hermes. Language and communication, Hermes' domains, are being manipulated *1984*-style by corporate interests using eco-propaganda, advertising, and *greenwashing*. One of the few hopes I have for humankind is for Hermes, the communicator, offering the possibility for easy and widespread dissemination of holistic messages and for a new vision for humankind, if we can develop one. Hermes leads the way or leads astray—it's our choice.

To develop a new vision, I propose that we create a team of experts from all fields who can communicate well with each other as they provide a deep analysis of our problems as a species and develop a plan all the world leaders can get behind. This team would include ecologists, psychologists, economists, spiritual leaders, scientists, technologists, educators, and indigenous peoples.

There are many innate ecological aspects in Jung's system and in the practice of Jungian analysis that could be part of this vision. Jung talked about the people in our dreams as "the little people within" and emphasized the importance of being in relationship with them. This is an ecology of the psyche, quite the opposite of the conquering ego position presented by Freud. Freud described the relationship with our inner world much as he described our relationship with the environment. Within us is the *seething caldron* of the Id requiring a vigilant defense against the polymorphous sexually perverse inner child. With regard to the environment Freud wrote the following:

> We recognize, then, that countries have attained a high level of civilization if we find that in them everything which can assist in the exploitation of the earth by man and in his protection against the forces of nature—everything, in short, which is of use to him—is attended to and effectively carried out [flood control, canals, agriculture, mineral extraction, and elimination of wild animals].[10]

Jung challenged us to unite our cultured side with "the two million-year-old man within," a goal that would help us use science and the arts to achieve an emotional, symbolic, and spiritual connection with nature.[11] It would bridge a connection with the Native Americans and their deep and profound sense of oneness with Turtle Island—the North American continent. This dovetails with Jung's challenge to Western society, including academia, to incorporate a sense of the numinous. Without this, Jung said, we will never have holistic systems.[12] Carl

Sagan, who as co-chair of *A Joint Appeal by Science and Religion for the Environment,* presented a petition in 1992 stating,

> The environmental problem has religious as well as scientific dimensions. ... As scientists, many of us have had a profound experience of awe and reverence before the universe. We understand that what is regarded as sacred is more likely to be treated with care and respect. Our planetary home should be so regarded. Efforts to safeguard and cherish the environment need to be infused with a vision of the sacred. At the same time, a much wider and deeper understanding of science and technology is needed. If we do not understand the problem it is unlikely we will be able to fix it. Thus there is a vital role for both science and religion.[13]

Deep ecology calls for the deepest possible analysis of our dysfunctional relationship with nature, and Jung offers this through his examination of the evolution of the God-image in the West.[14] Myths and religions help establish and maintain basic attitudes, values, perceptions, and behaviors, especially with regard to women, our bodies, sexuality and sensuality, and nature.

Humans emotionally, symbolically, sensually, and spiritually experience the basic dynamics of the universe, and, by definition, for our species to fully realize our niche, we have to connect to ourselves, others, and nature in this manner. This involves creativity and the arts and a proper focus in our educational and psychological systems.[15]

Consciousness and every layer of the collective unconscious can be scrutinized for dissonance with regard to our relationship with the environment.[16] At the **personal**, intra-psychic level, our relationship with the unconscious sets the pattern for our relationship with others and with nature, an example of scalar invariance in complexity theory. Our **family**, especially attachment issues with the mothering figure, can lead to an anxiety, an emptiness, and a narcissism that consumerism and fundamentalist religions prey upon. Our **national** myths of the cowboy and conquering the Wild West engender a conquering attitude towards nature and a religion of progress. Issues are compounded by the growing polarization in societies between believers and non-believers and the haves and have-nots. We are heading towards a dangerous period, especially in America, as it faces the archetype of decline—a problem for a country with an adolescent mentality epitomized by our myths of exceptionalism and the independent cowboy. Our hyper-independence makes us paranoid about any hint of socialism that many equate with communism. It is a revolutionary period (hexagram 49 in the *I Ching*) with the dangers of fascism increasing as economic, social, and environmental conditions deteriorate. The Judeo-Christian religion established core values in Western **culture** which have little connection with nature, the body, and sexuality. The Western Oedipal complex of human intelligence trumping the Great Goddess imaged as the Sphinx is poised to inflict the plagues of Thebes upon the entire planet and literalize John's apocalyptic vision.[17] Ecotheologian Thomas Berry described the Myth of Wonderworld as the myth of the West, now spread worldwide, as originating in John's Book of Revelation, the last book in the Bible. A thousand years of abundance and human perfections were supposed to precede the end of the created world. Humans decided to manifest the myth themselves when it didn't occur by divine grace. Berry writes, "The millennial myth was absorbed into, and found expression in, the modern doctrine of progress—which has seen humans trying to bring about this promised state through their own efforts by exploiting the resources of the earth."[18] Jung challenges us to unite our cultured side with the **primeval ancestor**, what he called "the two million-year-old man within," which is at the clan and tribal level of human relationships. Such a person would have a relationship with the **animal ancestor** foundation of the psyche like an indigenous person speaks of spirit animals. The deepest disturbance in our collective unconscious will be at the animal soul level, because for the first time in the history of life on earth one species will be responsible for eliminating twenty-five to thirty percent of the other species. And through the consequences of climate change we will decimate the basic requirements for *our* life as an animal: food, water, shelter, and a relatively stable climate.

Aldo Leopold described a science that deepens our appreciation of nature, helps us realize our ecological niche, and makes us aware of how we are destroying the environment.[19] We must realize that the climate change problem is a species problem, not just an American or European or Chinese problem. We must appreciate the unique niche of our species in nature as the only species able to use science and technology to violate the laws of nature and exceed the limitations nature brings about through restrictions of food and water and the spread of diseases. This makes it imperative for our species to be conscious and wise in our relationship with nature and oriented towards living sustainably.

From the more cultural perspective, our educational systems must make us more cognizant of our cultural evolution, the evolution of our religious forms, and the archetypal dynamics of the God-image within. Jung said we need more psychology, and famously added, "We are the origin of all coming evil."[20] We have to teach a psychology that educates students about archetypes, the shadow and projection, and how to live a meaningful life; Jung proposed individuation as the best antidote to consumerism.[21] The archetype of the provider side of the Great Mother, with her desire for stability, has captured our species—aided by the wonders of science and technology—giving us an abundance of food, clothing, shelter, cheap energy, and good health. The fatal flaw is our lack of wisdom and a lack of collective social and environmental consciousness.

Environmentalists and most scientists have been suffering from the Cassandra complex for several decades so the problem is not with science.[22] Jung's claim that big corporations are the modern day monsters provides an archetypal take on corporations as persons and the *Citizens United* Supreme Court decision.[23,24] The British Royal Society chastized ExxonMobil in 2006 for funding organizations deliberately trying to confuse people about climate change, attempting to convince the populace there was serious disagreement among scientists about the human factor in climate change. One ad agency was the same one hired by Phillip Morris in 1993 to create doubt that second-hand smoke can cause cancer as the Surgeon General's report in 1992 had indicated.[25] In a related story, I quote from the end of the 2012 Frontline program on PBS, "Money, Power and Wall Street": "It's very difficult to change gods. And in the modern age, our god was finance, except it's turned out to be a very cruel and destructive god."[26] A very real aspect of a paradigm shift will entail a re-visioning of the concept of corporations. They have the rights of a person but with no concern for children, grandchildren, or the seventh generation; their only goal is to maximize profits no matter what. Corporations and large financial institutions often are above governments and international politics. Without changing the rights of corporations, strict oversight of financial institutions, and the elimination of tax haven shell games, we are just rearranging the chairs on the deck of the Titanic—they will always be several steps ahead of us. I describe on my blog how I see the film *The Hunger Games* as an analogy to our present political situation veering towards fascism, defined as the union of corporations and government (JungianEcopsychology.com). This is conveyed in a quote attributed to Sinclair Lewis: "When fascism comes to America, it will be wrapped in the flag and carrying a cross" (not written by Lewis but expressing his sentiments).

It will take the paradigm shift Jung described as a *New Age* and *Age of Aquarius* for our species to face and address the frightful realities of current and future environmental situations, our collective sense of guilt for the damage we continue to do to the planet and to the poor and disenfranchised who initially will suffer the most from climate change, and for our demonic role in the coming extinctions of millions of species on the planet. "Fate leads those who follow her, drags those who don't." Jung said what is not brought to consciousness comes to us as fate. We can either consciously adopt an ecological perspective or let fate as ecological disasters eventually force such a perspective upon us, a perspective that will permeate all levels of human consciousness and behavior. To quote Jung, "We are beset by an all-too-human fear that consciousness—our Promethean conquest—may in the end not be able to serve us as well as nature."[27]

Nothing is currently being done that is big and bold enough to address the gestalt of conditions that are producing climate change, conditions at the personal, cultural, social, political, economic, educational, and spiritual levels. I am convinced that Jungian ecopsychology can make a significant contribution to this necessary dialogue. This has been the subject of my four volumes of *The Dairy Farmer's Guide to the Universe—Jung, Hermes and Ecopsychology*. Volume 1, *Jung and Ecopsychology*, examines the evolution of the Western dysfunctional relationship with the environment, explores the theoretical framework and concepts of Jungian ecopsychology, and describes how it could be applied to psychotherapy, our educational system, and our relationship with indigenous peoples.[28] Volume 2, *The Cry of Merlin—Jung, the Prototypical Ecopsychologist*, reveals how an individual's biography can be treated as an ecopsychological exercise and articulates how Jung's life experiences make him the prototypical ecopsychologist.[29] Volume 3, *Hermes, Ecopsychology, and Complexity*

Theory, provides an archetypal, mythological, and symbolic foundation for Jungian ecopsychology. I present Hermes as the god of ecopsychology and offer his staff as an emblem for ecopsychology.[30] Volume 4, *Land, Weather, Seasons, Insects: An Archetypal View*, describes how a deep, soulful connection can be made with these elements through a Jungian ecopsychological approach. This involves the use of science, myths, symbols, dreams, Native American spirituality, imaginal psychology, and the *I Ching*.[31]

Two promising areas are the Earth Charter that promotes "a sustainable global society founded on respect for nature, universal human rights, economic justice, and a culture of peace" and the Transitions movement dealing simultaneously with climate change and peak oil.[32,33] Lester Brown's *Plan B 3.0* offers an astute and comprehensive analysis of environmental problems and many promising possibilities for tackling them in a Marshall Plan style.

We have but a short time to bring about a paradigm shift—Jung's *New Age*—but the stakes are high. We are creating the conditions that will literalize John's dastardly vision of an apocalypse as he described it in the Book of Revelation.

NOTES

1. Ralph Metzner, "The Split Between Spirit and Nature in European Consciousness," *Trumpeter* 10 (1, Winter 1993): 2.

2. Jeremy Laurance, "Experts Fear Diseases 'Impossible to Treat,'" *The Independent*, Feb. 20, 2012. Accessed on Nov. 8, 2012, at http://www.independent.co.uk/life-style/health-and-families/health-news/experts-fear-diseases-impossible-to-treat-7216662.html.

3. Lester Brown, *Plan B 3.0: Mobilizing to Save Civilization* (New York: W. W. Norton & Co., 2008), pp. 69–75, 173–174.

4. Anthony Barnosky *et al.*, "Has the Earth's Sixth Mass Extinction Already Arrived?" *Nature* 471 (March 3, 2001): 51–57.

5. Ed Pilkington, "Climate Target is Not Radical Enough—Study," *The Guardian*, Apr. 6, 2008. Accessed May 31, 2009, at http://www.theguardian.com/environment/2008/apr/07/climatechange.carbonemissions.

6. James Hillman and Michael Ventura, *We've Had a Hundred Years of Psychotherapy and the World's Getting Worse* (San Francisco, CA: Harper, 1992).

7. James Hillman, *The Thought of the Heart and the Soul of the World* (Woodstock, CT: Spring Publications, 1992), pp. 89–130.

8. C. G. Jung, *Letters, Vol. 1, 1906–1950,* eds. Gerhard Adler and Aniela Jaffe, trans. R. F. C. Hull (Princeton, NJ: Princeton University Press), p. 285.

9. Neela Banerjee, "Tennessee Enacts Evolution, Climate Change Law," *Los Angeles Times,* Apr. 11, 2012. Accessed on Nov. 24, 2012, at http://articles.latimes.com/2012/apr/11/nation/la-na-tennessee-climate-law-20120411.

10. Sigmund Freud, *Civilization and Its Discontents,* trans. James Strachey (New York: W. W. Norton & Co., 1961), p. 39.

11. C. G. Jung, *C. G. Jung Speaking: Interviews and Encounters,* eds. W. McGuire and R. F. C. Hull (Princeton, NJ: Princeton University Press, 1977), pp. 396, 397.

12. C. G. Jung, "Answer to Job" (1952), in *The Collected Works of C. G. Jung,* vol. 11, eds. Herbert Read, Michael Fordham, Gerhard Adler and William McGuire, trans. R. F. C. Hull (Princeton, NJ: Princeton University Press, 1969), § 735.

13. Carl Sagan, "To Avert a Common Danger," *Parade Magazine,* March 1992, pp. 10–12.

14. Dennis L. Merritt, *Jung and Ecopsychology* (2012), vol. 1 of *The Dairy Farmer's Guide to the Universe—Jung, Hermes, and Ecopsychology* (Carmel, CA: Fisher King Press), pp. 54–70.

15. Merritt, *Jung and Ecopsychology,* pp. 109–124.

16. Barbara Hannah, *Jung: His Life and Work* (Boston, MA: Shambhala, 1991), p. 17.

17. Peter Redgrove, *The Black Goddess and the Unseen Real* (New York: Grove Press, 1987), pp. xiv, xv, xviii–xxix.

18. Nancy Ryley, *The Forsaken Garden: Four Conversations of the Deep Meaning of Environmental Illness* (Wheaton, IL: Quest Books, 1998), pp. 207, 208.

19. Aldo Leopold, *A Sand County Almanac and Sketches Here and There* (New York: Oxford University Press, 1949), pp. 201–226.

20. Jung, *C. G. Jung Speaking,* p. 436.

21. C. G. Jung, "Return to the Simple Life" (1941), in CW 18, §§ 1343–1356.

22. Cassandra offended Apollo and was cursed with the gift of prophesy, but no one would believe her.

23. C. G. Jung, *Dream Analysis: Notes of the Seminar Given in 1928–1930 by C. G. Jung*, ed. W. McGuire (Princeton, NJ: Princeton University Press, 1984), pp. 538, 539, 542, 543.

24. *Citizens United* was a landmark 2010 Supreme Court decision that overturned decades of restrictions on corporations and unions from contributing unlimited funds to political campaigns, claiming the restrictions violate First Amendment rights of free speech. Corporations are considered to be a person in this regard. The 2012 elections were the first to experience the effects of the new law of the land.

25. David Adam, "Royal Society Tells Exxon: Stop Funding Climate Change Denial," *The Guardian*, Sept. 19, 2006. Accessed Nov. 24, 2012 at http://www.guardian.co.uk/environment/2006/sep/20/oilandpetrol.business; and George Monbiot, "The Denial Industry," *The Guardian*, Sept. 18, 2006. Accessed Nov. 24, 2012, at http://www.theguardian.com/environment/2006/sep/19/ethicalliving.g2.

26. Thomas Jennings and Doug Hamilton (producers), *Frontline: Money, Power and Wall Street, Part Four*. Transcript accessed on Nov. 24, 2012, at http://www.pbs.org/wgbh/pages/frontline/business-economy-financial-crisis/money-power-wall-street/transcript-19/.

27. C. G. Jung, "The Stages of Life" (1931), in CW 8, § 750. Prometheus was the Greek Titan who stole fire from the gods for human use, enabling progress and civilization. His punishment was to be chained to a rock and have his liver pecked out by an eagle, the emblem of Zeus. The liver grew back by the next day and was eaten again, a scenario eternally reenacted.

28. Merritt, *Jung and Ecopsyhology*.

29. Dennis L. Merritt, *The Cry of Merlin: Jung, the Prototypical Ecopsychologist*, vol. 2 of *The Dairy Farmer's Guide to the Universe—Jung, Hermes, and Ecopsychology* (Carmel, CA: Fisher King Press, 2012).

30. Dennis L. Merritt, *Hermes, Ecopsychology, and Complexity Theory*, vol. 3 of *The Dairy Farmer's Guide to the Universe—Jung, Hermes, and Ecopsychology* (Carmel, CA: Fisher King Press, 2012).

31. Dennis L. Merritt, *Land, Weather, Seasons, Insects: An Archetypal View*, vol. 4 of *The Dairy Farmer's Guide to the Universe—Jung, Hermes, and Ecopsychology* (Carmel, CA: Fisher King Press, 2013).

32. The Earth Charter Initiative, "The Earth Charter." Accessed on Nov. 24, 2102, at http://www.earthcharterinaction.org/content/pages/Read-the-Charter.html.

33. www.transitionnetwork.org.

CHAPTER SEVENTEEN

HOW THE TREASURE OF COMPARATIVE MYTHOGRAPHY WAS LOST IN LATE TWENTIETH-CENTURY HUMANITIES

John Davenport

Introduction: Comparative Mythography

This essay focuses on a *tradition* of scholarship and thought that Carl Jung helped to develop and popularize which began in the nineteenth century and influenced his own thought. My main concern is with the significance of this tradition for religious studies rather than with psychological theories more narrowly understood. The decline of this tradition and attention to its topics in comparative mythology affects theology, religious studies, psychology, philosophy, literature, and many other disciplines in the humanities and social sciences.

The tradition is often called *mythography*, which stands for the science or study of myths. But it might be better named *comparative symbolism* given its enormous subject matter. It includes not only the study of sacred myths from all cultures and comparisons of related religious rituals, practices, and beliefs, but also the study of symbols, motifs, and plot patterns in heroic legends, fairy tales, great epics, and related genres of modern literature (e.g., medieval romance, religious poetry, and fantasy novels), as well as the historical development of imagery in religious and secular artwork of many kinds. Mythography began in the mid-nineteenth century when the birth of scientific linguistics, ethnography, archeology (and other related human sciences), and the global reach of European empires led a new generation of scholars to translate ancient Eastern texts and to gather and write down oral legends and traditional stories from cultures all over the world. These methods were also applied in Europe, supplementing the expertise in classical Greek and Roman mythology that loomed large in Western academia and pedagogy with improved knowledge of medieval sagas and legends (many deriving from Norse mythology) and the *märchen* or oral traditions of fairy tales blending tropes from Mediterranean and Northern European origins. In addition to the brothers Grimm in Germany and Perrault in France, linguists like Andrew Lang collected tales from every far corner of Europe, as collections like his *Blue Fairy Book* and others in the same series exemplify.

Myth Theory

In addition to all these branches, the mythographic tradition developed at two levels. From the late nineteenth century, the vast work of recording, redacting, and compiling myths and tales (mythography in its initial sense) was complemented by a succession of major *theories* about the amazing commonalities in symbols and narrative patterns among myths, legends, fairy tales, and religious imagery from around the world—then including biblical stories. So James Frazer scandalized Europe with his *The Golden Bough* which argued that Jesus's death fits the pattern of sacrificing a sacred king for the renewal of the land's potency. Frazer denied offering a full "system of mythology" based on the worship of trees or crops and suggested that actually "fear of the human dead" was "the most powerful force in the making of primitive religion."[1] The main implications of his work, however, were that religion has a naturalistic origin in the instinctive need to ensure fertility, and the magic potency that early peoples descried in various objects and phenomena arises from primitive belief in *sympathy*: like can influence like. Many other naturalistic theories followed: Max Müller argued that Indian religion began through personification of natural forces and that the primary function of myth is *atieology*—a pseudo-explanation of mysterious natural phenomena (such as the cycle of the seasons) motivated by the lack of any scientific explanation by reference to underlying mechanisms.[2] Malinowski, followed by Durkheim and Levi-Strauss, argued that myth and symbolic narratives developed primarily to serve social functions, holding societies together and working out the complex relations of culture and nature. Sigmund Freud found the origin of much religious imagery and ritual in wish-fulfillment and guilt over the Oedipal complex—originally in a literal act of slaying a father-chief in order to gain access to his wives. Contemporary sociobiological theories of religion have followed this search for natural causes in evolutionary rather than psychological theory.

Jung's Theory

By contrast, Carl Jung's account of symbols found in myths, legends, art, and dreams is much less reductionist. His theory of the archetypes is often misread as a naturalist one because his concept of the *collective unconscious* seems at first to describe a completely immanent source of religious ideas. In an early work, where he seems to be trying to justify his interest in mythic symbolism, Jung writes, "the whole of astro-mythology is at bottom nothing but psychology. Myths never were and never are made consciously; they arise from man's unconscious."[3] He rejects atieological explanations as relying on a rationalizing thought-process that would surely have produced wider differences in results across geographic space and historical time. Although his early works often give sexual interpretations of major motifs and symbol complexes, Jung sees the need for unity among one's different psychic aspects (a natural eudaimonistic *telos* going well beyond basic biological drives) as the truly fundamental motive behind mythopoesis.

Moreover, at the metaphysical level, Jung seems to be a Kantian; he insists that the expressions of the archetypes that we find in the symbols of myth, fairy tale, religious art, and dreams are only *phenomena*, pointing back to the hidden noumena.

> Whenever we speak of religious contents, we move in a world of images that point to something ineffable. We do not know how clear or unclear these images, metaphors, and concepts are in respect of their transcendental object. ... There is no doubt that there is something behind these images that transcends consciousness and operates in such a way that the statements

[about it] do not vary limitlessly and chaotically, but clearly all
relate to a few basic principles or archetypes.⁴

Thus we do not see or intuit the *numinous archetypes* themselves; "all we can do is construct models of them" and note their emotional power.⁵ The collective unconscious is then like the realm of Plato's forms; it is an experience-transcending dimension of realities that function as innate ideas to which we have only imperfect access. And although we may go "deeper into ourselves" to find them, the contents of this realm are emphatically *not* attributable to "our personal psyche; indeed they feel almost outside the body." As Jung puts it, "The ego is Here and Now, but the outside-of-the-ego is an alien There, both earlier and later, before and after."⁶ In other words, we can call this realm of the archetypes a part of *consciousness* only if we use that term in its now unfamiliar Transcendentalist sense, referring to a kind of Mind above individual minds. Hence, the ultimate origin of the archetypes is a mystery that Jung's theory does not purport to explain.⁷

This humility is the basis for the anti-reductionist approach of perhaps the greatest mythographer in the tradition, Mircea Eliade. It is also notably similar to John Hick's ecumenical interpretation of God as the Noumena Real to which all the main representations in historical religions point—the *ultimate* that Hick and Jung both follow Jewish mystics in calling the *Ens realissimum* (the ultimate reality). (This agreement is not surprising, because Hick is one of only a few philosophers of religion to take full account of the findings of comparative mythography and to wrestle with their implications.)

All the theories arising in this golden age of modern mythography from the mid-nineteenth century until about 1970 are similar in one crucial respect: they are all structuralist in the general sense that they look to a single hypothesis or small set of sources, functions, or basic ideas to explain the astoundingly universal figures, images, and patterns discovered in such a diverse range of material reflecting the growth of religious thought and imagination from its earliest origins until at least the scientific revolution (and even to today in art, dreams, and novels). That is crucial in understanding why their influence has declined (at least in academic disciplines, if not in popular culture) and, as a result, why scholarly concern about *the data or findings* that these theories each hoped to explain has faded so dramatically since the golden era.⁸ For, unfortunately, in the humanities and the most closely related parts of the social sciences, once certain theories start to be regarded as *passé*, that is often assumed (by a non-sequitur) to indicate that even *the phenomena they were meant to explain* can now be conveniently ignored in favor of other problems or issues more in vogue.

The Agenda Set by the Comparative Data and its Influence

My thesis concerns this change of attitude towards the *comparative findings* of modern mythography or symbol studies as opposed to the major explanatory theories of this data and the rival schools of interpretation they produced, which I will not assess here. By *comparative findings*, I mean not only the raw data first presented by ethnographers, psychologists, and art historians, but the clear commonalities across space and over time that emerge from a suitable juxtaposition or comparative presentation of the raw data. This involves at least a simple structuring or schematizing of the first literal reports of the phenomena, but such a comparative schematizing is far short of a theory that aims to explain the causes, sources, or functions behind these emerging commonalities. The comparative findings are the indications of manifold connections, perhaps of multiple types or levels, for which any adequate theory of the origin of religion and the development of mythic imagery and motifs found in traditional stories (with no named author) would have to account. So understood, the comparative findings of mythography constitute an immense body of evidence developed during the golden age, much of it presented to diverse academic and literate public audiences in the same major theoretical works that sought to *explain* these findings. For example, Jung presents a tremendous number of examples from his diverse genres in the process of comparing them in order to support theoretical hypothesis.

These comparative findings are obviously more important than any of the theories about them, such as Jung's account of the archetypes or Eliade's account of the sacred and profane. To our predecessors, they constituted a mystery of the first order. The universals discovered were so striking (sometimes even staggering or incredible), the range of them so wide, and the number of instances of each so large, that it was understood by everyone involved that making sense of them was a task of the highest importance, much like finding the grand unified theory is in physics today.[9] Without understanding how these universals arose, we could not really understand what human persons are, how culture works and ideas develop over time, what the religious dimension of human life amounts to, and perhaps other things too (depending on the theory). For example, the correct explanation of the universals of mythography might explain how persons can develop good identities or at least healthy psyches, or the root nature of meaning itself, or the basic forms of literature, or the most fundamental or original sense of several basic concepts studied in philosophy and theology. The mystery of these findings relates to *the origin of virtually everything that the humanities are about.*

Accordingly, the enormous significance of this comparative data (and the influence of theories about them) was felt throughout the humanities and social sciences well beyond the first half of the twentieth century. Argument and theory at this level held a particular power because it was received as an attempt to explain one of the *fundamental issues* for all human knowledge, a solution to which would have profound implications for many other areas of study and interpretative work. Thus, it drew together leading researchers from disciplines as diverse as anthropology, religious studies, ethnography, psychology, classics, history, literary theory, and philosophy into dialogues that our own current interdisciplinarity fad cannot hope to rival. For example, through the generosity of Olga Froebe, leading European scholars from several fields—Henrich Zimmer, Carl Jung, Martin Buber, Erich Neumann, and many others—gathered each year near Lake Maggiore in Switzerland to exchange finds. These Eranos conferences, and the resulting *Eranos Jahrbücher*, left future generations a treasure trove of comparative analyses; they provided the basis for Joseph Campbell's multimillion bestseller, *The Hero with a Thousand Faces*, which was perhaps the high point of this whole movement as part of popular culture (in the US at least).[10] Some of the best Eranos essays were translated and reprinted in six volumes of the famous and massive Bollingen Series, which published the works of Carl Jung in English, along with many other twentieth-century classics in comparative mythography, philosophy, and some works on art and literature. Produced by Princeton, it may be the most important single series of works ever sponsored by a philanthropic foundation. The Board room at Princeton University Press used to have a shelf containing the entire series, starting with the massive folio original of *When Two Come in the Name of the Father*, a volume on Native American sand painting. To see them all together, and try to imagine the sheer range of discoveries recorded therein, was a truly awe-inspiring, humbling experience.

It is widely assumed today, partly because of scientists like Richard Dawkins who know little of the history of ideas, that theories of evolution and biology, in general, were the main causes of modern doubts about religious beliefs so widely accepted in earlier centuries. Sometimes, Freud is grudgingly added as a second major force in this social change; however, I suggest that the findings and theories of comparative mythography were an even more profound source of doubt, for they altered the whole gestalt in which biblical stories were received and interpreted. Nietzsche (who influenced Freud) read new evolutionary ideas, but he was moved first and most deeply by studying myths from the viewpoint of the *new linguistics* of his time (and Schopenhauer's version of Hinduism); this was how he first came to the ideas of a slave morality, systems of rank, a sense of the sacred associated with cosmogonic power, and of course the figure of "Zarathustra" with his eschatological vision (inverted into an earlier cyclic paradigm in Nietzsche's own myth). Also, the biological theories that impressed Nietzsche did so mostly from the perspective of *vitalism*, which owed much to mythographic work at the time on *mana* and *orenda*. So it was that modern doubts about theological doctrines began more from the study of the *Vedas, Avestas,* and *Upanishads* than from Darwin.

The rejection of dogma, however, could still leave a sense of the transcendent or belief in divinity intact. Various mythographers offered naturalistic theories of the origin of religion on cultural or psychological (not evolutionary) bases, but Jung and many of his *Eranos* associates helped keep open other possible interpretations of cross-cultural universals. Although, to Nietzsche, the comparative evidence shattered old creeds of monotheistic religion, Pietist thinkers like Martin Buber were able to take such findings in a new spiritual direction.[11] Jung's work inspired developments in humanistic and existential psychology as well as the whole New Age movement. In literature, the study of mythology led to a new appreciation of medieval romance and even a new respect for Northern European (Norse) mythology and legends that had long been sidelined by the preference among Classics scholars for Mediterranean myth, art, and literature. Through the singular genius of Tolkien and a related circle of other religious authors, all versed in the data flowing from the *mythographic revolution* and highly resistant to naturalistic or reductive explanations of it, the entire genre of twentieth-century fantasy literature was born. In universities across the developed world, and perhaps especially in English-speaking nations, courses were offered with increasing frequency on mythology, folklore, children's literature, fantasy literature, comparative religious studies focused on religious symbolism, and Jungian psychology (and structuralist theorizing about these topics was ubiquitous). Rare was the non-science major who did not read the *Enuma Elish* or *Gilgamesh* and reflect on their implications for the nature of the Self or their similarities to certain biblical narratives.

How the Vast Comparative Findings of the Mythographic Revolution were Forgotten

Then something happened. During the 1980s, courses teaching primary myths and introducing students to the comparative findings of mythography waned. I do not think this was due to changes in student demand; when I was an undergraduate in the late 1980s, there was still strong student interest in such courses. Rather, scholarly interests shifted, and it was no longer the case that any aspiring scholar in religious studies, anthropology, or psychology needed to grapple with the comparative findings of mythography. I was surprised to meet a religion major at Yale in 1989 who, despite being an A-student, knew *nothing* of Jung's or Eliade's works and had not even heard of the term *eschatology*. Within continental philosophy as well, despite its focus on social dynamics and historical development, virtually no one now has even an elementary knowledge about the comparative data of mythography; it does not even occur to them to worry about it.[12] If they have even heard of the subject, they think of it as a superficial backwater of holistic thought worth no more serious scholarly attention than Wicca.

Why this happened is a large question that is not only unanswered, but even unasked. It seems to disturb hardly any teachers in humanities that a vast body of knowledge has just been forgotten, leaving the great questions it raised now largely ignored. How could an entire intellectual revolution lasting over a century simply be forgotten? This strange impoverishment was not a mere result of intellectual fashion, as if the comparative study of symbol and motif simply went out of vogue; in my view, it has three deeper causes.

First, writers involved in the postmodern turn often regarded the data on comparative symbolism as part of a *structuralist* anthropological method that they had somehow refuted (though they never bothered to address any of the classic works of comparative mythography beyond a few comments on Levi-Strauss). They found it easier to focus on issues of method, rejecting structuralist anthropology in abstract, rather than to come to grips with so enormous a body of results. Although Derrida famously refers to metaphysics as "white mythology" (i.e., pale, washed out mythology), by *myth* he only means Nietzsche's "mobile army of metaphors," not a body of stories with universal meanings that partly transcend the web of mythic signs.[13] Comparative cross-cultural similarities belie the extreme claims that Derrideans wished to make for *difference*; the potentially universal significance of some mythic figures is so clear a threat to post-structuralist dogmas that it was more convenient to push it out of view since refuting this challenge head-on would have required coming up with a rival theory to explain vast ranges of empirical evidence. Moreover, for many academics after WWII, an interest in mythology had become more suspect because so many fascist intellectuals tried to make use of Germanic myth. Thus, the most influential continental philosopher of the second half the twentieth century, Emmanuel Levinas, dismisses mythology as archaic mysticism, lacking the transcendence found in immediate encounter with the personality of others; although he appeals to "eschatology," it is a messianic ideal free of taint by any "positive religion."[14] For all the value of his ethical conception of alterity, he did not share Buber's reverence for pre-biblical spirituality, nor Rudolph Otto's recognition that religious symbolism records the human experience of an even more profound type of encounter with ultimate mystery, including promised eschatological goods.[15]

Second, while comparative mythology flourished despite the rise of logical positivist dogma in philosophy, analytic philosophy of religion began to revive in the 1970s by focusing on conceptual analysis and Christian tenets without much attention to the history of Christianity, let alone other religions across the world. Thus, at Notre Dame in the 1990s—the first home of such contemporary philosophy of religion—I vividly recall one very bright graduate student (from a Calvinist background), who is now a tenured professor, telling me that we could ignore all religion before Judaism because that was all just "devil worship." Analytic philosophers of religion now pay more attention to the history of Western philosophy, but most still see comparative religion as having little philosophical significance as their harsh rejections of Hick's religious inclusivism indicate.

Third, with the advent of cognitive psychology and advances in brain sciences, new and apparently more scientific approaches became possible in the areas of social science that had previously been interested in comparative sociology of rituals, myths, symbols, and fairy tales. Although bits of Jung's theories survived, e.g., in the typology of personality traits that was further developed in the Myers-Briggs type inventory, the central theory of the archetypes, with its apparent innatism, came to be regarded as mere untestable speculation. But in turning away from such *theories* within the comparative mythology/structuralist anthropology genre, practitioners forgot that the massive body of comparative findings was still highly important in its own right. Or perhaps they passed the buck, expecting folklorists in anthropology and colleagues in humanities to continue working on these findings in new theories of the development of myth, ritual, heroic sagas and fairy tales, and related art works. But scholars in the humanities, and especially in comparative literature, had come to regard comparative studies aimed at disclosing universal structures as outdated. Particularity, contingency, and embodiment, especially of *marginalized others*, is the privileged topic de jour; and anything smacking of Platonism is disdained as a vestige of colonialism (which, after all, taints the origins of modern mythographic studies).

This illustrates one tragic way in which paradigm-shifts in humanities are different from those in the sciences. There is much less cumulative development and memory of the main problems on scholarly agendas in the humanities; one movement tends to eclipse those before it entirely, like fads in clothing fashion (but without the vintage shops). Eliade himself suggested in *The Two and the One* that declining attention to the problems of mythography is due to increasing academic specialization, which makes large-scale, comparative work seem impossible to do with sufficient rigor. This is partly right, but still too generous. Rather, largely for *ideological* reasons, a crucial body of findings produced by scholarship in anthropology and religious studies has mostly slipped into oblivion. These findings, which may seriously challenge many dominant views regarding meaning, knowledge, and the significance of fundamental religious concepts, have fallen off the radar screen.

The effects of this decline on different areas of inquiry and popular culture are profound. To take just one example, Richard Dawkins offers a naturalistic account alleging that religion somehow evolves from natural selection because it helps promote group loyalties. His influential account does not consider Jung, Levi-Strauss, Eliade, Propp, Campbell, Zimmer, Buber, Otto, or Hick; he starts from a more simplistic concept of the religious phenomena that he hopes to explain. This makes the job easier for such sociobiological theories because the mythographic data suggest that religion developed through the persistence of certain basic *ideas* that seem to have no obvious source in sense-experience or evident survival advantage relative to other non-religious bases for kin loyalty. In short, sociobiological theorists of religion have almost no idea what primary religion actually was: they quite literally do not know *what* they are talking about, i.e., their purported subject-matter. Dawkins could not have gotten away with this in 1960.

Conclusion

Our challenge now is to renew attention to an enormous body of work that seriously calls into question many dominant views regarding the relations of meaning, symbol, metaphor, universal concepts, the formation of personal identity, and even alleged naturalistic origins of religion in general. We should all consider how serious work on comparative mythography could be revived in the humanities, how it could contribute to philosophy of religion and debates about the origin of religion, and how it might challenge the dominance of deconstructive views in literary studies.[16] The time is ripe for another paradigm-shift in which more global forms of shared religious consciousness become possible, beyond the alleged incommensurabilities of the postmodern view. Thankfully, what is said through myth, fairy tales, and their symbols—the most important part of which can be said in no other way—is no artificial construct of theory, but something of perennial significance that cannot be erased from human minds by the inattention of academics.

NOTES

1. See James Frazer, *The Golden Bough*, abr. ed. (1922; repr., Aylesbury and London: Hazell, Watson, and Viney Ltd., 1949).

2. An extreme example of this atieological story-form would be the *Just So Stories* of Rudyard Kipling.

3. C. G. Jung, *Freud and Psychoanalysis*, vol. 4, *The Collected Works of C. G. Jung,* ed. and trans. R. F. C. Hull (Princeton, NJ: Princeton University Press, 1970), § 477.

4. C. G. Jung, *Answer to Job*, CW 11, § 555. Jung's conception of the noumenal archetypes seems to be influenced by Leibniz's conception of innate ideas as patterns built into the individual essences of all things which embed each of their unique relations to everything else (each *mirrors* the whole from a unique viewpoint). In mental beings, these patterns will be manifested mostly as subconscious *apperceptions* that influence the shape of more conscious perceptions. Leibniz's monadology is a holistic metaphysics that would make a genuinely collective unconscious possible. And the monads seem to have been the model for Kant's noumena, so the similarity is not accidental.

5. Jung, CW 11, § 555.

6. C. G. Jung, *Mysterium Coniunctionis*, CW 14, § 410.

7. Jung even employs an analogy from quantum mechanics for this: "the very act of observation," or attempt at rational interpretation, "alters the object observed. Consequently there is at present no way of determining the real nature of the unconscious"; see Jung, *Mysterium Coniunctionis*, § 88.

8. I call 1850–1970 a golden era in part because of its amazing interdisciplinarity, as detailed below.

9. For example, consider the steps by which we can connect the archetype of the dragon with its separable head and tail, the witch figure (often sporting a head that can turn 360 degrees as if it were a separable part), the trickster archetype found in so many Native American myths, and the joker or fool—often depicted with clown-

like expressions mimicking those of archaic Mediterranean gorgons (some of which had snake-hair). At each junction, we have instances where at least two of the variations are depicted together in pottery, sculpture, drawings, etc., or are narratively linked, thus confirming their connections which spread out to form a web of interrelated symbols.

10. See the detailed history in William McGuire, *Bollingen: An Adventure in Collecting the Past* (Princeton, NJ: Princeton University Press, 1982), especially pp. 141–143.

11. See, e.g., Martin Buber, "Symbolic and Sacramental Existence in Judaism," in Joseph Campbell, ed., *Spiritual Disciplines*, vol. 4, *Papers from the Eranos Yearbooks* (Princeton, NJ: Princeton University Press, 1960): 168–185.

12. Last year we interviewed three leading scholars for a senior position in continental philosophy of religion. Only one of them knew anything of Jung or Eliade's work; the term *hierophany* meant nothing to the others. This is not to criticize them; they are all excellent scholars. It simply reflects the state of their field.

13. See Derrida, "White Mythology," in *Margins of Philosophy*, trans. Alan Bass (Chicago, IL: University of Chicago Press, 1985). I think Derrida's central error lies in assuming that *either* the "entire tropic system" of associations between words that we see in metaphors and etymologies determines the only meaning that words and symbols can have, *or* metaphorical and symbolic expressions are merely *ornaments* next to the pure ideas they are used to convey (pp. 221–223). Most mythographers would reject this as a false dichotomy. Moreover, ironically, Derrida's signature "concept of *différance*" seems to be derived from Plato's third-man paradox—see his reflections on "the metaphor of metaphor" (pp. 219–220).

14. Emmanuel Levinas, *Totality and Infinity*, trans. Alphonso Lingus (Pittsburgh, PA: Duquesne University Press, 1969), p. 23.

15. See Rudolph Otto, *The Idea of the Holy*, 2nd ed., trans. John Harvey (New York: Oxford University Press, 1958), pp. 34–38. Otto sees reductive-naturalistic mythographies as a "rationalization of religion" that are unable to account for the aspect of "mystery" found in the experience of divinity across cultures (p. 27).

16. I hold out some hope that this rebirth may be prompted by the publication of E. J. Michael Witzel's book *The Origin of the World's Mythologies*.

Chapter Eighteen

Walking the Streets
Non-Jungian Reflections on the Jungian Subject

Gustavo Beck

> ... let us keep our city on its feet.
> We dwell not only in rooms behind doors,
> in chairs at tables, at jobs behind counters.
> We dwell on earth also in the freedom
> of the legs that give freedom to the mind.
> —James Hillman, "Walking"

A Warning

Although this text will speak about the Jungian subject, none of the subjects involved in it are Jungian in the strict sense of the term; furthermore, whether or not they can be qualified as subjects or not depends very much on our epistemological frame of reference. It must be said, in fact, that this essay, in general, lacks any philosophical rigor in its usage of either concept. I, the writer of this text, am probably close to being Jungian, but I am not a Jungian. I read Jungian books, attend Jungian analysis and supervision, and discuss frequently Jungian ideas. I even indulge in certain practices which could be labeled as Jungian: I write down my dreams, exercise active imagination, and often use words like *archetype*, *psyche*, or *symbol*. Still, I have no formal training as a Jungian, neither as an analyst nor as a scholar. It is somewhat interesting that my friends and colleagues (and some of my students and even patients—in spite of my clarifications) do think of me as a Jungian. Of course, I am, after all, writing this for a Jungian audience—I expect this to be read by Jungians. The confusion is understandable. This is why it is important to insist: *I am not a Jungian.* My undergraduate degree is in psychology and my graduate degree in mythology; formally speaking, my Jungian training is, at best, indirect—enthusiastic but oblique, engaged but off the record, intense but unceremonious.

Perhaps quasi-Jungian papers like this one (and quasi-Jungian authors like myself) may find some solace in words written by a much more Jungian subject. In a recent paper, Thomas Kirsch stated that "the meanings of the word Jungian have expanded as Jung was read by a wider than purely clinical and insider audience."[1] "The word Jungian," Kirsch says, "is bandied about freely, as if it communicates something that as Jungians we immediately understand."[2] I confess that I am part of that wider audience which Kirsch talks about. Therefore, it is extremely likely that the word *Jungian* will be bandied in this text. Perhaps it will emerge more than appears necessary, although not so much because of an assumption regarding anything it might communicate, but rather as a result of the anxiety that this non-Jungian author experiences at the lack of referents when it comes to defining the term *Jungian*.

Regarding the term *subject*, I will keep using it somewhat capriciously simply because it services my argument. It is comfortable, and it will have all of us academics thinking that we know what we are talking about, that this thing that we are talking about is intellectually relevant, and that, even if we do not agree on what a subject is, we remain on the same page. My intention, of course, is to raise the possibility that we are not on the same page, neither as Jungians nor as academics—much less as Jungian academics. And as for the rest of the *subjects* mentioned in the essay (particularly my patients, my students, and my country), they are not Jungian or academic subjects either. I would much rather describe both them and myself as non-Jungian fellows, comrades, or even pals, but I will refrain from such a language for the time being because I am afraid that it might be frowned upon in a serious academic-Jungian conversation.

So there: consider yourselves warned about my non-Jungian status. The words I write today, although ambitious and perhaps even irreverent in their attempt at voicing their puzzlement, are modest and realistic about their possible place in the Jungian academic discourse. This is more the voice of an audience member raising his hand to ask a question than that of a scholar providing an educated answer to such question. Still, some questions must be asked—so let my hand rise, even if timidly so.

The Message

Warning issued, we move to the basic premise underlying this essay. The message is in fact so simple that it can be summarized in three words: *something feels wrong*. When I, the non-Jungian member of the audience, read contemporary Jungian literature and witness contemporary Jungian practice (particularly clinical practice), it becomes difficult to respond with words other than these: *something feels wrong*. This affirmation is the single cornerstone of any question posed by this essay, and thus will permeate every sentence of the text. *What* is the something that feels wrong? I do not know. *How* would I describe the feeling of wrongness? I am not sure. *Why* is this feeling qualified as wrong? It is impossible for me to say.

Still, I wish to use this as my starting point, for in spite of my utter ignorance about its nature, my wording does carry with it what I would describe as a passionate intentionality, and this should be acknowledged. To begin with, although I am in the dark about the *what*, *how*, and *why* of this something feeling wrong, I am absolutely clear about its *when*. The uneasiness that pushes me to express my feeling and to ask my questions arises precisely in the moment when all that I have read, wrote, discussed, and practiced, as a quasi-Jungian subject, comes into contact with my everyday life, particularly with my socio-historical context. The phenomenon that takes place when anything I have gathered about concepts such as symbol, individuation, transference, archetype, or the unconscious, enters the arena of my daily life (the newspapers, discussions on politics or economics, my weekly trip to the supermarket) can only be articulated by these three simple words that I will stubbornly reiterate: *something feels wrong*.

Note that I deliberately use the vague word *something*, purposely resort to the emotionally inclined verb *to feel*, and warmly welcome the value judgment that comes along when we qualify something as *wrong*. Yes, deliberately. I do not know why I put these words together, but it seems important to put them together, and thus I *want* to put them together, write them down, speak them up, and articulate them in front of a Jungian audience. This last aspect, the articulation, is what is most important in my passionate intentionality; what my autonomous determination wants is to tie together the vague something with the conscious feeling with the value of wrongness—most importantly, probably, it wants to make this tying together openly and explicitly. It desires for this *something that feels wrong* about what is Jungian to be set loose and felt in a public Jungian environment. What this text and this author want to do, in short, is to protest.

The Protest

The protest I wish to subscribe to today, however, is not just any type of protest, but empty protest, *kenosis,* which was described quite richly by James Hillman as the protest in which "you take your outrage seriously, but you don't force yourself to have answers."[3] This text, then, wishes to protest from within uncertainty; it wishes to be bold in its timidity. The hand that rises to ask the question might be shy and is certainly young, but it is also indignant and determined. Although I have insisted in separating myself from *being* Jungian, it is quite obvious that as a psychologist, and as an individual, I do have a connection with Jungian theory. I do not have a specific agenda, but my feeling of wrongness is crystal clear. The fury that fuels this text comes from the frustration that rises from muteness, from the feeling that Jungian theory—more specifically, Jungian theorists—either have nothing to say about contemporary social, economic, and historical issues, or simply choose to remain silent. Completely surrounded by armed conflicts, revolutionary movements, and social injustice, I find the shyness of Jungian contemporary theory to be inexcusably irresponsible. It feels wrong, as plain as that.

I shall not apologize for the visceral character of this protest, because what a protest such as this needs the most is to be unapologetic. Outrage has to be enounced with grounding humility, but also with fierce resolve. And the outrage expressed in this text, we must not forget, is aimed not only at psychological theory, but also at clinical practice. This author is raving against psychotherapy in general and at Jungian psychotherapy in particular, especially against the apparent lack of responsiveness from the part of Jungian praxis when facing contemporary socio-historical conditions. Save some exceptions, analytical psychology's systematic advocacy in favor of introversion and fantasy tends to alienate Jungian theory and practice from everyday social dynamics, particularly from public life. *Something feels wrong about this.* Jungian theory seems to isolate whomever it touches from everyday living—and the deeper the touch, the deeper the isolation. One of the things that feels wrong about the Jungian subject, in short, is its obsession with privacy, intimacy, innerness, and the corollary split from community that this engenders.

Such tendency towards inwardness, reflection, and individuality is of course not exclusive of Jungian psychology, but since this text is written for a Jungian audience, I shall circumscribe the problem to Jungians. It should also be acknowledged that this inclination is not accidental; it certainly has its purpose and its logic, and it is grounded in very elaborate theoretical principles such as individuation, complex theory, the Self, or the symbolic quality of life. The fact that it has a purpose, however, does not deny the fact that it also casts a shadow, and part of this shadow is a disconnection from the societal structures and historical contexts that surround these very elaborate concepts. Sometimes Jungian subjects, Jungian texts, and Jungian discourse, seem to perceive themselves as being outside of history and immune to contemporary social and economic systems. I want to emphasize here that this is not really an issue of Jung, but more an issue of Jungians, or of certain undercurrents of Jungian thought and practice. Andrew Samuels quotes Jung to illustrate how the initiator of Jungian thought himself, in fact, advises us to be mindful of historical context: "The psychologist cannot avoid coming to grips with contemporary history," said Jung, "even if his very soul shrinks from the political uproar, the lying propaganda, and the jarring speeches of the demagogues."[4]

I want to follow Samuels and push this statement somewhat further. "It is suspicious," Samuels states, "that depth psychologists concerned with the public sphere have not paid much attention to *themselves* as a cultural phenomenon."[5] What becomes crucial for me, as a non-Jungian subject who is interested in Jungian theory, is for Jungian psychology to *go public*. By this I mean that Jungian thought should step out of its habitual milieus, its usual safe spaces (the institutes, the reading groups, the consulting room, the workshops), and venture into everyday contemporary life: the life that happens in the city, in politics, in the markets, the parks, the prisons, the streets. And then, once it has gone public, I dare Jungian theory to remain silent; I challenge it to not protest and to remain in the margin. Let us see if muteness, shyness, or innerness can prevail then.

Furthermore, Jungian theory might benefit from stepping out of its usual frames of reference. If Jungian practice wants to come to its own, it needs to face the outer world as well as the inner. And the outer world is mostly non-Jungian. Jungian psychology, particularly in its practice and its community, tends to be too endogamic, incestuous, and close-minded. There is no confronting ourselves without confronting otherness, and it seems like due time for Jungian psychology to confront both. Hillman speaks about this encounter with the Other: "When you're with another person you're out of yourself because the other person is flowing into you and you are flowing into them, there are surprises, you're a little out of control."[6] That is what Jungian theory and Jungian subjects need: surprises, to be a little out of control.

The true surprises for Jungians, however, are to be found outside of themselves and certainly outside of their usual theoretical mindset. Jungian analyst Paul Kugler tells us how "Jung's most important contribution to the history of the subject in Western thought is his realization, as early as the 1920s, that within the personality there is not one, but two subjects."[7] "This superordinate other," Kugler says, "Jung called the self."[8] There is no time here to enter into deep discussion about the Jungian concept of the Self, but for the purposes of this essay it is important to say that this concept tends, *practically*, to send the Jungian subject in one of two directions: either into transcendence or into inner life (psychic experiences which may sometimes, in fact, coincide). Very seldom, however, does this notion of Self situate the Jungian subjects in the actual world where they live, in their social structures, their economic interactions, and their historical contexts. Perhaps, in fact, instead of speaking of Jungian subjects, I should shift to the term Jungian *Selves*. Yes! This is what this text is protesting against: Jungian Selves. Not the Jungian notion of Self, but the actual Jungian Selves that such a concept generates in people's everyday activities. It is these Selves that maintain Jungian subjects immersed in their own inner world or enthralled in transcendental autonomous fantasies. Jungian Selves are so familiar with inner or transcendental otherness, with interior multiplicity and with other-worldly tensions, that if they want to look for surprises they have to look for them not within but without, not beyond them but around them.

So that is my protest: *Jungians, come out of your Selves!*

Yes, Jungians, come out of yourselves. Come out of your books, your conferences, your consulting rooms, and your concepts. You know them too well. Come out and meet the world as it presents itself and not as Jungians read it. I am a non-Jungian Jungian, but I do have a Jungian Self, and writing this text is my coming out of it. For this protest is also against my own self (Self?). I am, after all, a clinical psychologist (and one that is influenced, yes, by Jung); therefore, I am as much in need of a Self-protest as is any Jungian. I protest against my Self for being a psychotherapist, I protest against my Self for embodying and acting out Jungian shadows, I protest against my Self because I took the time to come to this conference, because I invested energy in writing this paper, and because in spite of my fury I am impertinent and frivolous enough to read it to you. I protest against my protest, because my protest feels domesticated by psychological academy and psychotherapeutic practice; and I protest even more ravenously because, in spite of this domestication, the protest still feels important. This is *not* false modesty allied with *puer* reactivity; it is a professional reality-check induced by very real rage. "Therapy blocks this kind of protest," said James Hillman,

> it does not let these 'negative' emotions have their full say. Self-knowledge is the point of the emotions and the protest, not public awareness. Know *thyself*, know what you are doing before you know the issue, and know the meaning of an action before you act. Otherwise you are projecting and acting out.[9]

In spite of my discomfort, however, today I choose to articulate my protest. Firstly, as I said before, it feels necessary. Secondly, and most importantly, I have already protested in a much more concrete way. My protest, I am afraid to say, has been acted out already. Yes, acted out—in my clinical practice, several months ago.

An Inversion

I have spent several pages explaining my personal and theoretical position, but it is time now to stop explaining positions and begin describing what in fact happened. The essay I am reading is quite straightforward and practical; my intention is simply to share with you the experience of a walk I had through the streets of my hometown, Mexico City, as well as how such a walk came to existence. The walk took place on May 23, 2012 and involved, directly, only me and another person. Indirectly, however, it involved many more. That evening, my companion and I marched alongside thousands of other people during a protest against media manipulation in the Mexican presidential election. Most importantly for our discussion, this person who walked with me is my patient, and we walked together for exactly fifty-five minutes, the time usually allotted to his weekly therapy session within the walls of my office. This is what I have come to tell you: five months ago, a patient of mine and I walked the streets of our city, and we protested together against what we both perceived to be grave social injustice. We marched and voiced our shared sense of frustration. We laughed, spoke, yelled, and sang together out in the open: clinical sacrilege. The office walls were breached, the alchemical vessel was broken, the transference-countertransference dynamic was contaminated by everyday, social and political life. Quite irregular, I know.

Happily, irregularities do appear consistently in this story. So at least we have that. Usually, a paper like this would start with some clinical context, it would move from the logic of the consulting room to the logic of the streets. It would probably include some sketch of my patient's family history, his symptoms, diagnosis, and treatment plan. Most importantly, probably, it would delve into the transference and countertransference elements that are evidently present in our relationship. It would ask why a move like this made sense therapeutically, how this fits into the patient's usual behavioral patterns or emotional conflicts, or how the therapist is acting out this or that projection.

All this exists and is present in the process; my therapist quasi-Jungian Self is well aware of it and addresses it in the proper spaces for it. But this paper, strictly speaking, is not clinical, and thus does not need or want to explain itself clinically. Such an approach would again start from within, and what we wish to do today, let us remember, is to start from without. This paper cares little for my patient's psychological structure, the therapeutic relationship, or my countertransference as a clinician—all that shall remain within office walls. My starting point here is not the individual psychic realities that those walls are holding, but the social and political dynamics which hold those walls. Allow me to provide some outer, social context and describe the actual setting in which this particular psychotherapy was taking place at that time. And do not forget: this is still a case history, it is simply told from the outside-in.

A Spark, a Movement, and a Walk

In May of 2012, the Mexican presidential election was at its final stretch. Enrique Peña Nieto, candidate for the once all-mighty PRI party and who was heading the polls, visited the university where I teach—Universidad Iberoamericana—in order to give a talk. At the end of it, he was confronted by a group of students. Young people raised their hands to ask about Peña Nieto's handling of the Atenco crisis when he was governor of the State of Mexico. This case, according to the finding of the National Human Rights Commission, resulted in 207 victims of cruel, inhuman, or degrading treatment, 145 arbitrary arrests, 26 sexually assaulted women, and 5 foreigners illegally expelled from the country.[10]

Peña Nieto's response to the question was confident and resolute. Its content is somewhat secondary for the purposes of this text, so suffice it to say that it was received quite positively by some members of the audience and quite negatively by others—some perceived it as imbued with authority, others saw in it shades of oppression. The latter group started to heckle Peña Nieto in disagreement. The candidate was literally pursued on his way out of the university by hundreds of discontented students—his exit was somewhat rushed and not precisely elegant. All this was recorded and almost immediately reached social media. Many soon condemned the reaction of the students, which was minimized and characterized as belonging to a non-representative minority. Some politicians even questioned if those who had raised their voices were actually students or simply troublemakers sent by the opposition.

It was this interpretation that lit the fire. The young people who had protested at the university felt insulted by the response that the candidate gave to their question (the reply certainly did not satisfy them), but it was predictable and very much within Peña Nieto's usual discourse. What offended them most profoundly (and eventually moved them into action), however, was the subsequent trivialization of the issues they raised and the disdain with which their actions were handled by politicians and media. The fact that their status as students was put into question and that their collective voice was muted with insinuations of political manipulations was far worse for them than the rehearsed answer they received as a response to their original inquiry.

I happened to know several of the young people who protested that day. Many of them were my students. It was quite clear that, at the time, their protest was quite spontaneous and organic. There was no clear group identity or political ideology behind their dissent. They were certainly being political, in the sense that they were publicly voicing their views. But when this initial spark was ignited there was no particular political idea driving the students. Perhaps some individuals had clear political views, but *as a group*, they did not ask their question using, as a starting point, any specific ideological or political positioning. Much like me at the beginning of this essay, they simply *felt that something was wrong* and acted upon it. They sensed something, gathered around that sense, and gave it a voice. Subsequently, of course, the movement aligned itself with different political institutions and organizations. This paper, however, will not explore such developments either. This text is not about clinical psychology, but it is not about political science either. The only objective of this article is to defend that instant when something stirs and begins to move: the moment when the spark lights up, the bubble bursts, the inner and the outer come into contact, and a group of people, sensing that *something feels wrong*, decides to protest against it, publicly and communally.

What happened after this first moment was rather curious. Once the students started to sense that something was wrong, they organized themselves and, through the internet, created an eleven minute video in which 131 students appeared with their university identity cards, stating their names and student account numbers. "I am not a rioter; I am a student. No one trained me for anything." is what they said.[11] They simply wanted to reply to the politicians who had insinuated that they were not students and had been infiltrated as artificial rebels. The result was a video that went viral on YouTube, in which the students ratified their individual identities, but did so collectively. The video raised so much commotion that it soon began a social movement called #másde131 ("more than 131") and then #YoSoy132 ("I am 132"). The movement (along with the sense of something being wrong) grew quickly. The hashtag became the top trending topic on Twitter worldwide and remained there for several days. Soon several universities joined and, on May 18, a protest was organized. The protesters walked from Universidad Iberoamericana to Televisa, one of Mexico's most important television networks. The protest had the objective of denouncing the biases of mainstream media in the coverage of the election. These biases, of course, had been now experienced by the students themselves in the treatment given to the story that narrated the events that took place at their university.

It is crucial here to draw a parallel: just as I am not a Jungian, these protesters were not politicians. My words have psychological charge and involve psychological theory; their protests were of course political and had political consequences—but neither am I attempting to be a Jungian in my protest against Jungians, nor did they try to be politicians in their protest against politicians. The argument of this essay is that, although constructing psychological and political systems requires much skill and training, every human being is involved in both psychology and in politics, for any human being has both an inner and a public life. Not everyone is a psychologist or a politician, but any person's life is psychological and political. We, therefore, owe it to our Selves, and to other Selves, to respect our psychological and political senses. Hence, when *something feels wrong*, either within or without, this something, this feeling, and this wrongness should be addressed, both psychologically and politically.

Returning to our central story, by the time of this first protest, I was quite aware about the YoSoy132 movement. Several of my students were involved, and they updated me continuously about what they were doing. I also had two patients who played active parts in the movement (one of them was the patient with whom I walked), so I had a very strong sense of something moving and, of this movement generating some sort of connection between people. This patient, (whom we shall call John), in fact, asked me if we could change the session that week, because he had to attend some YoSoy132 organizational meetings. We switched our therapeutic session and saw each other Friday the 18th at 8 a.m., right before the first protest.

During that session, John told me that YoSoy132 was organizing a larger protest for May 23. This date coincided with our next session, and it so happened that the actual time of the protest coincided with our usual therapy hour. We had been talking about his involvement in the social movement for two sessions and I had kept a restrained attitude, although at times it was difficult to hide my enthusiasm. After the protest on March 18, it became clear to me that this enthusiasm was more than mere transference or personal political inclination; it had psychological elements, but it also involved real social aspects—something in the fabric of my country was starting to move. It was not only me who was moved by YoSoy132, and my being moved did not circumscribe exclusively to my therapeutic relationship with John. The outer and the inner were interpenetrating each other in more ways than one, and I anticipated the possibility of somehow participating in the movement. On Monday's session John was quite excited about the outcome of the first protest; he felt that something was "finally happening," and that "people were eager to be a part of it." There was a clear sense of momentousness. Something here was bigger than us, and this feeling encompassed both our unfathomable psychological depths and our unexplainable social context.

There was no way of confining this phenomenon to Jungian theory. This was not exclusively (not even mainly) about transference, inner conflict, individual neurosis, or individuation. This was, if you pardon my blasphemy, bigger than the Self—certainly bigger than the Jungian Self. And it was bigger than the Self because it was much smaller than the Self. It was much humbler, much more grounded, much more mundane. John, eager and shy, suggested something to me: "What if we do an 'out of the box' session? Why don't we have our next therapy hour during the protest?" My response did not require further inner reflection at the time. I had already thought this out carefully and discussed it with other clinicians, so I agreed almost instantly and simply set some rules. We were to meet at the usual time, and I would simply follow his lead during the fifty-five minutes of his therapy hour. Whatever happened during those fifty-five minutes would be his session. After that time, we would shake hands and part ways until next week.

We did meet. And our fifty-five-minute experimental session was indeed full of surprises. Thousands of people responded to the call for protest, not only in Mexico City but also all over the country. What had begun as a question in a university auditorium had turned into a nationwide social movement. In the midst of this ocean of people who danced and sang and screamed catchphrases against media manipulation, my patient and I were about to have a therapeutic hour.

Of course we did not talk about what we usually talked. We could hardly even talk. There was a lot of noise, people interrupted continuously, and we had to keep walking. We were not alone. We were not isolated. The city was there. Our fellow citizens were there and they demanded our attention. The inner work we had been devoted to for so long was now being called to break out of its innerness. We had barely walked fifty yards when a young man approached us. He was a student from a public university and was doing some research about the movement. He requested an interview and we gave it to him. He asked why we were there, why we felt the movement was important, and what we thought its place was in the Mexican scenario. We answered, and then we walked the street. Neither of us mentioned that we were patient and therapist, or that this was in fact our therapy hour. As we walked, we talked intermittently, some friends of John's joined us, and we ran into a student of mine and then into a man in his late sixties who thanked us (the young people) for giving him some hope in what had been for him times of despair. Things like these happened for fifty-five minutes. The world happened for fifty-five minutes. Life happened for fifty-five minutes. After this, we said goodbye, and met next week in my office as usual.

Today, John still attends therapy with me. Inner conflicts and neurotic patterns remain there, inside. We work this innerness continuously, through his struggles with his girlfriend, his job, and his family dynamics. Those inner struggles, after all, are also a form of life. The world is also *in there*. But something is different, I dare say. What has become clear to me as a therapist (and for John as a patient) is that such inner world is not separate from its outer context. These worlds are interconnected, and as a therapist it is my duty to work with them simultaneously. My therapeutic Self has lost the fear of the outer world penetrating the holy sanctuary of my office. I now welcome it. I invite it in. I challenge it to breach the walls. In the words of Andrew Samuels,

> Where the public and the private, the political and the personal, intersect or even meld there is a special role for depth psychology in relation to political change and transformation. The tragicomic crisis of our *fin de siècle* civilization incites us to challenge the boundaries that are conventionally accepted as existing between the external world and the internal world, between life and reflection, between extraversion and introversion, between doing and being, between politics and psychology, between the political development of the person and the psychological development of the person, between the fantasies of the political world and the politics of the fantasy world.[12]

Whether this decision was therapeutically correct or not, I still do not know. But the reason I do not know is partly that I do not bother with thinking too much about it. To my mind, its correctness or incorrectness is quite irrelevant. What I do know is that I had never felt such life—such outer life—within a therapy session. Protesting and walking the streets that day renewed my hopes not only in my country, but also in my profession. And what is more, it made it clear that my country and my profession are inextricably united and that it is my responsibility to be aware of my discipline's political, public, and social implications.

A Confession and an Invitation

This paper is a chronicle of me as a psychotherapist breaking four-fifths of the rules that I learned when I trained to be a psychotherapist—rules which I currently teach to my students and usually respect quite rigorously with my patients. Breaking the analytic container, tampering with the asymmetry present in the bond between psychotherapist and patient, and risking the relationship with my patient by exposing it to the outer world and by externalizing, outside of the consulting room, interests and feelings of my own are things that I tend to avoid, for the protection of both myself and my patients. This time, however, I broke the rules—my own intuitive form of protesting against the standardization of my discipline, I assume.

When I first shared this with my colleagues, there were two main reactions: one was that I was being foolish, the other one was that I was being courageous. I have spent several pages arguing why I do not think my decision was foolish. Now it is time to clarify that it was not courageous either. Being brave is not precisely one of my main character traits. So in order to take the decision of walking the streets and then in order to process it, I had to talk it out with several people and ask for some feedback. There were three pieces of advice that were particularly valuable; so valuable that I now want to share what I was told with every Jungian subject as part of my invitation to come out and relate to contemporary socio-historical realities.

The first advice I received came from liberation psychologist Mary Watkins, whom I emailed when the possibility of the session in the street arose. She replied with several questions, comments, and suggestions, but she closed her email with two words that grounded me instantly: *take time.* That is one thing the Jungian Selves can transmit to their patients, students, or colleagues: take time. Do not hasten; look around, notice. *Festina lente,* goes the old adage. Everything has its place—inside and outside, my Self and other Selves. Mary Watkins quotes Hillman's view of individuation: "Individuating begins with noticing, paying attention to the specifics of what is actually there so that it can become fully what it is."[13] Do our social systems not need more subjects that participate within them knowing how to take their time? Would this paced contact with the world not affect and enliven analytical psychology? There is more than one something in today's world (and in Jungian theory) that feels wrong and deserves attention. But such attention requires that we take time. When I challenge Jungians to come out of their Selves, I am not calling for impetuous revolution. I simply dare us to give space for new visions, or rather to submit our usual visions to public scrutiny and do a reality check that can only be provided by the world as it presents itself today. I do not wish for everyone to rise in arms; I simply want Jungians to view themselves as active participants in the world.

The second intervention came from a Mexican Jungian analyst, Rocío Ruiz, with whom I supervised this session very meticulously right after it took place. She listened to me very attentively, made several technical and theoretical remarks, but finished with a phrase that shook me to the core: "Well the bottom line is that, somehow, this pains you." This is something Jungian Selves can also do: allow people to become aware of pain that underlies the outrage and the protest—not only the individual pain or its archetypal pattern, but also the social and cultural expressions of such pain. I repeat: something *feels* wrong. The Jungian subject might not be the most qualified to determine whether there is something right or wrong with the world, but he or she is certainly capable of bringing forth the possibility of *sensing and feeling* wrongness.

And the only possible starting point for this, I am afraid, is within. Not within Jungian individuals, but within Jungian theory. If we were to see depth psychologists as a cultural phenomenon (as Samuels suggests), if we were to see them as a community, the critical questions become the following: What pains Jungians? What hurts them? What is the wound or the need that underlies the Jungian Self and its quest for innerness and for wholeness? What is the suffering that moves depth psychotherapists into reflection and imagination as their modes of action? And most importantly, what role does this pain play in contemporary social scenarios?

This brings me to the final piece of advice I obtained which came from Brazilian Jungian scholar Marco Heleno Barreto. With him I shared the idea of writing this paper and of attending this conference. He also listened to me keenly, and at the end of our conversation said to me, "What you must keep in mind with this paper is that you must include yourself in it." He was right. This paper is not essentially personal, but it would be absolutely devoid of any meaning if it did not have a strong conscious personal element. When the student movement began, its members used to be very emphatic about them being individuals that constituted a collective—not isolated individuals and not an undifferentiated mass. In contemporary times it is vital for people to operate communally without losing their individuality, and individually without losing their community.

Summarizing my confession, I (the non-Jungian Jungian subject) want to say the following: I intentionally and deliberately foster the emotional impact that comes with the feeling of something I cannot quite name being somehow out of place, askew, or potentially harmful. *And also I, a non-Jungian Jungian subject that attends Jungian events, reads Jungian books, and is perceived by many as a Jungian, do feel that something I cannot quite name in Jungian practice is somehow out of place, askew, and potentially harmful.* This feeling, even as a non-Jungian Jungian, hurts me and infuriates me. I also feel, evidently, that if we dare delve into what is out of place and askew, then what was potentially harmful becomes actively helpful.

Confessions public, one thing is still missing.

A Final Challenge

Jungians, come out of yourselves and face the outer, present world. Face social dynamics as they present themselves today. Face Twitter, the Internet, and the US presidential elections. Come out of yourselves and have some conversations with marginalized sectors of society; listen to the millions of people that live with less than one dollar a day; listen to the people who have (literally) never had a home; listen to the president of your country; listen to the presidents of other countries; listen to oppression; listen to injustice, and tell me what you hear; and listen to those who do not know what Jungian analysis is and to those who are not able to try it, either because they do not have the money or do not have the time.

Tell me what the world has to say about the word *Jungian*. Does it care? Could it care? Jungian, face any type of other. Face a Wall Street businessman, face a veteran, face an outraged student, face people who do not remember their dreams, and tell me what you see in their eyes. What shows up in someone's eyes when he or she looks at a Jungian? Face someone who does not care about Jung; face someone who is ignorant about Jung, or who is informed about him but finds his work trivial. But please, Jungian, face these others as a Jungian who is outside of Jungian turf. Feel social injustice and political abuse. Walk the street, Jungian, and tell me, doesn't something feel wrong? What do you feel, Jungian? Tell me what you feel, Jungian. Tell everyone. Go public, and walk the non-Jungian streets.

NOTES

1. Thomas Kirsch, "Reflections on the word 'Jungian,'" in M. Stein and R. A. Jones, eds., *Cultures and Identities in Transition: Jungian Perspectives* (East Sussex: Routledge, 2010), p. 190.

2. *Ibid.*

3. James Hillman and Michael Ventura, *We've Had a Hundred Years of Psychotherapy and the World's Getting Worse* (New York: Harper Collins, 1992), p. 104.

4. Andrew Samuels, *The Political Psyche* (London: Routledge, 1993), p. 5.

5. *Ibid.*, p. 11.

6. Hillman and Ventura, *We've Had a Hundred Years of Psychotherapy and the World's Getting Worse*, p. 41.

7. Paul Kugler, *Raids on the Unthinkable: Freudian and Jungian Psychoanalyses* (New Orleans, LA: Spring Journal Books, 2005), p. 70.

8. *Ibid.*, p. 71.

9. Hillman and Ventura, *We've Had a Hundred Years of Psychotherapy and the World's Getting Worse*, pp. 105–106.

10. Comisión Nacional de los Derechos Humanos México, *Recomendación CNDH sobre protestas en Atenco y Texcoco*, 2006, México. Accessed Nov. 23, 2013, at http://www.scribd.com/doc/184300359/Recomendacion-CNDH-sobre-protestas-en-Atenco-y-Texcoco-2006-Mexico.

11. *Cómo Nace YoSoy132, Video Original YoSoy131*. Accessed Nov. 23, 2013, at http://www.youtube.com/watch?v=hca6lzoE2z8 (my translation).

12. Samuels, *Political Psyche*, p. 4.

13. Mary Watkins, "Breaking the Vessels: Archetypal Psychology and the Restoration of Culture, Community, and Ecology," in Stanton Marlan, ed., *Archetypal Psychologies: Reflections in Honor of James Hillman* (New Orleans, LA: Spring Journal Books, 2008), p. 418.

Chapter Nineteen

Jung and Chinese Culture
Comments on Translations of Classic Chinese Texts, Jung's Commentaries and Conversations

Geoffrey Blowers

Jung's Confrontation with Yijing

By his own account, Jung's interest in Eastern philosophies began in the early 1920s shortly before his first meeting with the sinologist Richard Wilhelm. Jung described an idyllic setting at Bollingen, where, sitting under a 100-year-old pear tree, he began experimenting with the *I Ching [Yijing]* by bunching together, in arbitrary fashion, cut up reeds and "referring the resulting oracles to one another in an interplay of questions and answers."[1] His interest was sparked by two questions: the first dealing with the nature of the relationship between the random generation of the physical patterns and the *answers* contained in the text, and the second involving the *amazing coincidences* obtained between the oracle and his own thoughts. The search for answers to these questions was later to spur him to the development of key ideas in his theory of the psyche.[2]

Jung then met Wilhelm at Count Keyserling's School of Wisdom in Darmstadt. Keyserling's most known work, *The Travel Diary of a Philosopher,* published in 1918, was based upon his travels to India, China, Japan, and North America, a trip that encouraged his pursuit of Buddhism, occultism, and theosophy.[3] Keyserling's unsystematic philosophy stressed that the modern malaise arose from a loss of the spiritual core which defined each culture uniquely. From this loss, he discerned an urgent need for a synthesis of Eastern and Western approaches to life in order to cope with the grave situation facing modern man. These ideas gelled with Jung's thoughts and may have sparked his interest in Eastern philosophies in the early twenties. Jung was invited to lecture at Keyserling's school in 1927. He and Keyserling also corresponded. It is clear from the letters, as Richard Noll has observed, that Keyserling looked at Jung as a *quasi-guru* and sought his psychological advice about his dreams.[4]

In 1923, Wilhelm's translation of the *I Ching* appeared in German. Jung and Wilhelm were to become friends, and Jung would later write introductions to both Cary Baynes's English translations of Wilhelm's text in 1950 and to Wilhelm's translation of the Chinese alchemical text, *The Secret of the Golden Flower,* also translated by Baynes. Jung relied on these texts for his authority to make claims about Chinese culture and thought, to bolster his own theory of psychic functioning, and to lend support to his conceptions of the unconscious, archetype, and synchronicity. In a number of works, he made pronouncements on Chinese culture and its distinctiveness from that of the West using his own theoretical system for understanding it. His work has been taken by those Jungians interested in developing their ideas about Asia as a prototype for current-day discussions of the relevance of Western-based psychotherapy to the East.

Jung's essay on *synchronicity* was published in 1952.[5] In it, he employs the term to stand for the coinciding of a psychic and a physical occasion which have no causal relationship to each other, such as the conjunction of an outer event with a dream, vision, or premonition. He also used the term to describe the experiencing of similar or identical thoughts, or dreams, at the same time by persons in different places. Neither of these kinds of occurrence can be explained by causality. In seeking scientific support for the phenomenon, he drew upon three quite different kinds of evidence: the ESP experiments of J. B. Rhine, an examination of fortuitous marriage unions arranged by star signs, and the *I Ching*, only the last of which need concern us here.

In the *I Ching* Jung saw an instrument based solely on the notion that coincidence was self-evident and, hence, was not otherwise amenable to experimental analysis. It was made up of sixty-four hexagrams thought to have been devised by the mythic ruler Fuxi, around 3000 BCE, to ground a set of metaphysical or spiritual truths in some concrete reality by way of symbolization. Through a long line of scholarly interpretations, it has come to be seen as either a book of wisdom or a divination manual.[6] Divination in the *Zhouyi* is always deliberately performed and makes use of yarrow stick counting to find an oracle (cryptic written statement).[7] An oracle is attached to every hexagram and line. The diviner has to discover which oracle fits the situation. Six numbers are generated at random by counting yarrow sticks, and these six numbers refer to six lines that constitute one of the sixty-four possible hexagrams.

Jung referred to a consultation of the *I Ching* as an *experiment-with-the-whole* in which no restrictions are imposed, so that it is given "every possible chance to express itself."[8] According to Jung, the constructed hexagram functions as a symbolic carrier of a specific meaning and is coincident with what is supposedly in the mind of the one seeking a consultation. The basis for this phenomenon, he believed, was the activation of archetypes, which he presupposed can manifest themselves not only in the individual psyche but in material events as well.

Jung and the Tao

Jung also sought support for his theory of synchronicity in Wilhelm's translation of Lao Tzu's *Tao Te Ching*. *Tao* has had many translations. Arthur Waley translates it as *way*, Jesuit missionaries as *God* or *logos*, but Wilhelm translates it as *meaning (sinn)*.[9] Lao Tzu thought of it as *nothing* by which he meant, according to Jung's interpretation of Wilhelm, that "it does not appear in the world of the senses but is only its organizer," as the following quotation brings out:

> We put thirty spokes together and call it a wheel;
> But it is on the space where there is nothing that the utility of the wheel depends.
> We turn clay to make a vessel;
> But it is on the space where there is nothing that the utility of the vessel depends.
> We pierce doors and windows to make a house;
> And it is on these spaces where there is nothing that the utility of the house depends.

Therefore just as we take advantage of what is, we should recognize the utility of what is not. [Ch. XI][10,11]

This Chinese view, thought Wilhelm, pointed to a *latent rationality*, or hidden logic, suggesting that *reality*, comprising a material universe and a set of non-material organizing principles, is conceptually knowable.[12] Jung assumed that the function of both the *Yijing* and the *Tao Te Ching*, was to reveal their principles through reading or *confronting* their texts. Thus, the readings would meaningfully inform the psychological interpretation imparted by the reader. As Stephen Karcher points out in his essay on Jung and the *I Ching*, "Jung maintained that the *I Ching* was the speaking person."[13] But, as the German Tibetanologist, Anagarika Govinda (Ernst Lothar Hoffman), has noted, there is a simpler explanation of oracular consultations: "a clearly formulated question generally contains or calls up the answer from our depth-consciousness. The oracle lies in ourselves. The *I-Ching* only helps to evoke it. It is a psychological aid to self-knowledge."[14] In other words, where books are used as the divining instrument, the oracular statements, often couched in ambiguity, stimulate the mind to make its own choices. On this account, Zhouyi is not a fortune-telling instrument, but rather a work that promotes self-cultivation (understanding). For Jung it was essentially "a psychological procedure" and his interpretations were biased.[15] As the Sinologist Richard Rutt concludes, "Had he not wanted to write his foreword, or had he known about the work done on *Zhouyi* by the Chinese scholars of his day, he would have interpreted the oracles quite differently."[16]

The Secret of the Golden Flower

In 1928 Wilhelm sent Jung his translation of the Taoist alchemical text, *The Secret of the Golden Flower*, and asked him to write a preface.[17] Wilhelm's translation was based on an eighth-century CE Chinese treatise emanating from an esoteric Taoist movement known as The Order of the Golden Elixir, devoted to enhancing and maintaining life through yoga and meditation. The text was also influenced by Buddhist thought with its emphasis on the illusory nature of life and the quest for *nirvāna*.[18] Jung was to describe his first encounter with this book as the event which shook him from his sense of isolation (after his break from Freud) and confirmed the ideas of the psyche he was developing at the time. Yet "what Jung did not know," as Thomas Cleary, translator of a much later version of the same book, made clear, "was that the text he was reading was in fact a garbled translation of a truncated version of a corrupted recension of the original work."[19] Cleary argues these assertions in an interesting way, but there are those who remain skeptical because he does not allow other scholars to examine the textual evidence for his claims.[20] While Cleary's edition came sixty years after Wilhelm's, they both point out in the introductions to their respective translations that as the text appeals to those of differing religions without causing them to renounce their fundamental beliefs, it is "a powerful treatise on awakening the hidden potential of all humans beings."[21]

In a letter to Wilhelm, Jung referred to his *Commentary* as "a European reaction to the wisdom of China," the aim of which was to "build a bridge of psychological understanding between East and West."[22,23] At the same time, he warned European readers of the work not to see it as a panacea for their psychological ills. Jung believed it was "only in combining insights from the East with a highly developed intellectual function of Western psyche, that a full understanding of psyche will be achieved."[24]

East-West differences then were to be explained in psychological terms (as was his whole approach to the texts), and he generally avoided examining in any depth the metaphysical assumptions upon which the original texts were founded, feeling they were beyond his competence. At such times he felt it necessary to "bring [them] to a level where it is possible to see whether any of the psychological facts known to us have parallels in, or at last border upon, the sphere of Eastern thought."[25] This last statement he claimed in a psychological commentary he was asked to write on another Tibetan text: Evans-Wentz's 1939 edition of the *Tibetan Book of the Great Liberation*. This work is attributed to Padma-Sambhava, a monk who brought tantric Buddhism to Tibet in about 747 CE. The *Great Liberation* is *nirvāna* achieved through the practice of inward contemplation under the belief that the only reality is mind or consciousness and that matter is mind-made. Also, all minds are manifestations of the Absolute or One Mind. Jung had earlier written a psychological commentary to Evans—Wentz's translation in 1927 of *The Tibetan Book of the Dead (Bardol Thödol)*.

The content of this work, which seemed less palatable to Western minds than the *Great Liberation*, dealt with facing up to death and the art of dying with the belief of reincarnation. It was a book of instruction for the dead and the dying as their souls embarked on a journey of forty-nine days from death to rebirth. Jung, anticipating the difficulty of the strangeness of this for a Western reader, chose to deal with it solely in psychological terms congenial to his framework. Since "the world of gods and spirits is truly 'nothing but' the collective unconscious inside me,"[26] he claimed, it was possible to understand the narratives of the journey of dead souls as descriptions of the dissolution of the ego allowing "the soul to enter a form of psychosis and torment."

Although Jung has had support for this view, in, for example, John Beebe's response to William McGuire's account of the Jung-Wentz relationship, at the time, his psychologically reductive account of the *Bardol* brought him his critics.[27] Lama Anagarika Govinda, in a review of Evans-Wentz's edition of the book (to which he also supplied an introduction in its third edition), contrasts Jung's approach with that of Evans-Wentz himself, who was at pains to present the text from the standpoint of Northern Buddhism. To describe yogic experiences in terms of Western psychology, Govinda said, was to "bring [them] to a plane where they lose their meaning and thus deprive them of their only value."[28] Govinda never met Jung, as Evans-Wentz did in 1938 when he attended the Tenth International Medical Congress of Psychotherapy in Oxford. There, Jung spoke of being unable to solve the problem of reincarnation. He described to Evan-Wentz some dreams he'd had of moving corpses, which he interpreted as symbolizing his own past corpses.

Jung also dreamt of an ancient graveyard where a tomb, dated 1830, had a corpse whose arm touched Jung's, seen as a symbol of his own corpse or that of an ancestor. Evans-Wentz then asked a question: "May we not be our own ancestors reborn?" to which Jung, after some considerable thought, gave no affirmation.[29] He was, however, able to agree with Evan-Wentz's view of the nature of reality as that which "transcends both science and philosophy as we know them, being neither this nor that, neither existence nor non-existence."[30]

Jung's Position

In the texts briefly mentioned here, Jung's approach was to highlight the psychological significance of Eastern philosophies to Westerners by pointing to what he felt the West lacked: an integration of the functions of consciousness with scientific explanation. A post-enlightenment world has increasingly marginalized consciousness, reducing it to an epiphenomenon of brain activity in the belief that the universe is monistically materialistic. But for Jung, the reality of the world depended upon the presence of a knowing subject—consciousness is not "an accidental by-product of the material world but in … a crucial sense is the very condition of its existence."[31] By not integrating mind into the general worldview, the West has caused a split of science with religion, which has not occurred in the non-Christian world of the East. Materialism is not a *fact* but a metaphysical hypothesis; Jung thought of it as "a symbol for something unknown, which you might as well call 'spirit' or anything else."[32] From such a perspective, science fails to falsify a religious worldview. But religion, according to Jung, is also at fault for trying "to retain a primitive mental condition on merely sentimental grounds."[33]

Critics of this position argue that Jung himself was constrained by his insistence on a duality of object-knower which prevented him from appreciating that in yoga practices, for example, it is possible to achieve a transcendence of this duality.[34] This is also the position of those in the transpersonal psychology movement who stress the importance of a spiritual dimension in which it is possible to transcend the merely mental realm of the individual ego.[35] This understanding grew from those psychologists originally associated with the work of Abraham Maslow, who himself had postulated the phenomenon of the *peak experience*—a rare unplanned moment when the individual reaches a new level of activity and awareness of the self's possibilities.[36] Such a going-beyond one's normal everyday boundaries led some to the view that the transcendence was spiritual, and, therefore, could be reached by self-cultivation. The latest and best known proponent of this position is Ken Wilbur.[37] Jung is sometimes quoted as being a forerunner of this perspective. Yet those who see a continuity between Jungian and transpersonal psychology can be countered by the actual arguments of Jung vis-à-vis the Eastern philosophies with which he was acquainted.

Conclusions

Jung would appear to have misunderstood some aspects of Eastern religions and philosophy, in part because of his reading them through the filter of questionable translations and also because of his need to impose his own framework. Nonetheless, his hermeneutical approach was innovative and inspiring to many who came later.[38] Where others have sought comparisons between Eastern and Western thinking, and prematurely judged the outcome, Jung seemed clear that they represented two halves of our potential existence, each side being in a state of deprivation due to its neglect of the other. And while he was also suspicious of Westerners seeking therapeutic salvation in Eastern practices (since he saw this happening at the expense of examining their shadows), he was insistent on not prescribing different psychologies for East and West, in spite of their different ways of seeing. He claimed

> there is only one earth and one mankind. East and West cannot read humanity into two different halves. Psychic reality still exists in its original oneness, and awaits man's advance to a level of consciousness where he no longer believes in one part and denies the other, but recognizes both constituent elements of the one psyche.[39]

Jung's reservations, like all his comments, are historically locatable. Against them, there has been since his time a flourishing of contact with the East—everything from "new age wisdom seekers to the formalised dialogues between theologians, philosophers and psychologists."[40] He thought that the Chinese would have no need of Western psychotherapy given that they have recourse through yoga practices to a Taoist outlook which prevents them from getting to a state in which "the pairs of opposites of human nature [were] so far apart that all conscious connection between them was lost. There has been growing recognition in China of psychological problems at the state level.[41] This has resulted in formal recognition of the profession of "counsellor."[42] Since the mid-1990s, programs run by outside groups for the training of Chinese doctors in psychoanalytic psychotherapy have been established in several major Chinese cities.[43] There have been several international conferences sponsored by the German-Chinese Academy for Psychotherapy (GCAP), the Freudian International Psychoanalytic Association, and the Jungian International Association for Analytical Psychology. An Institute of Analytical Psychology has been set up in Guangzhou and IAAP training groups exist in Taiwan and Hong Kong.[44] This has resulted in a new openness to Buddhism, mediation, yoga, Chinese medicine, and therapeutic techniques. Even if there still remains the thorny question of the West's dominance in terms of its "conceptual framework dictating all the time the nature and direction of the exchange," and while Chinese psychologists have not openly taken up Jung's question of a difference of mind in approaching the Western psychotherapy/Eastern philosophy divide, there are those who are intent on scientifically investigating psychology and counseling from an indigenous perspective.[45,46]

Whether Jung's prophecies, that East and West should find solutions to their psychological problems in their own respective systems, are shown to be correct will depend on the answers to the provocative questions he raised.

Earlier versions of this paper were read at the Second International Conference on Humanistic and Transpersonal Psychologies and Psychotherapies Oct. 17–21, 2003, Qufu, Shandong; the International Forum on Chinese-Western Cultures and Human Spiritual Development Dec. 19–21, 2003, Beijing, China; and the C. G. Jung Institute, Zürich in February 2011. The author acknowledges the University Hong Kong in supporting this work through HK-China travel, small project, and UDF grants; the ETH-Bibliothek, Zürich for copies of its Wilhelm-Jung letters; and Ms. Tonja Fong for translating them.

NOTES

1. C. G. Jung, *Memories, Dreams, Reflections* (London: Collins and Routledge & Kegan Paul, 1963), p. 342.

2. In *Psychological Types* he drew on the Taoist conception of opposites.

3. For a full account of Keyserling, see Walter Struve, *Elites Against Democracy* (Princeton, NJ: Princeton University Press, 1973), pp. 274–316; and Richard Noll, *The Jung Cult* (Princeton, NJ: Princeton University Press, 1994), pp. 92–95.

4. Noll, *The Jung Cult*, p. 95.

5. C. G. Jung, "Synchronicity: an acausal connecting principle," in *The Collected Works of C. G. Jung*, vol. 8, ed. and trans. Gerhard Adler and R. F. C. Hull (Princeton, NJ: Princeton University Press, 1973).

6. There are many versions and commentaries of this text in English. I have drawn here on two: Wei Tat, *An exposition of The I-Ching or Book of Changes* (Hong Kong: Dai Nippon, 1977); and Richard Rutt, *Zhouyi: The Book of Changes, a new translation with commentary* (London: Curzon Press, 1996).

7. *I Ching* is the common name referring to the composite work together with commentaries and ancient text; *Zhouyi* refers to the ancient core document derived from the Bronze Age comprising the period.

8. Jung, CW 8, § 865.

9. Cited in footnote 1 of Jung's letter to Wilhelm, September 10, 1929 in C. G. Jung, *Letters, Vol. 1: 1906–1950*, ed. and trans. Gerhard Adler and R. F. C. Hull (Princeton, NJ: Princeton University Press, 1973).

10. Jung, CW 8, § 920.

11. Arthur Waley, *The Way and its Power: A Study of the Tao Te Ching and its Place in Chinese Thought* (London: Allen and Unwin, 1934).

12. Richard Wilhelm, *Chinesische Lebensweisheit* (Nabu Press, 1971).

13. Stephen Karcher, "Journey to the West: C. G. Jung and the Classic of Change," *Spring: A Journal of Archetype and Culture*, Fall/Winter 1999, p. 5.

14. Anagarika Govinda, *The Inner Structure of the I Ching: The Book of Transformations* (San Francisco, CA: Wheelwright, 1981).

15. Fu Hsi, King Wen, the Duke of Chou, and Confucius, *I Ching or Book of Changes*, ed. and trans. Richard Wilhelm and Cary F. Baynes with foreword by C. G. Jung (Bollingen/Princeton University Press, 1950), pp. xxvi.

16. Rutt, *Zhouyi*, p. 55.

17. Published in 1929 as *Das Geheimnis der golden Blüte*; the English translation by Cary Baynes with Jung's preface first appeared in 1931.

18. J. J. Clarke, *Jung and Eastern Thought: A Dialogue with the Orient* (London: Routledge, 1994).

19. Dongbin Lü, *The Secret of the Golden Flower: The Classic Chinese Book of Life*, ed. and trans. Thomas F. Cleary (San Francisco, CA: Harper, 1991), p. 3.

20. I am grateful to an anonymous reviewer for this point.

21. *Ibid.*

22. Jung to Wilhelm, September 10, 1929.

23. C. G. Jung, "Commentary," CW 18, § 75.

24. *Ibid.*, § 56.

25. C. G. Jung, "Psychological Commentary on *The Tibetan Book of the Great Liberation*," CW 11, § 788.

26. *Ibid.*, § 857.

27. John Beebe, "Response to William McGuire," *Journal of Analytical Psychology* 48 (4, 2003): 447–452.

28. Lama Anagarika Govinda, *Mahabodhi Society Journal,* August 1954, cited in Ken Winkler, *A Thousand Journeys: The Biography of Lama Anagarika Govinda* (Longmead, Dorset: Element Books, 1990), p. 126.

29. Winkler, *A Thousand Journeys*, p. 70.

30. *Ibid.*, p. 71.

31. Clarke, *Jung and Eastern Thought*, p. 127.

32. Jung, CW 11, § 762.

33. *Ibid.*, § 763.

34. For a good account of these see "Criticisms and Shortcomings" in Clarke, *Jung and Eastern Thought*, pp. 158–178.

35. Read, e.g., Introduction in Donald Moss, ed., *Humanistic and Transpersonal Psychology: A Historical and Biographical Sourcebook* (Westport, CT: Greenwood Press, 1999).

36. Arthur Hastings, "Transpersonal Psychology: The Fourth Force," in Moss, *Humanistic and Transpersonal Psychology*, pp. 192–208.

37. Wilbur's first major work *The Spectrum of Consciousness* in 1977 was a synthesis of Western psychology and Eastern religions.

38. See, e.g., Robert Walker Gunn, "The Experience of Emptiness in the Process of Self-Transformation in Zen Buddhism, Christianity and Depth Psychology as Represented by Dogen Kigen, Thomas Merton and Carl Jung, with Donald Winnicott and Heinz Kohut" (Ph.D. diss., Union Theological Seminary, 1997); and Mindy McAbee, "A Comparison of the Theory and Practice of Jungian, Archetypal, and

Buddhist Psychology from a Nondual and Postmodern Perspective" (Ph.D. diss., Pacifica Graduate Institute, 1999).

39. Jung, CW 8, § 682.
40. Clarke, *Jung and Eastern Thought*, p. 181.
41. Dongbin Lü, *Secret of the Golden Flower*, p. 87.
42. Report in the Ministry of Labour and Social Security's China Employment Training Technical Instruction Center, details of which can be found at http://ms.osta.org.cn/nvqdbApp/htm/fenlei/ecGzs_Zy-6728.html; See also, http://english.people.com.cn/200503/21/eng20050321_177575.html.
43. See G. Blowers and T. Yuan, "Psychoanalysis in China," in A. de Mijolla, ed., *International Dictionary of Psychoanalysis*, vol. 1 (New York: Thomson Gale, 2005), pp. 285–287.
44. Reported in the IAAP Newsletter, 24, 2004, p. 13.
45. *Ibid.,* p. 191.
46. See in particular, C. L. W. Chan, F. Fan, S. M. Y. Ho, and A. M. P. Wong, eds., *Chinese Culture and Counseling* (Beijing: Ethnic Publishing House, 2002); and S. M. Y. Ho, W. M. Lee, and S. M. Ng, eds., *Theory and Practice of Indigenous Counseling Research in Chinese Speaking Communities* (Beijing: Ethnic Publishing House, 2002).

Contributors

Teresa Arendell, Ph.D. is a Jungian analyst living and practicing in Maine. She is Professor Emeritus from Colby College, Maine, where she taught sociology. She specialized in and conducted qualitative research; presented papers at professional conferences for the thirty years she spent in academia; published numerous peer-reviewed articles covering topics of family, gender, sexualities, women and aging, family, and social policy; and authored three books on family, divorce, and social policy. Her current work focuses on Jung, Nature and Psyche: The Wild, Wildness, and Wilderness, and on Jung as phenomenologist. She's conducted workshops and lectures in the fundamentals of Jungian theory and practice, dream interpretation, mother-daughter relations, archetypes and cultural and individual complexes of aging and being aged, sense of place, the American cultural complex of wilderness, and nature, psyche, and place. She's an active participant at the Boston C. G. Jung Training Institute where she serves on multiple committees. Experiencing the natural world and activities with her grandchildren are among her greatest delights. TeresaArendell.com.

Gustavo Beck, M.A. is a psychology professor at Universidad Iberoamericana (Mexico City). He is also a translator of books and essays on psychology and the humanities, and a clinical psychologist with a private practice in Mexico City.

Geoffrey Blowers, Ph.D. [B.Sc. (Sheffield), M.Phil. (Sussex), Ph.D. (HK)] is currently Director of Studies and the Research Office at Hong Kong Shue Yan University. He is co-editor with Alison Turtle of *Psychology Moving East: the status of Western Psychology in Asia and Oceania* (Westview, 1987), co-author with Kieron O'Connor of *Personal Construct Psychology in the Clinical Context* (Ottawa/Montreal, University of Ottawa Press, 1996) and has published papers on the history of psychology and psychoanalysis in China and Japan. He was twice President of the Hong Kong Psychological

Society and is currently its Registrar. He is also Founding President of the Hong Kong Institute of Analytical Psychology.

Joseph Cambray, Ph.D. is President of the International Association for Analytical Psychology. He has served as the U.S. Editor for The Journal of Analytical Psychology and is on the Editorial Boards of The Journal of Analytical Psychology; The Jung Journal: Culture and Psyche; and the Israel Annual of Psychoanalytic Theory, Research, and Practice. He is a faculty member at Harvard Medical School in the Department of Psychiatry at Massachusetts General Hospital, Center for Psychoanalytic Studies; adjunct faculty at Pacific Graduate Institute; and former President of the C. G. Jung Institute of Boston. Dr. Cambray is a Jungian analyst in Boston, MA and Providence, RI. His numerous publications include the book based on his Fay lectures, *Synchronicity: Nature and Psyche in an Interconnected Universe*, and a volume edited with Linda Carter, *Analytical Psychology: Contemporary Perspectives in Jungian Psychology*. His most recent papers include "Cosmos and Culture in the Play of Synchronicity," Spring Journal, 2012; "Jung, science, and his legacy," in International Journal of Jungian Studies, 3:2, 110-124, 2011; "L'Influence D'Ernst Haeckel dans le Livre Rouge de Carl Gustav Jung," in Recherches Germaniques, Revue Annuelle Hors Serie, 8, 41-59, 2011; and "Moments of complexity and enigmatic action: a Jungian view of the therapeutic field," in Journal of Analytical Psychology, 56 (2) 296-309, 2011.

John Davenport, Ph.D. is Professor of Philosophy at Fordham University. He teaches and writes on ethics and political philosophy, moral psychology and agency (including free will, autonomy, and love), existentialism, and philosophy of religion (including comparative religion and myth). With Anthony Rudd, John co-edited the 2001 collection, *Kierkegaard after MacIntyre*, and the new collection on *Love, Reason, and Will: Kierkegaard after Frankfurt* (Bloomsbury, 2015). John has authored several other essays on Kierkegaard, including four recent articles on the structure of existential faith and selfhood in *Fear and Trembling* and other works. He published a monograph on motivation and volition titled *Will as Commitment and Resolve* in 2007, and *Narrative Identity, Autonomy, and Mortality* (Routledge, 2012). In addition to articles on global governance, he has recently published an article on "A New Existential Model of God: A Synthesis of Themes from Kierkegaard, Buber, Levinas, and Open Theism," in *Models of God* (Springer, 2013).

Harry Wells Fogarty, M.Div., Ph.D. is a Jungian Analyst in practice in New York City. He also serves as a lecturer in psychiatry and religion at Union Theological Seminary, New York, and as a faculty member for the Jungian Psychoanalytic Association (JPA) and the Philadelphia Association of Jungian Analysts (PAJA). His publications include "The Secret of Achebe's Lion: Making Meaning of the Chronicity of the Intolerable" in *Journeys, Encounters: Clinical, Communal, Cultural, Proceedings of the Seventeenth International IAAP Congress for Analytical Psychology*, ed., Pamila Bennett; "A Jungian Perspective on Transcendence and Symbolization," *Issues in Psychoanalytic Psychology*, vol. 30, no. 1, 2008; "The Ethical Attitude in Analytical Practice" in *Proceedings of the Fifteenth International IAAP Congress for Analytical Psychology*; and "Poisons and Panaceas in Analytic Training" in *Destruction and Creation: Personal and Cultural Transformations*, ed., Mary Ann Mattoon.

Tiffany Houck-Loomis, M.Div., Ph.D. is an analyst-in-training with the Jungian Psychoanalytic Association (JPA) in NYC; a part-time professor in the areas of Philosophy, Religious Studies, and Psychology; and the Director of the Doctor of Ministry program in Pastoral Care and Counseling at New Brunswick Theological Seminary. Her publications include "Broken Silence: An Interdisciplinary Study on Formed, Unformed, and Reformed Inherited Trauma," a chapter forthcoming in an edited volume through Duquesne University Press (2015); "When Fast-Held God Images Fail to Meet Our Needs: A Psychoanalytic Reading of Job Chapters 6 and 7," in Pastoral Psychology (2013); and "Good God?!? Lamentations as a Model for Mourning the Loss of the Good God," in the Journal of Health and Religion (2012).

Margaret Klenck, M.Div., L.P. is a Jungian Analyst in private practice in New York City. She is a graduate from the C. G. Jung Institute of New York, and holds a Masters of Divinity from Union Theological Seminary. Margaret is a past President of the Jungian Psychoanalytic Association in New York, where she also teaches and supervises. Margaret has lectured and taught nationally and internationally. Recent publications include the opening essay in the second volume of *Jung and Film*, edited by Chris Hauke and Luke Hockney, which she co-authored with cinematographer Tom Hurwitz, ASC, and the entry on Jung in the newly revised, *Psychoanalytic Terms and Concepts*, published by Yale University Press.

Tara-Marie Linné, M.S.W., L.C.S.W. is an independent scholar in NYC. She is nationally certified by the National Association of Social Workers and clinically licensed in four states. She received her B.S. in psychology from the University of Virginia and a Masters in Social Welfare from UCLA. She pursued post-graduate training through the Washington School of Psychiatry and conducted a private practice in Washington, D.C. She served as V.P. Legislative Affairs for the Greater Washington Society for Clinical Social Work and has been a member of the Washington Society for Jungian Psychology and Phoenix (AZ) Friends of C. G. Jung.

Farzad Mahootian, Ph.D. (Ph.D. Philosophy, M.S. Chemistry) teaches the Global Liberal Studies core at New York University. He has taught philosophy, science, and humanities courses for over twenty-five years. His research focus is the relevance of myth and metaphor to the history of philosophy and the sciences. Recent publications include "Jung and Whitehead on Intuition: An Interplay of Psychological and Philosophical Perspectives," with T. Linné in *Rational Intuition: Philosophical Roots, Scientific Investigations*, eds., L. Osbeck and B. Held (Cambridge, 2014); and "Metaphor in Chemistry: An Examination of Chemical Metaphor," in *Philosophy of Chemistry: Growth of a New Discipline* (Springer, 2015).

Mark E. Mattson, Ph.D. is Associate Professor of Psychology at Fordham University where he served as Associate Dean of Fordham College at Lincoln Center from 2009 to 2014 and as Associate Chair of Psychology for 14 years. He is a cognitive experimental psychologist with interests in the history of psychology at Fordham and in New York City, in errors and their implications for musical performances and theories of action and intention, and in the functions of autobiographical memory. His most cited article so far is his first: Erickson and Mattson (1981) on the Moses illusion.

Dennis Merritt, L.C.S.W., Ph.D. has a doctorate in entomology from UC-Berkeley, an MA in Humanistic Psychology from Sonoma State, and a diploma from the C. G. Jung Institute in Zürich. He is in private practice as a Jungian analyst in Madison and Milwaukee and author of the four volume *Dairy Farmer's Guide to the Universe—Jung, Hermes, and Ecopsychology* (2012-2013). His blogs on "Hunger Games," guns and the American psyche, and climate change are found at JungianEcopsychology.com and articles on sense of place and using the I Ching in an analytic setting at EcoJung.com.

Frances M. Parks, Ph.D., A.B.P.P. is a clinical psychologist and graduate of the C. G. Jung Institute Zürich. She has served as an administrator and faculty member in academic training programs. Clinical and analytic issues in aging are current areas of focus in her work. She is also exploring parallels in the experience of opera and the analytic process. She served as president of the Washington State Psychological Association and is a member of the C. G. Jung Institute of Seattle and of the Inter-Regional Society of Jungian Analysts.

Susan Rowland, Ph.D. is Chair of MA Engaged Humanities and the Creative Life at Pacifica Graduate Institute, CA, and formerly Professor of English and Jungian Studies at the University of Greenwich, UK. She is author of a number of books on literary theory, gender, and Jung including *Jung as a Writer* (2005); *Jung: A Feminist Revision* (2002); *C. G. Jung in the Humanities* (2010) and *The Ecocritical Psyche: Literature, Evolutionary Complexity, and Jung* (2012). She also researches detective fiction with the book *From Agatha Christie to Ruth Rendell* (2001) and, forthcoming, *The Sleuth and the Goddess* in Women's Detective Fiction.

Martin A. Schulman, Ph.D. was the Editor of The Psychoanalytic Review for sixteen years. He served on the Boards of Directors of the National Psychological Association for Psychoanalysis (NPAP), the Council of Psychoanalytic Psychotherapists (CPP), the International Federation for Psychoanalytic Education (IFPE), The South East Florida Institute for Psychoanalysis and Psychotherapy (SEFIFPP), and the Harlem Family Institute, as well as the Editorial Boards of Psychoanalytic Psychology (Division 39 of the APA) and Psychoanalytic Books. He has coedited *Failures in Psychoanalytic Treatment* (IUP) with J. Reppen, *Way Beyond Freud* (Open Gate Press) with J. Reppen and J. Tucker, and *Sexual Faces* (IUP) with C. Schwartz. He has just completed with R. Kaplan a book on working with ultra-orthodox religious patients. He is a committed Freudian (OMG).

Jennifer Leigh Selig, Ph.D. is the founding chair of the Jungian and Archetypal Studies program at Pacifica Graduate Institute. She is the co-editor and author of several books, including *Reimagining Education: Essays on Reviving the Soul of Learning* (2009); *The Soul Does Not Specialize: Revaluing the Humanities and the Polyvalent Imagination* (2012); *Integration: The Psychology and Mythology of Martin Luther King, Jr. and His (Unfinished) Therapy With the Soul of America* (2012); and *A Tribute to James Hillman: Reflections on a Renegade Psychologist* (2014).

Jay Sherry, Ph.D. teaches history and psychology at Long Island University–Brooklyn. He has presented his research on the life and work of Carl Jung in a variety of psychoanalytic publications and venues, most recently at the Freud Museum in London. His book *Carl Gustav Jung, Avant-Garde Conservative* (Palgrave Macmillan) received a 2011 Gradiva Award; he is now writing a book about the Jungian strand in American Modernism. For more, visit www.jaysherry.com.

William J. Sneck, S.J., Ph.D. an alumnus of University of Michigan, taught Pastoral Counseling at Loyola University, MD, as associate professor (1985–2000), and currently serves as the associate director for Jesuit Center, Wernersville, PA, as well as adjunct associate professor for Loyola Univ. in MD. He has authored *Charismatic Spiritual Gifts: a Phenomenological Analysis* (University Press of America, 1981); "Jung: Mentor for Pastoral Counselors," in Research in the Social Scientific Study of Religion, 18 (2007), 35—51; and "Carl Jung and the Quest for Wholeness" in Robert J. Wicks (ed.) *Handbook of Spirituality for Ministers*, Volume 2 (Paulist, 2000, 196—213.)

Ann Belford Ulanov, M.Div., Ph.D., L.H.D. is the Christiane Brooks Johnson Professor of Psychiatry and Religion at Union Theological Seminary, a psychoanalyst in private practice, and a member of the Jungian Psychoanalytic Association (NYC) and the International Association for Analytical Psychology. With her late husband, Barry Ulanov, she is the author of *Religion and the Unconscious*; *Primary Speech: A Psychology of Prayer*; *Cinderella and Her Sisters: The Envied and the Envying*; *The Witch and The Clown: Two Archetypes of Human Sexuality*; *The Healing Imagination*; *Transforming Sexuality: The Archetypal World of Anima and Animus*; by herself she is the author of *The Feminine in Christian Theology and in Jungian Psychology*; *Receiving Woman: Studies in the Psychology and Theology of the Feminine*; *Picturing God*; *The Wisdom of the Psyche*; *The Female Ancestors of Christ*; *The Wizards' Gate*; *The Functioning Transcendent*; Korean edition of *Our Religion and the Unconscious*, Fall 1996; Korean edition of *Primary Speech*, 2000-2001; Korean edition of *Cinderella and Her Sisters*, 2002; *Religion and the Spiritual in Carl Jung*, 1999, reissued as *Spirit in Jung*, 2005; *Finding Space: Winnicott, God, and Psychic Reality*, 2001; *Attacked by Poison Ivy, A Psychological Study*, 2002; Italian edition of *Cinderella and Her Sisters*, 2003; *Spiritual Aspects of Clinical Work*, 2004; Czech edition of *The Female Ancestors of Christ*; *The Unshuttered Heart: Opening to Aliveness and Deadness in the Self*, 2007. *The Living God and the Living Psyche*, 2007; *Madness and Creativity*, 2009.

Ann Belford Ulanov is the recipient of an honorary doctorate from Virginia Theological School; an honorary doctorate from Loyola Graduate Department in Pastoral Counseling; an honorary doctorate from Christian Theological Seminary; the Distinguished Alumna Award from the Blanton/Peale Institute; the Vision Award from the National Association for the Advancement of Psychoanalysis; the Oskar Pfister Award from the American Psychiatric Association for Distinguished Work in Depth Psychology and Religion; the Distinguished Contribution Award from the American Association of Pastoral Counselors for Distinguished Work in Depth Psychology and Religion; the Gradiva Award for best book in Psychiatry and Religion 2002 from the National Association for the Advancement of Psychoanalysis for *Finding Space: Winnicott, God, and Psychic Reality*.

Frederick J. Wertz, Ph.D., a professor at Fordham University since 1985, has written on the philosophy, theories, methodologies, and history of psychology as well as empirical research on various topics. He is the co-author of *Five Ways of Doing Qualitative Analysis: Phenomenological Psychology, Grounded Theory, Discourse Analysis, Narrative Research, and Intuitive Inquiry* (Guilford Publications); former editor of *Journal of Phenomenological Psychology and Bulletin of Theoretical and Philosophical Psychology*; former President of APA Society for Theoretical and Philosophical Psychology and APA Society for Humanistic Psychology and the Interdisciplinary Coalition of North American Phenomenologists; and 2014 Rollo May Awardee for pioneering work in humanistic psychology from the Society for Humanistic Psychology.

Beverley Zabriskie, L.C.S.W. is a Certified Jungian Analyst in New York City and a founding faculty member and former President of the Jungian Psychoanalytic Association (JPA). Her recent publications include "Time and Tao in Synchronicity" (2014) in *The Pauli-Jung Conjecture and Its Impact Today*; "Psychic energy and synchronicity" (April 2014, Journal of Analytical Psychology); "Synchronicities: Riddles of Time and Emotion" (2012) in *The Playful Psyche: Entering Chaos, Coincidence, Creation*; "The One and Many Souls of New York" (2010) in *Psyche and City: The Soul's Guide to the Modern Metropolis*; "When Psyche meets Soma: the question of incarnation" (2006) in Corrigal, J., Payne, H., and Wilkinson, H., (Eds.) *About a Body*. She also authored "A Meeting of Rare Minds" (2001), the Preface to *Atom and Archetype: The Pauli-Jung Letters*. She is a frequent national and international lecturer: bevzab@aol.com.

INDEX

A

Academy, Jung and, 116, 121, 122, 165–172
Achúcarro, Nicolás, 55
active imagination, 22, 127–129
Alsberg, Carl L., 55
analysis, empirical, Jung vs. Freud on, 25–26
analytical psychology, 138
  deep ecology and, 225–229
  key features of, applicable to LES, 143–147
analytical psychotherapy, transformative process in, 149
archetypal symbolism, 143
Arendell, Teresa, 8
Arendt, Hannah, 203–204
atieology, 246

B

Bair, Deirdre, 78–79, 81
Banks, Sir Joseph, 87
Barreto, Marco Heleno, 274
Beck, Gustavo, 9
Beebe, John, 282
Belford Ulanov, Ann.
  See Ulanov, Ann Belford
Bergson, Henri, 70
Berry, Thomas, 224, 225, 237
Bible, as symbol, 194–196
biblical scholarship, 7
  threat of unconscious and, 192–194
Big Bang model, 92
Bigger, Charles, 205, 206
Bleuler, Eugen, 37, 39, 80
Blowers, Geoffrey, 9
Boas, Franz, 82, 92
Bohr, Niels, 6, 40, 82, 132, 139, 152

Bonpland, Aimé, 88
Bowen, Margarita, 89
the bridge, Jung and, 172–175
Brooke, Roger, 207
Brown, Lester, 240
Brown, Schuyler, 191
Buber, Martin, 250, 251, 253, 255

C

C. G. Jung Institute, 6, 121–123
Cambray, Joseph, 5, 135–136, 142-143
Campbell, Joseph, 250, 255
Caputo, John, 209
Carey, Nessa, 95
Casey, Edward, 226–227
Chinese culture, Jung and, 277–285
the *Chora,* 208–211
Cleary, Thomas, 281
close reading, 126–129
collaboration, 155
collective shadow, 131
collective unconscious, 82–83, 247
common factors research, 118
comparative symbolism, 8, 245
complementarity, 6, 139–141
complex adaptive systems, 93
conceptual knowledge, theory and, 26–28
Cosmos: A sketch of a physical description of the universe (Humbolt), 90–92
counter-transference, 41, 152
creative evolution, 70
creative fantasy, 172
Crisp, Quentin, 101
Cunningham, Andrew, 86–87

D

The Dairy Farmer's Guide to the Universe—Jung, Hermes and, Ecopsychology (Merritt), 233, 239–240
Damasio, Antonio, 94
Darlington, Thomas, 59
Darwin, Charles, 89–90
data, Jung vs. Freud on use of, 22–24
Davenport, John, 8
Dawkins, Richard, 251, 255
deep ecology, 8, 224, 236
  analytical psychology and, 225–229
Deloria, Vine, 225
dementia praecox, 37, 78–79, 80
Derrida, Jacques, 209, 253
determinism, 17
Deus Absconditus, 7, 176
Deus Absconditus (Jung), 204, 211
dreams, 17
Duino Elegies (Rilke), 205
Dunn, T. Joseph, 58
Durkheim, Émile, 82
Dutch Hunger Winter, 95–96

E

ecological unconscious, 8, 226
ecology, 88
ecopsychology, 233–234
Edelman, Gerald, 44
Eder, David, 102
Einstein, Albert, 40, 46, 82
Eliade, 248, 254, 255
Elsberg, Charles Albert, 59
emotion
  kinship, 44
  psychic energy and, 43–46
empirical analysis, 25–26
Empirically Supported Treatments (EST), 117
Empirically Validated Treatments (EVT), 117
empty protest *(kenosis),* 262
entrainment, 135, 143
epigenetics, 94, 95
Eros, 143
Evidence-Based Medicine (EBM) model, 117
evidence-based practice, 5, 115–118
  future of, 118–119
Evidence-Based Practice in Psychology (EBPP), 117
Exercises, Ignatian, Jung and, 215–222
experimental science, psychology as, 16
Extrovert/Introvert, 144

F

Fisher, Erik, 133
Fishman, Daniel B., 119
Flexner Report, 59
Fogarty, Harry W., 7–8, 9–10
Fordham lectures, 15, 37, 41, 65, 77–79, 101–102.
  See also Jung, Carl Gustav
  accomplishments of Jung with, 3–4
  as exposition of new way of doing science, 166
  group photo, 51–54
  historical context of, 1–2
  honorary degree recipients at, 54–55
  Jung at time of, 1–2
  Jung's attacks on Freud in, 17–18
  other non-Fordham instructors at, 55–56
Fordham Medical School, 59–60
Forster, Georg, 87, 88
Franz, Marie-Louise von, 131–132, 144
Frazer, James, 246
free association, 22
Freud, Sigmund, 247
  Jung's break with, 15–16, 41–43
  Jung's letter to, after Fordham lectures, 2–3

tension and break between Jung
  and, 18
Froebe, Olga, 250

G

Gaia Theory, 224
Galison, Peter, 134
Garside, Charles Zeh, 58
German Romanticism
  ecological perspective and, 94–95
  return to scientific research and, 94
  science and, 86–93
Gieser, Suzanne, 86
God
  death of, 203–204
  God after, 204–205, 211
  images of, in *The Red Book,* 175–181
  Jung's references to, 165–166
Goddard, Henry H., 56
The Golden Bough (Frazer), 246
Govinda, Anagarika (Ernst Lothar
  Hoffman), 280, 282
Graef, Charles, 58–59

H

Haeckel, Ernst, 88
Halperin, David, 191
Hansen, James, 233
Harvard lectures, 42, 43
Head, Henry, 54–55
Healy, William P., 59, 60
Heisenberg, Werner, 132
Hick, John, 248, 254, 255
Hillman, James, 91, 116, 124, 229,
  234, 264, 265
Hinkle, Beatrice, 5, 65–67, 69–71
Hoffman, Ernst Lothar (Anagarika
  Govinda), 280, 282
Hoffman, Irwin, 154
holistic studies, reemergence of, in
  contemporary science, 93–96
Holmes, Gordon, 55
Hooker, Sir Joseph Dalton, 89

Houck-Loomis, Tiffany, 7
Humboldt, Alexander von, 5, 82,
  87–93

I

I Ching (Yijing), 9, 277–280
Ignatius, 215–222
ignorant observer, 134
imagos, 24
individuation, 105, 127, 143, 183,
  238, 273
  process of, 44, 106, 139, 207, 217
infantile sexuality, 17
instincts, 27
interactive expertise, 134
International Psychoanalytic
  Association (IPA), 38

J

Jacoby, Mario, 142–143
Jacoby's diagram, 142–143
James, William, 38, 70
Jameson, Frederic, 104
Jardine, Nicholas, 86–87
Jaynes, Julian, 40
Jelliffe, Smith Ely, 58, 61, 77–78
Jones, Ernest, 39, 102
Joyce, James, 174
Judging/Perceiving, 144
Jung, Carl Gustav, 250, 255.
  See also Fordham lectures; *The Red
  Book* (Jung)
  Academy and, 165–172
  accomplishments in Fordham
    lectures, 3–4
  break with Freud and, 15–16
  at Burghölzli Hospital, 80–81
  Chinese culture and, 277–285
  concentric diagram of psyche, 145f
  cutting off ties to Freud, 41–43
  dreams of, 79–80
  first phase of scientific writing in
    career of, 79–81

Beatrice Hinkle and, 65–67, 69–71
influence of physics on, 39–40
interview with Teller, 67–69
last years of, 131–132
letter to Freud after Fordham lectures, 2–3
medical studies of, 80
mentors of, 38–39
Modernism and, 104–107
positive attitude towards Freud's principles by, 19–21
Post-Modernism and, 107–109
pre-modern romanticism and, 110–111
psycholanalysis and, 19–21
religion and, 165–167
Tao and, 279–280
tension and break between Freud and, 18
theory of archetypes of, 247
at time of Fordham lectures, 1–2
Jungian ecopsychology, 8, 239–240

K

Kant, Immanuel, 131
Karcher, Stephen, 280
Kearney, Richard, 204–205, 207, 210
Keller, Catherine, 209
kenosis (empty protest), 262
Keppler, Carl, 59
Kernberg, Otto, 154
Kille, Andrew, 191
kinship emotion, 44
Kirsch, Thomas, 122, 262
Knauer, Alvyn, 55
Kraepelin, Emil, 55, 80
Kristeva, Julia, 209
Kugler, Paul, 264

L

laboratory case study, 147–148
laboratory engagement studies (LES), 133–136, 139

key features of analytical psychology applicable to, 143–147
origins of, 134–136
psychotherapy vs., 151–153, 156
transformative process in, 149–151
Laing, R. D., 111
Lambert, Michael, 118
Lamborn, Amy Bentley, 7
Lang, Andrew, 246
Lao Tzu, 279–280
latency, 17
Leopold, Aldo, 237
LES. *See* laboratory engagement studies (LES)
Levinas, Emmanuel, 207, 253
Levi-Strauss, 247, 253, 255
Lewis, Sinclair, 239
libido, 3, 17, 28, 40, 47, 168, 173
Liber Novus, 83, 172, 216, 219, 220–221
Linné, Tara-Marie, 6
Logos, 143
Lovelock, James, 224
Luborsky, Lester, 118
Lyell, Charles, 89

M

Mahootian, Farzad, 6, 135
Maloney, William J. M. A., 58–59
Manoussakis, John, 206, 210
Maslow, Abraham, 283
materialism, 283
Mattson, Mark E., 5, 9-10
May, James V., 55
McCluskey, Thomas, S. J., 59–60
McGuire, William, 282
Merritt, Dennis L., 8, 233, 239–240
Messer, Stanley B., 119
midstream modulation, 135
Mills, Jon, 103
Modernism, Jung and, 104–107
Müller, Gerhard, 90

Müller, Max, 246
mythography, 245–246
   comparative findings of, 249–252
   golden age of modern, 248–249
   ways comparative findings of, were forgotten, 252–255
myths, Jung's theory of, 247–249
myth theory, 246–247

N

Naess, Arne, 224, 226, 228, 229
Nature, 8, 224–229
Neumann, Erich, 250
neurosis, historical development of theory of, 136
"new kind of knowing," 7, 199–200
Nicholl, Roy H., 58
Nietzsche, Friedrich, 251, 253

O

observation, as cornerstone of psychoanalysis, 20
the Open, 205–206
Oswald, David, 205–206
the Other, 206–208
Otto, Rudolph, 253, 255

P

Pacifica Graduate Institute, 6, 123–126
Pally, Regina, 43
Parks, Frances M., 5–6
Pauli, Wolfgang, 40, 85–86, 153
Peña Nieto, Enrique, 267–268
Penfield, Wilder, 56
personal equation, 167–172
physics, influence of, on Jung, 39–40
positivism, 132
Post-Modernism, Jung and, 107–109
post-secularism, 204
Pragmatic Case Studies in Psychotherapy (PCSP), 5, 119
pre-modern romanticism, Jung and, 110–111

projection, 146–147, 150
Propp, Valdimir, 255
Psyche, 224
psyche, 8, 42, 47, 110–111
   as interactive process, 45–46
   Jung's concentric diagram of, 145f
   Jung's theory of, 136–139
psychic energy, 39–40
   emotion and, 43–46
psychoanalysis
   Jung and, 19–21
   Jung vs. Freud on, 21–22
   observation as cornerstone of, 20
   post-modern, 108–109
   science and, 29–31
   theoretical postulations of, 26–28
psychoanalysts, academic psychology and, 16
psychoanalytic concepts, 27
psychoanalytic theory, 27–28
   complexity, paradox, and change in, 29–31
   science and, 28–29
psychology
   academic, psychoanalysts and, 16
   as experimental science, 16
The Psychology of the Unconscious (Jung), 77, 137–139
psychotherapy
   LES vs., 151–153, 156

Q

quantum theory, 85–86, 132, 168
Quinlan, Frances J., 58

R

Ramachandran, V. S., 94
The Red Book (Jung), 6, 90, 93, 165, 168, 170
   Jung's God-images in, 175–181
   new view of science and, 83–86
regression, 17

research method, 21
responsible innovation, 133, 155
Richards, Robert, 91
Rilke, Ranier-Maria, 205
Rogers, Carl, 118
Rollins, Wayne, 191, 196
Rosenbaum, Erna, 153
Rosenzweig, Saul, 118
Roszak, Theodore, 8, 226
Rowland, Susan, 6, 189
Rubin, Seth, 119
Ruiz, Rocío, 274
Russel, Colin K., 56
Rustin, Michael, 104, 154–155
Rutherford, Ernst, 81
Rutt, Richard, 280

S
Sagan, Carl, 235–236
Samuels, Andrew, 102, 125, 263–264, 272
schizophrenia, 80, 137
Schore, Allan, 135
Schulman, Martin A., 5
science, 139–143
    around 1912, 81–83
    German Romanticism and, 86–93
    ideal of value-free, 132
    psychoanalysis and, 29–31
    The Red Book and new view of, 83–86
    reemergence of holistic studies in contemporary, 93–96
    theory and, 28–29
Science and Technology Studies (STS), 132–133
The Secret of the Golden Flower (Wilhelm), 84–85, 280–282
Seed, John, 228
Selig, Jennifer Leigh, 6, 189
Seminar Notes (Jung), 215–222
Sensing/Intuition, 144
Shamdasani, Sonu, 78, 85, 123, 137

Shedler, Jonathan, 118–119
Sherry, Jay, 5
Sneck, William J., 6–7
Socio-Technical Integration Research (STIR), 133
    midstream modulation of, 134
Sorapure, Victor Edgar, 58, 59
Storer, Horatio, 54, 60
stream of consciousness, 70
symbols, Jung's account of, 247–249
synchronicity, theory of, 40, 92, 278, 279

T
Tacey, David, 225
Tao, Jung and, 279–280
Tavistock lectures, 42, 145f
Taylor, Eugene, 4
technoscience, 139
teleology, transference as, 40–41
Teller, Charlotte, 5, 65–67
theory
    conceptual knowledge and, 26–28
    research and, 28–29
The Theory of Psychoanalysis (Jung), 16, 37, 136, 137.
    See also Fordham lectures
therapy. *See* psychotherapy
Thinking/Feeling, 144
Thompson, J. J., 81
Tillich, Paul, 166–167, 168
trading zones, 134
transference, 42, 44, 46, 106, 141f, 142, 143, 146–147, 152
transference relationships, 141, 144
    as teleology, 40–41
transformative process
    in analytical psychotherapy, 148
    in LES, 149–151
transformative research, 148–149
two-person psychology, 108

U

Ulanov, Ann Belford, 6, 193–194, 196–197
   discussion of chapter by, 187–189
   unbarring Sheol, 192, 196–200
   unconscious, threat of, biblical scholarship and, 192–194

V

von Franz, Marie-Louise, 143, 144, 153

W

Waddington, C. H., 95
Walls, Laura Dassow, 90–93
Walsh, James J., 56–58, 59
Watkins, Mary, 273
Weismann, August, 94
Wertz, Frederick J., 4, 10
White, Victor, 167
White, William Alanson, 56, 78
Whitehead, Alfred North, 144
Wilbur, Ken, 283
Wilhelm, Richard, 84, 277–278, 279–281
Willer, Stefan, 94
Wink, Walter, 191
Wolff, Toni, 122
Wood, David, 228
Word Association Test, 166

Y

YoSoy132, 9, 269–270

Z

Zabriskie, Beverley, 4–5, 85
Zhouyi, 279, 280
Zimmer, Henrich, 250, 255

CPSIA information can be obtained
at www.ICGtesting.com
Printed in the USA
FSOW04n1024040916
24605FS